In the Shadow
of the Volcano

In the Shadow of the Volcano

One Family's
Baja Adventure

Michael Humfreville

Sunbelt Publications
San Diego, California

In the Shadow of the Volcano

Sunbelt Publications, Inc.
Copyright © 2006 by the author
All rights reserved. First edition 2006

Edited by Jennifer Redmond
Book design by W.G. Hample & Associates
Cover design by Leah Cooper
Project management by Jennifer Redmond
Printed in the United States of America

Sunbelt Publications, Inc.
P.O. Box 191126
San Diego, CA 92159-1126
(619) 258-4911, fax: (619) 258-4916
www.sunbeltbooks.com

09 08 07 06   5 4 3 2 1

Library of Congress Cataloging-in-Publication Data

Humfreville, Mike.
  In the shadow of the volcano : one family's Baja adventure / by Mike
Humfreville.— 1st ed.
      p. cm.
   ISBN-13: 978-0-916251-75-8
   ISBN-10: 0-916251-75-6
  1. Baja California (Mexico : State)—Description and travel. 2.
Humfreville, Mike—Travel—Mexico—Baja California (State) I. Title.

F1246.2.H86 2005
917.2'2—dc22

                                                        2005030812

Contents

Part 1

Newlyweds
Find a Life

A Difficult Decision

Mary Ann and I were married in 1973. We had a small house in La Crescenta, California, and both of us worked at NASA's Jet Propulsion Laboratory (JPL) in Pasadena. I was a support engineer; Mary Ann was in procurement. Neither of us made much money, somewhere around five dollars per hour. Work was stressful then, just as it is now. We had only taken a week for our honeymoon, and when we returned, we quickly refocused on our work and went hard-charging back into the JPL scene. We never really got away from it long enough to bond as a couple.

One Sunday, after a hearty party on Saturday night, we drove into the Angeles Crest mountains forming the northeastern limits of the Los Angeles basin. Stopping beside a remote stream running through a narrow gorge westward, we walked beside the crystalline chilly water talking and remembering the night before.

There was more to life than working as intensely as we both did. While we were talking I began working on a mid-range plan that would give us a focus over the months ahead and would also serve to give us the one-on-one time we needed. I suggested to Mary Ann that we sell one of our cars, save every penny we could for a number of months, and take a year away from work for a major trip. We could start in Mexico, specifically Baja California, spending several months in the summer in a warm place where the living requirements were minimal, then continue to Europe or wherever we decided.

Mary Ann balked immediately. Where did I come up with this stuff?

"Right," She said. "Who will make the house payments, and what would we do with Rochie and Dulcie? And what would we do for work when we decide to come back?"

"We rent the house, we take the dogs, and we leave work so much in demand they can't wait to rehire us."

"And what car do we sell?"

"Yours …"

Several short months later we did just that and in that order. We said good-bye to our friends and families, stuffed our Toyota Land Cruiser beyond capacity, called the dogs, and headed into our first shared challenge. Over these months we formed the basis of a relationship, rocky as the Baja roads at times and smooth as the early morning Sea of Cortez at others. This time and these experiences coming early in

3

our relationship have held us together through many extraordinary events. The trials of Baja gave us a focus on matters important to us without being tugged into the unending dither of a country that really does work *too* hard. But we knew it didn't have to be Baja California. It could be anywhere that grabbed your heart...

The Middle of the Story

I woke at 5:30. It was difficult to sleep once it became light. The sun wasn't up that early but when the darkness of the night relaxed the muscle of morning, animals began looking for food.

What actually woke me were the flies.

I lay in our bed on the sand, looking out of the thatched walls of the hut toward the islands, hoping for another moment or two of sleep. But I was hoping for the impossible. Several flies landed at once on my face, like they'd planned the maneuver, and my reaction brushed them away. I sat up, picked up my left sandal and waved it wildly in every direction, my arm outstretched, at anything flying I could reach. The flies dispersed for a moment, then gathered again undeterred. My eyes focused outside the hut, on the bay.

The water was smooth, without a single ripple. The bait fish were quiet at this early hour; nothing stirred on land or sea, except the flies, of course. The offshore islands two to three miles away in the south end of the bay were already hot, dry, and barren, with only a few cacti to collect the little moisture in the air. From the north I could see a vee of pelicans approaching in formation, heading for the open water and a day's fishing for survival. They passed just a few meters above the hut and I could hear the wind rushing through their wings. There was no better way to wake up.

I grabbed my fishing pole and walked the few feet to the edge of the bay, cut a small piece of mostly dried, rotting octopus we had caught for bait the day before and cast my line out into the still water. As the lure struck the still surface several baitfish jumped, surprised at the impolite intrusion. As the weight pulled my bait to the bottom, about five feet deep at this distance, I knew I would likely hook a cabrilla, trigger or puffer fish within a few seconds. I was not fishing for pleasure, rather for six or eight of the two- or three-pounders, which I would clean and fry or boil, adding garlic and salt to make dog food.

Our two dogs, Rocinante and Dulcinea (named for Don Quixote's steed and lady, in that order) were standing beside me at the edge of the bay—the magical water through which they could see minnows swimming and off the surface of which they could see two canine companions. Rochie and Dulcie pawed at the mysterious, reflecting liquid during the few minutes it took me to bring in the fish I needed and together we walked back to the hut.

The sun was rising above the lower islands in the bay. Intensely bright golden orange shafts of light streamed from the moist cumulus clouds hovering above the islands and warmed the colors of the ragged desert and sparse beach flora rugged enough to survive the harsh climate. The sun was wonderful in its interaction with our surroundings but not to my body. By my small weather station, mounted on a board and tied to the side of our hut, it was, at six a.m., already ninety degrees and ninety-five percent humidity.

This was the beginning of our second or third week at the bay. The two of us were falling into a predictable swing, an easy and comfortable lope of day-to-day survival. Our first week had been the busiest, filled with several major undertakings: finding a location that would provide maximum comfort for the summer, near a supply of required goods: simple foods, a source of potable water, and a not-too-distant place to buy a simple meal or beer and socialize occasionally. English and tourists were not required but neither would they be a problem.

The Beginning of the Story

Originally, we'd started looking for a place to spend the summer in a remote area on the west coast of Baja, between El Rosario and Black Warrior (Guerrero Negro). Wanting to be isolated from civilization, we thought we might settle near one of several tiny fishing villages in that area.

Our first nights were spent south of the tiny fish camp of Santa Rosalillita on a beach of steep sand dunes, two hundred yards from the ocean, where the evening air was cool and we could hear the Pacific breakers pounding the beach. On the second night we were surrounded by a pack of coyotes, and worried about them attacking the tent (a few years later we would know better). Regardless, I slept with a revolver by my side. In the middle of the night a dense fog crawled up onto the beach. When I got up to scare the coyotes off, Rochie and Dulcie took off and disappeared in different directions and we could only wait for them to return to camp. The fog hovered around until midmorning the next day.

At the edge of the fishing village there was a small adobe house, deserted for what looked like several years. It had no roof but could be covered with some poles and palm fronds or tarps. We'd spoken to a family nearby and they said that the owners would be gone for some time and we could use it as our own. But by noon it was still damp and foggy, something we'd seen along the central desert's west coast many times before. It hadn't bothered us as tourists, but as potential residents it was too damp and dark. We continued further south along the Pacific side of the peninsula.

The coastal roads in that area were still nothing more than sandy tracks running along the shore here and there to bypass a bad swatch of sand or dark lava. Our old Land Cruiser had been beaten almost to death on its many previous trips along the peninsula. We had replaced the original engine with a small Chevy V8 in a common conversion, but I had paid a hundred dollars for the very used engine and we had not done the best job of mounting it in the Toyota. The net result would have been comical if it wasn't so frustrating. Every few hundred miles we had to stop and clean the spark plugs, which were drowning in oil and wouldn't fire. The engine ran better at the beginning of this trip than it did at the end, but even then was burning two quarts of oil for every tank of gas. Our entire trip included the constant struggle to keep the poor truck operable.

Thus we limped into El Tomatal, on a volcanic point jutting several hundred yards into the pacific. The compact, tiny village was stuffed into a pocket in the rocky shore, with a natural harbor in which several *pangas* were bobbing at anchor in the rough water. El Tomatal was an inviting place to stay for an extended period, but there was no site close by the community that was remote enough for us. Also, the weather was similar to Santa Rosalillita. After several days of wandering the west coast we were not making much progress. Breaking camp, we drove back to the newly completed transpeninsular highway and turned south, stopped at a local ranch offering *comidas y sodas* on the out-skirts of El Rosarito.

We had eaten at this ranch many times before. It sits on a small bluff just north of El Rosarito, on the east side, just before a long slow dip in the road drops to the ugly fifty-kilometer run into Black Warrior. This restaurant had always had a great selection of dishes, from *carne asada* to lobster. I had wondered when I first visited, back when everything was dirt and dust and traveling a few miles took forever, how they obtained their supplies for a restaurant. What I overlooked was the fact that in my travels I was moving in a different circle than the locals; I was moving as quickly as I could to make it as far down the peninsula as my time permitted, seeing as many new sights as possible in the shortest time. The locals, *por el otro mano*, were simply maintaining their status quo. There I was in the middle of the peninsula, looking south for days on end while the pacific coast or the Sea of Cortez was, in either an easterly or westerly direction, only a few kilometers away. Fresh fish, even lobster, which reproduced furiously on the remote, rocky sections of the peninsula's coastline, was almost within walking distance.

The restaurant was a twenty-five foot square room loosely attached to the house of the restaurant owner. The walls were covered with faded photographs the subject of which was truckers and hunters. The older ones showed many men with their kill of mountain goats and lions from the nearby hills. It was surprising to see rifles in many photos, because of the strict rules opposing weapons by a government always afraid of revolution. Other photographs showed men standing beside their trucks. The older of these shots included only smaller trucks. On my first trip down the peninsula I had been hitchhiking and had the good fortune to ride most of the way on the passenger side of a *Servicio Particular* truck driven by a gentleman, Epifanio Ybarra, who hailed from San Ignacio. In the early days the roads had been dirt and did not allow larger scale transport. But there were a few more recent photos, since the transpeninsular highway had been paved the year before, of eighteen-wheelers. How the world of Baja had changed overnight!

We asked what was available and ordered. I opened up our map. As far as our immediate housing situation was concerned, our biggest problem was the weather. If we were going to survive for an extended period in this environment we had to find a location that required minimal external support. The west coast in the central region of the peninsula was too damp, even in the summer. We sat eating *huevos con machaca y verduras* and reviewing the map. From the 1960s I knew that there was nothing on the hundreds of miles of eastern coastline from San Felipe to Santa Rosalía that had anything that we were looking for. But my mind was locked into the days before the highway had been built. Those were the days when I grew up in Baja, days where the average achievement after sixteen hours of driving was maybe fifty to a hundred miles. In those days I had always hot-footed it as far south down the peninsula to get as close to the tip as possible. Our current situation was completely unlike those trips. We were looking for a place to live. With this newly-surfaced thought in mind we looked at the map again. In the direct center of the long and rugged coastline we'd been ignoring was Bahía de los Angeles, the Bay of the Angels. The locals at the restaurant volunteered their high regard for the beauty of Bahía de los Angeles.

One of our friends from JPL, Skip Reese, had traveled down to the bay several times in the late 1950s and early 1960s. Years before, over lunch at the Lab, we had listened to his tales of the fishing, sea life, offshore islands, and a tiny slow-paced fishing village settled around the remains of a mine that gave up its ghost during the last Mexican revolution. In those days I had never considered the bay as a potential destination because, when the road was dirt, my depth perception was always set further south, to the old colonial towns down on the peninsula that were influenced by the Jesuits in the 1700s and had, I thought, more character.

But now, as we sat in this rancho finishing our *machaca* and instant coffee with tinned evaporated milk and flies everywhere, I began to realize that Bahía de los Angeles was the one place we should investigate. It also fit with the poor condition of our truck, as it was fairly close by. From Skip we already knew the general weather: *hot*. The village had been there since the time of the building of San Borja, a Jesuit mission, forty-five kilometers inland, in the 1760s. Bahía de los Angeles was used as a supply point to San Borja and later supplied the mines near San Borja and ten kilometers south of the bay, at Las Flores. I sensed that it was a supply point still, a small Guerrero Negro (a town on the Pacific side from which the entire central peninsula was provisioned).

At that moment, finishing our rancho lunch at the north entrance of El Rosarito, about fifty kilometers from Guerrero Negro, we were the same distance as the crow flies from Bahía de los Angeles.

Locating Bahía de los Angeles

The peninsula, a long and gangly piece of land, did not suffer from a lack of information, local or distant, even without electricity or telephones. We asked the owner of the ranch about Bahía de los Angeles and listened to his answers with an ear tuned to our simple wants. It was a remote place, with remote provisions (where in Baja did this description not fit?). The weather was very hot and the sea life was plentiful. We finished our meal, chased the flies off the tin of milk for the hell of it, climbed back into the Land Cruiser and headed north for the junction with the dirt road that tied Bahía de los Angeles to the transpeninsular highway. Little did we expect that a major influence was about to enter our lives.

At El Rosarito we fueled up from a local rancher with five-gallon *latas*, siphoned and measured carefully out of the larger drums of gasoline, then made a U-turn and headed north up the peninsula. We drove past the westward turnoffs we had explored during the previous days, past those long, low, west-facing valleys full of acacia trees and their yellow blossoms, the few adobe ruins, and endless cacti: cardón, ocotillo, cirio… We drove along the narrow crested route of the paved highway, foreign in its own land, and dropped down into the wide valley south of Punta Prieta. We passed the military outpost and did not enter the village, but continued another seven kilometers to the turnoff, where we stopped to stretch our legs and let the dogs wander. On the northeast side of the road there was a ranch that sold sodas and food. On the southeast was a ranch with an impressive collection of damaged and rusted cars and trucks; we learned many years later that this was the Sheriff for the entire central peninsula, an area covering many thousands of square kilometers of land.

We collected Rochie and Dulcie and considered the road to the bay.

This was where the macadam stopped, so to speak. We observed the trailhead of a road, sixty-six kilometers long and twisting, that culminated on the edge of the Sea of Cortez at a village that had been host to many Cochimí in the sixteenth century, tempted the pearl hunters of the seventeenth, and served as a supply point for the development of San Borja over two hundred years ago. The road would lead us to a village that had also served provisions to the mines of San Borja and Las Flores. And, attractively, the road was not paved.

It is a difficult thing to imagine wanting a dirt road rather than a paved one. But I had poked and prodded this peninsula my whole life. The old dirt transpeninsular road was one of a kind. It carried you back in time, while transporting you through the equivalent of the Sahara. From seaside at San Quintín, through the 4000-foot mountains south of El Rosario, the central desert, to the southern state of Baja California Sur with her small majestic remnants of the ancient merger between elements of Europe and Mexico, to the great escarpment of Loreto above the plains of La Paz, and south to the East Cape and land's end at Cabo San Lucas, the transpeninsular highway covered it all.

Baja was the inverse of southern California's immersion in a fast-paced lifestyle in which I lived with ten million others of my kind. It was a forced introduction to a much slower, harmonious way of life. It was where the United States had come from. The most wonderful and memorable single thing about that old dirt track was that a person could grow lonely on it. A hundred times I had wandered down this road, alone or with a friend, but without encountering any other for days at a time, and had worried that a problem would happen with the truck that I could neither hear for all the noise nor fix for lack of spare parts. I could be days on the road and wanting to touch some other friendly life form and I would round some small corner and find, stopped in the middle of the road, some single axle duel rear wheel delivery truck with "*Servicio Particular*" written by hand on the doors. The driver, covered with grease and dirt from the axle and roadway, would be beside one of the rear split rim wheels, patching his non-spare tire and I would stop my small truck and jump out of the cab and offer him some assistance and he would be glad to see me, just glad to have another person there with him.

In the mid-1960s it became evident that the road would someday be a fact. The Mexican government had a crew that traveled the thousand kilometers of dirt, placing "*Arriba y Adelante*," "upward and onward" posters to a cactus every ten kilometers or so, alongside the old dirt track. Progress was inevitable. It was an assumed improvement for the locals. The initial grading of the virgin desert began in several places at the north, center, and southern portions of the central peninsula. The disruption to the barren desert was inconceivable, as the devastation to a land that becomes evident after a war. I had looked forward to there being a single lane of asphalt moving south along this skinny turf, but what I had failed to realize was that in order to create a road it must be raised from the floor beneath it to protect the asphalt. This requires the movement of massive amounts of dirt from the sides of the road toward the center. Also, once the road is built, it is not a desirable trait to have the vegetation retaking the terrain it has recently lost. This leaves the highway department, many hundreds of miles distant, to re-wage its war by sending troops back to constantly deforest the sides of the road for a hundred feet or more on both sides.

So, then, suddenly in the early 1970s, small and isolated segments of pavement appeared in the central peninsula. The pavement was a foreign element in the harsh desert, clashing with the soft tones of the sand, rock, cactus, and sky.

But at the junction of the road to Bahía de los Angeles there was simply the pavement continuing straight ahead and a well-traveled dirt road forking east toward the Sea of Cortez.

By the time we reached this point it was midafternoon. We were tired from the long drive and ghostlike from the endless dust that flooded the truck, covering our bodies with powder and matting our hair. At this latitude the sun was taking its toll. Although the road was long, it was smooth, covered with sand and dust rather than the decomposed shale and granite of the roads earlier that day. We made good time, climbing gradually over the first few kilometers and making a wide southward swing and dropping into a wide arroyo, Llulluay, and climbing back to the rising plateau and continuing eastward.

About a mile before the arroyo there is another dirt road, heading north. There was no reason for it to be announced, and thus it wasn't. It leads to a *tinaja* used by the Indians, the Cochimí. These natives survived here in the sixteenth and seventeenth centuries, before the Jesuit Friars treaded their way north from southern Baja. The Cochimí were generally peaceful and numbered perhaps forty thousand throughout the southern and central peninsula. They lived in small bands, were nomadic, and built no structures except an occasional arched mound of earth to interrupt a winter night's wind. The Cochimí lived by eating lizards, snakes, mice, birds, rabbits, and a number of native plants. Their favorites of these were the sweet *pitahaya*, the fruit of a particular cactus found throughout the central desert, which the Indians ate raw when ripe. The Cochimí cooked the agave plant, which grew a meter or more tall and which they would uproot and throw whole into a fire, roast for many hours and peel and eat like an artichoke, coveting the tender inner leaves.

The favorite time of year for the Cochimí was when they made their visits to the *tinaja*, in the mid- to late spring when food was most plentiful in this severe environment. The *pitahayas* were at that time ripening and the other edible plant life was tender, before the unbearable heat and dryness of the endless summer settled in. Many small bands of Cochimí came together during these abundant desert times. The Cochimí gathered at the *tinajas*, places where tiny artesian springs encouraged their silvery liquid to the surface and where the terrain was suitable to allow the water to remain there, standing, running, trickling to provide life to a few lucky seeds, plants, and weeds that had the good fortune to stand in the path of this moisture for a brief moment, before it evaporated or returned to the earth. Foraging around the *tinaja* was better than average and, while the small supply of water and food held out, the bands hung together and, I imagine, caught up with the news from distant family members, births, deaths and who knows what else. I knew nothing of the language used to communicate but I had no trouble envisioning these uncomplicated people building fires, gathering food, cooking, eating, and sitting on the dusty earth together sharing their harsh and savage experiences since the last meeting. I wished I could have been amongst them.

The bands remained grouped until the food or water was exhausted, then dispersed back to their individual nomadic areas, changing locations every few days and continuing their search for food. I suspect there was no concept of leisure, except at these *tinajas*, in the late Baja spring.

We were presently blessed with that same late spring. Our truck continued through the unending dust and heat, through the beds of dry, arid watercourses, along plateaus, through gullies, up and down hillsides of lava. Eventually we made a sharp, blind turn to the south and could see, stretching before us, many kilometers of low valley with a few cattle. Still completely barren desert, it was of a physical configuration not as unfriendly as that which came before it. We passed along the western edge of this valley. A cooling wind was moving here, along a sharply climbing range of hills to our immediate west. After several kilometers the road returned again to continue east and began a long climb. From the south another dirt road forked into our own.

This road led the ancient traveler here from the Mission of San Borja. The mission was built in the 1760s as the Jesuits walked and muled their way north, arguing with the Cochimí, twisting them into conditions of living unfamiliar and unwanted by the Indians or by any other tribe more civilized than the Europeans with their odd god and their arrogance. In the course of a few decades the lonely friars and their love-starved soldiers had brought influenza and syphilis to the Indians, diminishing their numbers from tens of thousands to a lost and beaten tiny percentage of that number. And all this in the course of several score and a few years, from 1700 until the time the Jesuits were ordered to return to Europe, suspected of stealing from the Crown.

Not anxious to lose a potential source of revenue, Spain was quick to replace the Jesuits with the Franciscans, who continued to force the Indians to conform in the most ridiculous ways to the standards of people ignorant in the ways of the desert. By the time the Europeans patience and hopes of fortune departed the peninsula, the Indian blood was so thin that it would never recover.

In small and familial ways, the manners of the Cochimí remain.

Every year at the mission San Borja, itself a *tinaja* of the pre-Jesuit days, a gathering is held. There the families from many thousands of hectares around gather at the water hole to continue their celebration of life and continuance. Hundreds of people come from all over the central part of the peninsula to visit, to lay eyes on old friends and enemies, to eat and drink, to expose their strongest and their weakest attributes to each other. For who but a strong person can expose his weakest elements to his enemies?

Here, at the Mission San Borja, in the fall of every year, the tradition of the *tinaja* continues. The blood of the Cochimí, perhaps diluted in its purity with the mixed blood of Europe, has found continuance. In this annual gathering the people of the central desert have built their empire with no need for walls; there is no need to protect what no one else wants. What the Cochimí found in their time, the current residents have also found. This desert is so peaceful and so isolated, so hard to achieve and so barren that it remains incontestably the land of those who are able to exist upon it. But it is special—there is no other place like it. It is an awesome feeling to walk where so few others have walked and then only over such great distances of space and time.

The road to Bahía de los Angeles, from the turnoff at the highway to the Mission San Borja, remains straight, continuing to climb a high and wrinkled plain, wandering eastward toward the Sea of Cortez. After several kilometers the road reaches a saddle in a low range of hills.

As we approached the crest the blue of the gulf was visible below, and what had seemed like a continuation of the eastern peninsula was soon revealed as islands in an azure sea. The entire breadth of the bay was visible. Angel de la Guarda, the second largest island in the immense gulf, is a backdrop for the smaller islands punctuating and protecting the wide mouth of the bay, taming the rougher waters of the outer Sea. As we continued over the crest, the islands could be identified, the size of the bay brought into proportion.

The bareness of the desert surrounding us was violent. From this distance there was no form of life other than cactus. Our map indicated a village at the southwestern shore of the bay, but neither a sign of man, nor a village or road was seen in the distance.

The road continued eastward, down the decline toward the gulf and, just past kilometer sixty, climbed a small hill and turned southward. We passed a few abandoned sunburned shacks, then a larger number, perhaps thirty in all, until finally the whole village was in view. The road wound slowly down the trailing edges of the mountains toward the sea. Huge mounds of orange-pink scallop shells lay nearby, in pairs of tops and bottoms. Several vultures labored heavily from the dusty roadbed and lifted upward into the thermals, to announce our approach from the north.

Like the road that had carried us there, the village was covered with dust. Dust and heat and, now, the humidity of the gulf seeped down upon us. The sea shimmered in the distance, and vision seemed blurred from the heat radiating off the seared earth, reflected upward to further heat the air. The road settled to sea level and the full impact of the humidity wafted through the open windows of the Land Cruiser.

There were a few outbuildings on both sides of the road. On the left were an airstrip, dirt and sand hacked from the desert, and shoreside weeds and aquatic plants. On the right was an adobe building with a thatched roof, housing the Armada (the local navy, provided to search every plane that lands on the airstrip). The road dead-ends into another, running to and away from the water. To the right the road is straight and climbs to the base of a 4000-foot mountain immediately behind the village. On this street are several adobe homes and a small market, Dos Pinos. But we turned left from the junction, toward the water and into an area surrounded with a low block wall, but open and inviting. There was a small Pemex gasoline station. Awaiting fuel at the station was an odd assortment of airborne and earthborne craft. Mostly airplanes were in this line, mixed with a few cars and trucks. The planes awaited the higher octane that would lift their finely tuned engines into the heated, buoyant air and carry them to the comfortable and secure environs of Alta California. The vehicles were waiting too, for the fuel that would carry them over the rocks, sand, mountains, and valleys of different routes north.

A set of formidable stone buildings with a raised large patio amongst them stood to our right, a few hundred feet from the bay. The large buildings that housed the *tienda* and *restaurante* also included, on the opposing side of the L, one of the numerous residences of a family we would come to know well over the decades, the Díaz family. After arranging for a meal later that evening, we reconnoitered the surrounding area. We spent that night in one of the Díaz bungalows on the beach, and had dinner with a few Americans and locals. It had been a dusty, bone-jarring, and trying journey. Surely there was a place to recompose ourselves here, in the village of Bahía de los Angeles. Tomorrow perhaps we'd find it.

In Search of Turf

The following morning we had coffee at the Díaz ranch and headed immediately out in search of an isolated beach.

From the village of Bahía de los Angeles, a poor quality dirt road continued south along the bay. Two kilometers past town this road passes behind a hill containing an old mine and narrow gauge railway that was operative years ago, and then rejoins the coast of the bay. There it passes through a steep escarpment, a wide and severe runoff from the 1500-meter mountains, Bahía de los Angeles and Santa Ana, lifting almost vertically out of the bay. Along this two-kilometer stretch of ocean there are many small and sandy intrusions into the land, and rocky points protruding into the bay. The road ran parallel to the beach, a hundred meters inland, and a few small side roads offered access to the beach. We explored several of these and one was more attractive than the others; it left us in a runoff at the beach with a patch of sand twenty meters square and on a rise immediately above the highest tide line. This was to be our home until we decided to leave.

We set our tent up in the dry gully and looked over the surrounding area. Amongst the sand and desert rocks and scrub there was little to build a hut from, but never having built a hut my mind was open to anything. This was a safe site, elevated several feet above the surrounding desert. The sand seemed best for building a hut, as it was softer to sleep on than the rocky terrain. So we decided that this was the place. We would look for building materials tomorrow.

I had been feeling mildly sick most of the day. As time passed I realized that I had probably eaten something that was bad, and was coming down with a case of something unpleasant. Once we were at rest the thing that didn't like my body was in a hurry to get out. It attacked from all directions and I spent two days alternating between lying in the sweltering tent trying to die and running for the arroyo we had designated as the toilet. Time was foggy and vague. Pain mixed with heat and thirst and sweat and filth. Fortunately, someone in our travels had recommended Lomatil for problems of the type I was experiencing, and I had started these small blue wonder pills early in my discomfort. By the beginning of the second bad day I was already beginning to recover. By evening I was nearing normal and could move about.

Hut Construction

The third day we scouted the surrounding areas for building resources. Across the south end of the bay were a number of palm trees and some fallen fronds. Inland, to the west, someone was working to improve the road from the junction to the Bahía; many cirio cacti lay uprooted and drying in the desert. We decided to frame our hut with this long, gangly cactus and cover it with the palm fronds. Several days were spent driving in various directions, retrieving whatever was available and would serve to build the small quarters. Burying the uprights a foot apart, one of us would dig a hole with our hands in the sand (we had no shovel) and the other would wait for the best moment and shove the large end of the cirio into the hole before it filled itself in. Then we would weave the smaller, more flexible cirio trunks horizontally between the vertical ones.

It took us three days to complete this effort and our hands were soon bloody pulps from the thorns of the cirio. We tied palm fronds to the outside of the irregular framework we had built, and when we ran out of fronds we used cardboard from old boxes, blankets, layers of newspaper and anything else that would prevent sunlight from invading our private space, but allow as much air flow as possible.

The only thing we could imagine needing protection from was the penetrating sun, and when we were done we had a sun-proof single room measuring about twelve feet by seven feet. An opening, which served as a door, was in the center, facing east toward the water and the warming morning sun. To the left of the door was a place where we could open our sleeping bags for the night—during the day the bags would be rolled up, allowing access. To the right, against the back wall, was the kitchen. A three-foot shelf supported a camping stove. Against the wall to the right of the door was another simple shelf of crates and plywood where we kept our supplies. Here we stored canned food we had brought, not knowing what supplies would be available, along with vegetables, meat, and fruit. Flour and dry goods were stowed in an unused ice chest under this counter, to keep out the mice and bugs. A niche or two above the shelves held gas lanterns.

As we stood back, realizing that we had built a house, we couldn't help but be pleased at our creation. Rochie and Dulcie had already settled into the shade of the hut, out of the slanted rays of the afternoon sun. We arranged our few supplies in their places and it was a home. As the afternoon turned into evening we puttered, arranging and rearranging our things. When we were done the sun was falling behind the Bahía and Santa Ana peaks. We lit the lanterns and sat outside on the beach. The air was moving slightly, silently. Small ripples in the water lapped at the shore. The pelicans were cruising toward the north end of the bay for the night in a pattern they had been following for as many years as they had existed, thousands in this place. Their wingtips felt the surface of the water as they glided, centimeters above its surface. As the sun set behind us and the glow left the sky and ocean, the lanterns cast their yellow light onto both the beach and us, sitting, watching these events unfold before us for the first time.

There was no question in our minds that we had searched for and found the very best place on the peninsula to spend some quiet time. There would be trials, not the least of which would be the extreme heat and solitude that neither of us was accustomed to. But we had started and finished this house together and we could face the next challenge as it happened. Tonight we had a new home to sleep in.

The Bucket

We had no fresh water except for cooking and drinking. In the early weeks the ocean water was cold.

One evening, like others before, we were walking on the beach as the sun set behind the western mountains and we spotted a green five-gallon bucket that had floated up and was resting on its side in the sand above the tide line. In that environment, it wasn't something I could pass up, so we carted it back to the hut.

The next day, while we were scrounging the desert for extra materials for the hut, we brought home two eight-foot branches of a Palo Verde or some such tree. Both were forked on one end. I dug two holes in the sand, four feet apart, while Mary Ann placed the branches in, forks up and I filled in the sand at their bases. With an ice pick and a rock, I punched a number of small holes in the bottom of the bucket. Then we ran another branch through the handle of the bucket and laid it in the forks of the two upright poles. We had an instant shower. It had no running water, of course, but whenever we wanted to bathe in warm water we would heat seawater in a large tub over the fire pit and transfer it to the bucket while one or the other of us stood beneath. It was primitive, but it worked just fine.

After using the shower for a few days, we found that we couldn't get the sand off our wet feet before we dried. Firing up the old Land Cruiser, which we had named Tortuga (tortoise), we drove up to La Gringa at the north end of the bay. We filled up the back of the truck with the smooth round beach pebbles there and carted them back to the hut and lined the sand under the bucket with gravel. Our shower was perfected.

Twenty-five years later, with Camp Gecko now in full swing, Mary Ann and I drove down to our old stomping grounds to visit with Doc and see what he thought about the new guy on the gossip platter, the Escalera Náutica. *Doc ended up giving us a tour of his campground. He had made a few minor changes to the configuration of the beach. We told him that we had lived here a long time back, but we couldn't place exactly where the hut had been.*

"There's one thing I've never understood." Doc said. "It's some small stones on the beach." He walked a few yards away to the place where the stones were located.

Both Mary Ann and I immediately recognized that these were the smooth La Gringa stones we had brought to our hut so many years before. It was everything that remained, from the beginning of our lives together on what was then a quiet beach, but it was as much as we needed. We just looked at each other and at Doc in amazement.

Sometimes in life we may think that everything we accomplish is soon meaningless. But in that moment we had changed the world.

Settling In

Over the next days we began to fall into the life that would occupy us for the next months. We put the finishing touches on the fire pit and lined it with rocks. There was never a need for a fire for warmth, but every other day we would heat a washtub with seawater over the fire for washing clothes. We ran clotheslines to a number of nearby bushes from the corners of the hut.

Gathering mud from a nearby lagoon, we planted a variety of seeds beside the hut, where they were shaded part of the day. Nothing resulted; the soil was no doubt too sandy and saline. We experimented with making our own tortillas, but with no cool water I couldn't form the *masa* to the proper consistency and it always ended up sticking like glue to everything it touched. This is clearly a gringo problem; the Mexican ladies did it all the time. I tried on several occasions over the months but never developed a technique. I always ended up flinging the dough to the fish, enraged and cursing to the befuddled pelicans and gulls that constantly held fast to the shore in front of the hut.

We tried to live off the rich bounty of the ocean and the vegetables we could get in the village. We experimented with the fish caught from shore. Cabrilla was flaky white meat but wasn't long on taste. Triggerfish was dog food, they were disgusting to look at and so tough-skinned they were nearly impossible to clean. Luckily we never tried to cook puffer fish, as they are deadly (we didn't know that at the time). From the shore we didn't catch the more interesting delicacies we would later appreciate: octopus and squid, clams and mussels, crab and lobster. Sometimes we would tire of seafood and break down and open something canned that we had brought with us.

Over time we began craving something doughy. Luck supported our needs.

The Box

Often in the evenings as the heat and sun's intensity dropped, Mary Ann and I walked down the shore toward Rincón at the south end of the bay. The breeze off the water was cooler and Rochie and Dulcie would run forward, looking back, wanting us to watch them, so we did. There is really very little to distract you in that peaceful environment, which was just what we wanted. Small crabs were scurrying toward the water as our feet fell, making shallow indentions in the sand, marking our way to the hut when we turned back, whenever we chose, and yet leaving no lasting impressions. There were no neighbors in those days between the village and the Díaz cattle ranch.

A fish carcass was there along the shore. I picked it up and tossed in into the water where its nutrients would serve again. We stooped over the water in the evening reflections, staring at the submerged carcass, a foot out from the shoreline. Rochie joined us. Soon small minnows were attacking the flesh of the dead triggerfish. Rochie was fascinated. He saw his own reflection on the surface, and was confused. When he started pawing at the surface, I wasn't sure if he was chasing the fish beneath or attracted by the beautiful dog above. His paw hit the water and the twin images were gone. So was Rochie's interest. In a flash the thought-provoking moment of fish and dog that he was so intensely into disappeared and he was off down the beach, catching up with Dulcie.

We continued our walk, encountering a metal box washed up on the shore. How could it float? I wondered. I had no answer, but there it was. Even at this remote place we often encountered items swept by the winds and tides to these shores. We learned to place greater value on castoffs here than we did in other places. We stopped and the dogs idled in racing circles around us at a distance. The box, about thirty inches deep, was unlidded and measured perhaps fourteen inches wide by five inches high. What could we do with this? I wondered. We continued our walk, but on the way back to the hut I picked up the box and carried it back home with us.

After so many months living by the shore of the bay we were missing many things. Several of them were food groups. We had traveled across the peninsula to Guerrero Negro to buy the vegetable seeds that we had planted in the impotent sands by the hut. I had driven old Tortuga to the lagoon and carried back saline mud that had also proven dysfunctional for fostering life. At least the kind we wanted. All we were eating was fish and canned foods. There was little offered in the village in those days.

One morning I'm up early and have caught the fish for dog food for the day, and I almost trip on the metal box. I realize how we can use it. I clean and cook up the dogs' favorite garlic triggerfish and cabrilla, serve them and set to my task. I measure the opening of the elongated box with twigs broken off at lengths and carve a piece of a washed-up orange crate, a lid, to those dimensions. I attach it to the metal box with two small pieces of chain, holding the new door in place but allowing it to open upward. Then I take old Tortuga back to the lagoon with a large tarp in the cargo area and fill the tarp with the oozing goo of the lagoonbed. I return to the hut and dig a second small fire pit in the sand, lining it with slop from the lagoon. I construct a mud structure twelve inches above the fire pit and place the box on top. We cover the sides and top of the box with a thick layer of mud. Then we wait.

After two days the mud had fully set and cracked in numerous places. We decided to try it out. Mary Ann whipped up some concoction that included flour, water, leavening and a few other simple ingredients. I built a fire in the new pit and closed the door to the box sitting atop.

"What temperature do we want?" I called.

"I don't know. Maybe 350."

She stirred the flour. I stirred the coals. Our souls were stirred at the thought, thirty minutes into our future, of what we would be eating. Mary Ann put dollops of her mixture into a muffin pan we had been fortunate to bring with us on this adventure. We popped the tray into the box and closed the cover. The sides of the wooden lid smoked as they came into contact with the metal box. Every few minutes I opened the door just a little to see how the muffins were rising—just a little, just so, now pillowing, now turning a perfect golden. And then we were consumers once again, of tasty baked paste in this remote place we loved so fully.

We walked from time to time, just us four beasts along the beach, scanning the shoreline for other flotsam and jetsam. Whenever we spotted an object that might prove useful we adopted it. You just never know when something you stumbled upon might turn up to be useful. In utility, did we fulfill the box or did it fulfill us? Together we made each productive and useful.

Mary Ann and I were learning a lot about each other with our quiet time there, during that summer in our hut of thatch and on our beach, alone. We learned about our selves and our environment—about life and death in the natural world. We learned about relationships and the limits of love and animosity, about richness and poverty, aloneness and togetherness. We learned to talk to each other and ourselves. We learned how to face into our shared future and just say "We will deal with this and win!"

Poor old Rocinante—he never did figure out how things worked. Whenever he reached out to touch his magic fish or his own image, his paw would touch the calm surface, and his whole big picture, whatever that was, would begin to fade.

Sight and Sound

Life is routine and almost uninterrupted in this environment. We read: novels, nonfiction, everything we had brought with us. I even tried to work through *Don Quixote*. I only made it halfway. Real excitement was a car or truck passing on the road to the south end of the bay, a few hundred meters inland. We would hear the engine when it was miles away and walk to the nearest sand dune to spy it on the road. There was a small ranch belonging to the Díaz family a few miles south and it was usually their truck we would see passing. If they saw us they would wave. Regardless, we would wave back. We were not lonely, but we were always happy for a visitor or some outside entertainment. As we slowly settled into the lifestyle we found that we were working at a different pace. In some unidentifiable way we slowed down. Our days were filled with routine tasks and no outside pressure, no challenges except those from our own choices. Surviving a windstorm in the middle of the night, or shoring up the hut to keep it from blowing over is a whole different animal than giving a technical presentation to a roomful of authorities.

Our surroundings were completely natural. There were no sounds except those of the wildlife, the wind, the sea. We went months without even listening to recorded or broadcast music. (Now, years later, I wonder how we could not have missed the emotion of music so much that we wouldn't have found a way to play it.) Everything in our lives was natural and simple, we were returning to basics.

Producing food by fishing and simple baking in our homemade oven, we bathed and washed clothes in seawater heated by burning collected wood. Walking on the beach, we learned the habits of the sea and began to understand the complexity of tides. We watched the sea life that, day and night, passed through our shared environment. Just by the sounds we began to identify the events surrounding us. Enveloped in a rich new culture, we began to recognize what now seems so basic: the difference between a coyote and a wild dog's howl; the difference between a sea gull's cry and that of a tern. Over the months we learned the differences between the sound of the blowholes of bottle-nosed dolphins and smaller whales that passed near the shoreline in the night. We could tell how far offshore they were and the purpose of their visit, food or entertainment. (Even to trained ears, the midnight sound of a nearby pelican hitting the water in a dive for bait still sounded like a blow from a distant whale.)

We began to realize that animals require entertainment and get bored just as humans do. I had read an article stating very authoritatively that animals *less than human* (who assigned this hierarchy?) had no sense of humor or of play. By immersing ourselves in their environment, I was seeing that, while there was certainly an *eat or be eaten* caution amongst animals and they never fully let their guard down, animals played too. Play may not have meant the same to them as it does to humans, but humans possibly should rethink their understanding of play.

To us, play means the complete abandonment of caution, a time to completely relax and enjoy humorous frivolity, alone or with others, peers, parents or other trusted and unthreatening entities. While I believe we think of play as a necessary relaxation, we don't think of play as a learning process built into our total integration with all life. Play to other animals is both daring, possibly humorous, challenging and dangerous, and what else I can't imagine, but more. It is not an escape from the process of learning, rather a continuation of it. Regardless of what I've read, I'm convinced that animals other than humans do play.

But I don't think it is the removed play that humans conceive, where threat is removed from the equation.

Over time, I came to identify the birds that flew over our hut just by the sound of their wings. The brown pelicans were the easiest because they were the largest and flew the lowest. Their pattern was also the most predictable because they migrated to the steep cliffs at the north end of the bay as the sun set over the Bahía and Santa Ana mountains, looming behind the hut, and returned to the south end to fish before the sun rose over the gulf in the morning. The steep drop from land to sea at the north end allowed them the updrafts of air that crashed sharply into the rising cliffs from the flat bay to give them buoyancy in the early morning.

Daily, I awoke to the sound of the pelicans flying a few feet over our hut. As the night faded, in my half sleep, I could hear the wings working the air, could sense the individual birds flying in formation, that pelican wedge I had seen so many times, could nearly feel the tug of the muscles and tendons that moved the wings up, then down, then up, then down. In my half-awake state I could visualize the feathers undulating as their wings pumped, almost hydraulically, the barbs of their feathered vanes bending beneath each pulse of their wings and feel the lift of the downthrust and the fall of the recovery of the wing to the top of the cycle, to be repeated again. I could even feel the tug of the wind as one pelican spelled another as leader of the wedge where the rush against the wind was greater, and the relief of the leader, as he was replaced, and moved to the back of the pack.

Throughout the days, our world was filled with the experiences of a natural world of heat and dust, of humidity, of windstorms, and of days so tranquil you'd turn your body into the slightest movement of air as relief from the heat. The sea life filled many hours. Sitting on our shoreline we watched the endless passage of birds, seals, dolphins, bait, and whales.

When the hottest part of the day was over, we would fix dinner. It was best to cook and eat before it was dark. The darkness meant that we would light the kerosene lantern and the false light, even at that low intensity, was a magnet for every bug within a mile. We usually ate something we had caught and a starch and sometimes a vegetable. The vegetable might be whatever was available fresh in the village, or canned. But the climate was so hot that we didn't need a lot to eat.

As the sun set, we would sit and watch the dogs come to life from the shadows and cooler places in the earth and play in the water and on the damp sand. The pelicans wedged toward the north end and the masses of bait working the bay in front of us threw thousands of tiny concentric circles on the surface of the red, orange, and yellow, otherwise glossy ocean. The human sounds were not foreign to this scene, they were part of it. Our sounds were only soft voices and quiet footsteps in the sand and over damp rocks.

In the evenings we tried to read by the single kerosene light but, particularly on still nights, it was difficult because the bugs were attracted to the light. As soon as we could settle in for the evening we would turn off the light. In the dark there was nothing to do but sit and listen to the sounds of the bait stirring the sea's surface, a few birds working the bait, the small waves and the wind, maybe sea lions barking. As the evening wore on, the dolphins and often a stray whale blew thirty meters offshore, passing in the thirty-foot-deep water, back and forth, eventually moving on. Perhaps we were not enough entertainment for them. Gradually the larger animals quieted, including us, and we would roll out our sleeping bags on the sand inside the hut and listen to the night sounds as we fell asleep. All night long the natural world worked its restoration on the day; the muscled bodies rested while the minds worked to integrate the events of the day into their own realities. In the morning an entirely fresh picture had been painted and we were refreshed, cleansed, and ready to tackle the new challenge, wondering what new marvels would be revealed to us.

Often during the day, and occasionally at night, winds crashed into our peaceful world. The winds were always unpredictable below the heated mountains, meeting with the cooler air from the sea. We were still learning to cope with their unannounced visits. At least once a week we'd get slapped with a blow that would last at least the entire day. We secured the lightweight gear inside the hut and went about our activities pretty much as usual.

Occasionally it blew hard enough to churn the sea surface into horizontal spumes of water that would rise from the crests of the wild waves and blow across the ocean and onto the shore. The sand stung our bare legs as it blew across the land. In these stronger blows, the walls of the hut, being buried only in eighteen inches of sand, would creak and tilt with the wind. We would fortify the uprights with additional sand, rocks, or cirio cactus poles. Inside, with the walls groaning due to stress from the gusts of forty or fifty miles per hour, the equipment and utensils we had suspended from the walls and ceiling rained to the sand. It was an earthquake of sorts, particularly since you didn't know how bad the wind would get before it tapered off.

It usually peaked before it could cause too much damage, so we learned to live almost normally with these winds when they happened during the day. Occasionally they came in the middle of the night. Waking from a sleep to loud, gusting, shaking, noises, the invisibility of the night compounded our inability to get a grip. We would often have to stand, holding things together until the worst passed. The next day we would shore things up stronger than before, but the next wind would be bigger than the one it followed. We learned how to tough it out and also that all things would pass.

Mike and His Mountain

One morning, about a month after we had settled in, a man appeared on our beach. We had not heard sounds to announce his arrival, which was unusual because it was so quiet. He hailed us from the beach and we walked down to see who it was. A tall, lean man, with light skin tanned like leather, he spoke English. His name was Mike, and he had a small house on the outskirts of the village; he had heard that there were Americans living here and wanted to look us up. We saw he had arrived on our beach in a kayak, which accounts for the fact that we didn't hear him. He was a sort of naturalist who distilled his own water from a homemade evaporation device, and baked bread from wheat flour he milled himself. We offered him a soda or beer, but he said he drank only water. The only water we had to offer him was local and hot, to which he was accustomed. Mike had lived in the village for many years, and climbed the peak (Cerro Santa Ana, directly behind our hut) several times a year, even in the summer. When he did this he left the bay at four in the morning in order to reach the thousand-meter-high peak before it was too hot.

He was an older guy, maybe fifty, and I could imagine him climbing Mike's Mountain, tanned and breathing so heavily that his ribs protruded, glistening with sweat, pulling himself up the steep mountain path foot over foot. Mike told us that he kept water at the top in a special place. It sounded like a good idea just in case you ever wound up there. When I asked why he went there, it was like the question didn't make sense to him. But I don't like exercise for its own sake and he felt exercise was vital to his well being; it would never occur to him to ask why he was hiking to the top of some mountain. He was just doing it.

Mike was a good guy and he came to visit us almost daily for some weeks. He had retired from an aerospace firm in San Diego and we shared ideas that probably would have shaken the industry just because they were so simple, having been conceived in this restful environment. It's interesting, once again, to see how a person's mind looks for whatever it has been missing. Our minds were missing the complexities of our previous lives. We needed mental processes.

Patricio's Mail Service

Once the hut was complete, we had more free time. We read several hours a day. We wanted to write to our friends and family but there was no mail service beyond Ensenada, three hundred miles north. Patricio, who operated the Pemex station for the Díaz family, told us he would give our letters to anyone who was flying out to a destination where there was postal service. We also found that the Díazs had a post office box in Ensenada and that we could receive letters there; whoever was near Ensenada would stop and check the box and bring any letters to Antero Díaz's office at the bay. While this was basic, it worked. It meant that we could receive letters about three weeks after they were posted in the U.S. This gave us incentive to write and we filled pages with experiences and details we were anxious to share. The mail allowed us some form of connectivity to our now-fading previous lifestyle.

Patricio had run the Pemex station in the bay for many years. (He continued to run it until it closed in the mid-1990s.) Patricio was a sly fox with the trick of always separating you from a small amount of your money. Operating his own calculator at lightning speed, he apologized for the inevitable and frequent errors in the calculations of the Pemex pumps as his fingers flicked over his own machine, equally erroneous. His addition was always in his favor just enough that most customers were unaware or at least would not balk. But Patricio was so steadfast in his self-serving calculations that I occasionally had to speak up and have him correct his figures. Many others did likewise. It was beyond me how he could be so widely recognized as a minor rule bender in his own small community and not be ashamed. I was naïve to think that all people shared my concerns.

Over time I thought I had Patricio pegged and could avoid his cheating ways. But he showed me how little I knew. When he heard we were taking a trip north he asked us to post a number of letters he had collected.

We'd been at the bay for about a month, without ice and with no ability to cool food or drink, and decided we would head to Ensenada in search of a way to cure this problem. We had heard from the locals that the electricity had been extended from Ensenada to San Quintín. Hidden amidst this information was the clue that there might be a number of used refrigerators that operated on liquid petroleum gas (LPG) on the market as their owners replaced them with the more efficient electric models. This was encouraging news and we hastened to depart before these appliances were sold elsewhere or retired to the nearest *barranca*. So we spent a day or two preparing for our trip in old Tortuga.

Our last stop on the way north was to fill up our gas tanks and visit Patricio. As we completed these two tasks, Patricio handed me a thick stack of letters and asked if I would post them in Ensenada. I took the stack, pleased that I could contribute to the process that I had taken advantage of. I would mail these letters in Ensenada and some happy folks would hear from long-lost loved ones. Many more important things passed between then and our arrival in Ensenada, and I had almost forgotten the letters when they fell out of my pack and I went off to post them. In a last-minute check, I flipped through the whole stack. Patricio, the good-hearted crook, had set me up once again. He had charged everyone that gave him a letter the price of a stamp. Then he had cleverly placed stamps only deep enough in the pile that the unstamped letters would escape my notice. Here, in Ensenada, a far distance from the bay, Patricio knew that I would spend my own money to post the letters; he would benefit from pocketing the difference. What a bum! If he had spent as much time adding quality to his services as he did cheating everyone he might have been a rich man.

Sad Realities

Our trip to Ensenada was a big event. It was about a month after we had built the hut and we were planning to buy a propane refrigerator and some clothing. We spent time getting ready and making sure the hut was as securely tied down as possible. There was no way to close it; it had only an opening for a door and nothing to close. But there was no one within miles and the few villagers were not about to bother us. On the night before our departure we went to bed early in the evening, looking forward to an early start, somewhat sad to be leaving our tranquil private beach for the hype of the city four hundred kilometers north toward another home.

We were up at first light of morning and threw our packs into the old truck. We climbed aboard and I turned the key in the ignition and could imagine the flow of electricity threading its way through all those small wire junctions, covered with dust, rust, oil, all damp from the humidity. I was amazed when the engine even tried to turn over. Tortuga bucked and swayed as the old Chevy engine cranked, working to catch a spark on its long and arduous journey from the battery. Just when I knew it was not going to start, it suddenly sprang to life and a great gust of exhaust spit out the tailpipe and lifted gently upward into the clear morning air. I feathered the throttle and the engine settled into an uneven sputtering idle. Mary Ann called to the dogs, hiding from the sound of the engine's odd noises and my swearing, and they warily jumped in. I put the old truck into first gear and eased out the clutch pedal. We moved forward in the soft sand and crawled out of the track to the road that led to Bahía de los Angeles.

While we had been in the bay only a month, it had been a time of great change. Our relationship with each other and our world had been forever influenced by the recognition of the earth and the universe so big and powerful that we could never return to our previous environments and feel the same as we had before. A month filled with such extremes might well seem a full year. In some ways I felt like we were deserting a lifestyle, when, in fact, we planned to be gone only two or three days, one day up and one day back. We had lived in isolation through so many events it seemed that we were coming out of a bubble, heading for some foreign, unknown place. While we missed society, we had our hands full at the bay, immersed in a self-imposed process of isolation and experimentation, and we were committed to that learning experience. It was almost like we were turning our backs on our new life just as we were getting started. In spite of both of our individual concerns about leaving, we really wanted something to keep food and water cold.

The road leaving the bay travels westward from the Sea of Cortez, heading inland into the higher desert, through a series of deeply worn, seaward-running gullies in the escarpment sweeping from the Sierra de San José y Calamajué range to the sea. The shore was hot and humid. As we labored inland heat and humidity were trapped in the airless depressions gouged by infrequent but torrential rains flooding into the folds of earthen fans. The air was nearly too thick and hot to inhale. The terrain shimmered, vibrated in the heat. The air from the engine made the cab even hotter and images untruthful to the actual road danced on the hood of the truck. Even in the shade the metal of the doors and dash were too hot to touch.

Sweat poured down my face, underarms, and chest. Mary Ann, using a cloth she had dampened before we left the hut, wiped the sweat off my face. When I looked at her across the seat of the Land Cruiser, it was easy to appreciate the effort she had made. It was too hot to think. My thoughts were clouded.

We were looking forward to seeing people and being in a social element again, but I couldn't get over the thought that we were deserting our home and lifestyle only a month into it. I felt that we had established a self-supporting mechanism for a newly married couple. I don't mean that we had or needed rules, rather that we had simplified our life to avoid too many overwhelming interruptions until we had formed into a single element. I wondered if Mary Ann felt the same. It was not something we could have talked about before, I was just realizing it as we drove off through the heat and dust. And sometimes talking only takes away from the depths of a reality.

Over the time we had been at the bay we had silently and unknowingly assumed what were to become our roles in our life together. These were, I'm sure, forged by the way we were individually raised by our respective families, and by our own uniquely formed personalities. Over our time on the beach we had each had our own accomplishments without outside direction or social pressure. We were allowed to choose our activities from a set of those which needed doing plus anything we could imagine. We had done this without consciousness.

It made me proud—I thought of us as independent and that was pleasing.

After traveling a few kilometers along the runoff erosions, the road rose to the level of the surrounding desert and a small breath of air moved through the open windows of the cab. The sun continued pulsing through the roof of the Land Cruiser and the dust floated through the windows and floor vents. Following the road, I was driving through a fog of heat and grime. The further we got from the beach the more the humidity dropped and the heat and dust increased. The weather station on the dash told me the temperature was now over one hundred degrees with forty percent humidity. As we drove inland the temperature increased and the humidity decreased even more. I constantly checked the water and oil gauges for nominal readings as we continued our gradual climb to the center of the peninsula.

By the time we reached the junction of the bay road with the transpeninsular highway, the spark plugs' tips were covered with oil from the blow-by of the old engine. We stopped to correct this problem with a process we had down pat. Using a deep socket and ratchet wrench, I removed each plug and handed it to Mary Ann. She cleaned the tip of the first plug with a small wire brush while I removed the second plug, and so on. We had done this many times over our time at the bay. Soon we were back under way.

From the junction, the road was paved both north, toward Ensenada, and south, toward La Paz. It had been four weeks since we had driven on a paved road and it was an opportunity to check the truck out for engine problems that could not be heard on the dirt roads.

On the pavement we couldn't hear anything new, so the oil consumption problem continued to be our biggest worry; but it was an inconvenience rather than a show-stopper, for the moment, anyway. The rest of the day we traveled north, past the turnoff for San Felipe and the east coast road at El Crucero, then Nuevo Laguna Chapala, Rancho Sonora, Los Tres Enriques, San Agustín, Santa Cecilia, El Progreso, and through the red and rocky mountains into El Rosario and on to the Pacific Ocean. The temperature dropped one degree every mile from the 1200-meter summit of these coastal hills to the level of the sea. As we neared the Pacific coast and dropped into the valley of El Rosario, the vegetation changed noticeably. We had transitioned from the desert region, home to the cardón, cirio, ocotillo, and so many other cacti, to the California region, hosting the vegetation familiar to those of us from southern Alta California: coastal sage, chaparral, and low brush.

When we arrived in El Rosario it was seventy-five degrees and foggy. From El Rosario the drive was three hours on the pavement to Ensenada. The most striking change was the encroachment of farming into the barren desert as we continued north. Twenty kilometers south of San Quintín we were driving past light brown ploughed fields that were used for dry land farming. A few miles north we were seeing more green irrigated acreage filled with regular rows of corn and other vegetables. Farming equipment was more in use than in past years. Several wells and pumps had been imported with the slow and irregular extension of electrical power from the border region.

Once we neared the Valle de San Quintín the narrow paved road widened and the traffic increased, mostly with trucks hauling produce from the valley to the hungry mouths of towns to the north, including those in the U.S.

Between San Quintín and the smaller villages of Vicente Guerrero, Camalú, Colonet, San Vicente, and Santo Tomás we passed the smaller family farmers that rely on the seasonal rains and the limited supplies of water from the west running creeks formed by the runoff of the Sierra San Pedro Mártir and Sierra San Miguel. Here people survived or failed on a family-by-family basis and it was rewarding to see water flowing through the bottoms of the creeks at the north end of each village. The people would be fed this year, at least.

Finally we were nearing Ensenada. As we passed through Maneadero we met with traffic, exhaust, dogs and children running, drunks staggering in the streets. After being on our own so long it was confusing to be in the midst of this much action. In Ensenada we found a hotel along Avenida López Mateos and, careful to shake off the dusty debris from our trip before entering our room, stretched out to rest before facing the town.

The trip, including several stops to clean the spark plugs, had taken the better part of the day. It was now evening and we bathed, changed clothes, and went out for dinner.

The tourist streets of Ensenada surrounding our hotel were alive with nightlife. It was Friday and people filled the streetside cafés, bars and shops. It was exciting but a little unnerving.

When we had moved to the bay it had taken us time to adjust to the quiet lifestyle. We had eased into it with all the activities required, including building a hut, and fallen into a lifestyle that occupied our time during the first couple of weeks. When we had finished the first major tasks and settled down, we were aware that time was a different commodity at the bay than it had been in our previous lifestyle. We had adjusted to the slower pace and were happy alone with only each other.

After accepting that change and integrating with the physical environment of extremely rural living it was a shock to re-enter the hype of tourist Ensenada. I couldn't shake the feeling that somehow I had sold out by coming here, that I had deserted something, left something behind that I wanted to keep and could never recapture. I kept reminding myself that we were only here overnight and would be going back the next day or the day after.

We walked along the busy sidewalks talking and looking through the windows at many things we didn't have any use or money for. Furnishing a hut in the sand does not involve too much frill. Wandering through the main tourist area, we found a side street running east toward the native quarter and walked until we had left the tourists behind and were among the locals.

Many of the shops were open and had inexpensive clothing and sandals. It was interesting to see the native *mercados*. We bought several print shirts and a pair of pants for a few pesos. We realized that the items we were buying would only be used at the bay; they were things that seemed to fit our lives there which didn't belong anywhere else. The local part of Ensenada is much larger than the tourist part and is even more filled with people on the move. But it was not as aggressive as the tourist sector. There was a lot of shopping going on but not on any schedule or with the same perceived necessity. If a sale was to be made a bargain had to be found. Nothing was imminent.

We wandered throughout the streets and found the few items we needed. Mostly we were replacing things that were old to begin with and were more quickly spent by washing in the hard seawater. Throughout this part of town there were vendors with mobile carts on many corners selling cut fruit of every color in tall glass cups, frozen *paletas*, flowers, tacos, and hot dogs wrapped in bacon and served with jalapeños. Men rushed to make deliveries, salespeople called for your attention and smells of cooking food radiated from the myriad small cafés and restaurants.

Walking through the streets, I began to sense a change. I felt I was a part of this scene, whereas I hadn't felt that way in the tourist sector. I wondered if maybe I was just used to the pace of Mexico more than of the U.S. tourists. Or maybe more accustomed to Spanish over English. But I suspected it was the *force* with which the tourists attacked their objectives, and the shared respect with which the Mexicans dealt with each other.

We retraced our steps to the tourist quarter. We were getting hungry and if I wanted one thing it was a quality meal in a quality atmosphere. I knew of no better for either of these in Ensenada than El Rey Sol. Situated on a key corner of López Mateos, the Sun King had reigned as the highest quality restaurant in Ensenada for many years. For me, it wasn't that the food was supreme or that the service was tops; they might have been, but I am no judge. What I liked about El Rey Sol was that it set its sights very high. It wanted badly to be the fanciest and highest quality restaurant in town, in an old money sort of way.

We walked back through the busy American-littered Mexican streets to the restaurant where we waited a few underdressed minutes and were gracefully seated at a table in the main dining room. The atmosphere was wonderful, not pompous, but almost. The tables were covered with good linen on top of which were placed abundant quantities of silver knives, forks, and various spoons in several locations. Pressed linen napkins were inserted into silver napkin rings and polished glasses for red, white, and dessert wines were positioned at each setting. While we weren't completely comfortable in our very casual jeans and sandals, we fit well enough with the other bohemians that one found in south-of-the-border towns. We relaxed with a glass of white wine and ordered escargot and considered the menu. The snails worked well with the thick and chewy local wine. Fresh bread and unsalted butter added their touches.

Around us were an assortment of comfortable Mexicans, both locals and visitors, Europeans on tour, Americans wanting to spend money and a few of us just wanting very badly to be pampered. This was an interesting collection of individuals, some ethnically intermixed, couples of seriously different ages, and all dressed in their own styles and traditions. Many conversations were pursued across the frontiers of tables and ages and races and monies, and voices were raised and lowered in subtle tones as subjects shifted like the seas of our bay. How could I have questioned our brief re-injection into society? Here we were surrounded with something so basic to my life I could only think of it as an element. How could we survive without other voices? Here, at El Rey Sol, a wondrous event was underway, a party where we dreamily floated from one laughing group to another more serious, leaving each, respectively, laughing and contemplating, but each affected by our observations of their patter and us by theirs. This was what I was best at. How could I live without it?

Maybe this was the reason we'd found the bay in the first place, then subsequently had not wanted to leave. I was trying to understand my feelings and sort them out but was interrupted by our very able waiter who was asking if we had decided on our dinner.

We ordered filet mignon, making certain it came from Mexico, and a bottle of Cabernet Sauvignon wine from the Santo Tomás Vineyards we had driven through earlier this day. This filet from a Mexican steer is superior to any filet that we Americans can offer. While it is not as silky as the smaller American cut, it is more savory and still extremely tender. It is typically served wrapped in an aromatic slice of bacon. El Rey Sol placed a daub of Béarnaise sauce in the center of the filet as a crown. This was not difficult to get excited about. As the unaccustomed food and wine and company performed around us we succumbed to the temptations of the evening. For dessert we ordered a rich *flan* and Port wine, and gently entered late evening in the midst of many revelers with unique uniforms.

As the party at El Rey Sol broke up, we paid and said good-bye to our partners-in-meal. It was now late and we walked through the quieting streets, west to the fish market on the pier and the beach, where we had learned to be comfortable and at rest. We sat on the sand and I returned to my focus on the lively time of the earlier evening at El Rey Sol.

In my mind I was coming to a fork in the road. Alone, we were a couple forming a relationship. Could I give what was necessary to cause this to set? Or was I a social flirt that enjoyed wisping through life, full of myself, longing for numerous short-term relationships, with little long-range impact? I didn't want to cause myself to make a decision. Nor did I want Mary Ann to feel my tension and confusion. We were different people and we had different needs. But I wanted to know my own and our direction. I think she did also.

Sitting on the sand, with her head on my arm, with a warm evening behind us we were comfortable and filled with the day. Our conversation worked down to our future:

"I'm enjoying what we're doing tonight."

"Me too," she said.

"It's nice to be with people again, where we can share their thoughts and experiences and sometimes just listen to the table next to us and overhear their conversation and become, privately, part of it. And it's nice to share interests with others."

"But it's also nice to have something only to us."

"Right," I said. "Where we're living gives us freedom from others and from the pressures they create. But when we are here with others, I miss society. It's confusing because we can't have it both ways." I went on.

"I love you and can't wait to get back to the bay. I saw something in myself earlier tonight that I didn't like. I saw a salesman and I saw an outgoing person. I'm not that way when it's just you and me, alone on our beach. It bothers me because I'm not sure this image works with our relationship. You're a natural person. You are yourself above all else. When you're alone, with me, or around others you are constant. What am I? I can't even answer that question myself. How could I ask you? I like lots of people and I identify with them almost immediately. Within ranges, if someone I like likes something, then so do I. My opinions change with the company I keep. I don't mean that I have no standards, you know that I do. But I enjoy being around people enjoying almost anything. I enjoy being alone for these months because, not only is it helping us understand our relationship together, but also because I am getting to know myself. It's much easier without all the noises of work, parties, extended family, outside rules and whatever else clutters up a relationship."

How can two lives intertwine in the confusion and fuss of contemporary society? Before Baja we lived in the midst of a continuous traffic jam. The bay had offered us the opportunity to build a relationship upon our basic needs, depending on each other for complete physical and emotional support. Our more social side places demands on the practical and financial issues. How do we fix this? I really don't know. What I do know is that we will most likely leave here in a few months, maybe a year at most, and return to the society we left. We were raised in the U.S. and our permanent, at rest position will probably remain there. In the meantime, I want to learn as much as I can, about myself and about my wife and about the people around us, and about how to make a relationship between two people sustainable and survivable. I don't want us to get deeper into this relationship only to have it fall apart in a few years, with a couple of kids who'll suffer because we didn't think and plan and ensure that we were going somewhere together.

It was cool and dark and we were alone on the beach. Here on the Pacific the waves were much bigger than on the Sea of Cortez side and they crashed on the shore. At the bay there were usually no waves but just quiet lapping between the water and beach, the quiet tinkling sounds of the smooth round stones of Las Cuevitas.

We sat without talking for a while, the wine wearing thin, enjoying the remnants of a warm evening in the cooling air. We could look back from the beach and see the activity of the town, couples walking along Avenida López Mateos and Boulevard Lázaro Cárdenas and the side streets, shops closing for the night. Faint music came from the cantinas, slowing as the night progressed from hot rock to steamy slow dances. We listened to the sounds of the town that were now so foreign to us and yet not unfriendly or unwelcome. It was clear that we were in the midst of an experience rush—we were stretching ourselves and I think we were both proud of it. Whatever we were experiencing was going to influence us individually and together for the rest of our lives.

Much of the west coast of Baja is subject to summer fogs and cool evenings. This was the case tonight. We stood and brushed the sand off of each other and walked down to the pier and fish market. Many vendors were preparing fish tacos for customers, laying out condiments: diced cucumbers, Mexican mayonnaise, marinated onions, cilantro, lime, *pico de gallo*, guacamole. Groups of people were sitting in folding chairs beside tables and bars, drinking beer and eating tacos. We walked out to the end of the pier and then back, and along the beach and toward the town and the hotel, talking, holding hands, thinking about our future.

There really wasn't a way to know where our relationship would go from here, or for us to control what happened with our lives in the future. There were no guarantees. What we had was a chance to make the best of what we wanted. We had chosen a different path than many others. Personally, I have always been convinced that anything unique is better than anything routine. It would take a long while, but we would just have to wait and see where our paths led. Both of us were at peace.

Walking through the town, most of the businesses and restaurants were closed or closing. A few cafés poured coffee for a few tiring guests and the streets were calming from the business of the evening. The fog was getting heavier. Bugs circled the streetlights, and I felt the foreign dampness of the cool west coast air.

While looking at the displays through the windows of the closed shops along Avenida López Mateos, Mary Ann took my hand. We were content. When we reached the hotel we were still warm with the events of the evening: the dinner, the beach, the town in the night. Inside the rooms, we closed the shades against the cool air, leaving the windows open. We modeled for each other the clothing we had bought that day, then undressed and went to bed. Later in the night, unable to sleep, I thought that every experience has the potential of becoming a disaster or a prize. Mary Ann and I had collected some unique experiences recently and we were on our way toward more. In my eyes, that built character. Neither of us would be wrong to do that, regardless of whatever faced us later in life. I was pleased to be where we were and looking forward to the morning and our continuing choices.

The noises during the night were strange and kept us from sleeping soundly, something to be expected after the solitude of our isolated beach. Ensenada was full of forgotten noises: truck airbrakes, car horns, late music from a rowdy bar, a drunken fight, a police siren. We had been away from so many sounds for so long that they weren't part of what we expected. By morning we were tired but ready to get up and get underway with the day.

We never discussed it afterwards but I know we had both been obliged to consider our futures and our relationship on this visit. We were returning to paradise to continue forming the basis of a new family, a bond that would hold, sometimes strong and sometimes not, through trials and pains, the brightness or glory and the inky blackness of despair that would last us through our lives to an unforeseeable end. Unnamed children would result from this union. We would be responsible for their early lives. They would depend on us, play with friends, attend school, mature, and eventually leave our family home to marry and bear children of their own. After it was all done we would have only each other. It was more than symbolic when we turned the truck around and headed south, together.

Return to the Bay

Our plan was to follow the road back in the direction of the bay until we saw the power poles end. There we hoped to buy a cheap LPG refrigerator, because people always prefer electricity over LPG. We followed the same chain of villages, the pearls of the west coast, in the reverse direction we had come the day before. Around Colonia Vicente Guerrero, north of San Quintín, the poles stopped. We stopped at a hardware store and asked where would be a place to find a used refrigerator. The shopkeeper told us about a community center where we might ask. This proved true and we were soon en route to the house of a family with one for sale.

We located the house, parked and walked to the door. There was no need to knock, as the resident family and the whole neighborhood were aware of the arrival of two gringos. A man met us at the door. When I explained that we were looking for a refrigerator he smiled and welcomed us in. It took a minute to realize that we were actually looking at a refrigerator, and that it was really an old one. But it was on its top, upside down. And there were flowers growing out of the bottom, which was, at this point, the top.

We collected ourselves enough to realize that there was no way out of this situation without asking about those things that made no sense to us. The man told us, in a manner that made me assume we should have understood from the beginning, that older gas refrigerators can develop some kind of "bubble" that prevents them from cooling properly. Standing them on their tops for a period of time fixes the problem. While I didn't even have a concept of the problem or its cure, I had been told this before. As we stood gawking at the flowers, the man assured us that it worked just fine; it just had to be burped every so many years. Right.

I have never bought a major appliance, albeit very used, with greater misgiving. We were hundreds of hard miles from home and buying a very used but sensitive device that was positioned upside down with flowers growing from its underside. How could we go wrong?

But the man was convincing and I have never known a Mexican to be able to meet you eye-to-eye and tell so tall a tale. So we believed him and closed the deal and I paid him forty dollars and, with qualifying instructions about not leaving it in a horizontal position for long, he helped us load the refrigerator into the back of the truck. And off down the road we went. In El Rosario, the last outpost going south, we picked up a forty-gallon LPG tank and had it filled. There was no room in the bed of the truck, so we chained it onto the front bumper, on top of the winch and toolboxes. By now the truck was pretty well loaded down. As we geared up and headed south I could see the temperature of the engine was higher that normal. It continued to rise slowly for the next hundred or more kilometers and, by the time we reached the friendly family living at El Crucero, the dirt road heading toward the east, we were running very hot. This is a bad situation in the desert.

I pulled off the road and up to the house where years before I had met the owner, with my old friend Epifanio. My mind flooded with memories of him and our time at this remote ranch, and of the many times I had passed this way since Epifanio had died.

An unfamiliar man left the doorway of the ranch and came toward the truck. I climbed out of the cab and asked him if he had water from his well that I could use to fill my radiator. He said that they had little water and that the well was dry. From the back of the truck I pulled several gallon bottles of water we'd kept for just this problem. The radiator didn't take much, so we left him with what water remained in our supply, keeping only a small reserve. I realized that the problem that was causing our engine to overheat was not a shortage of water; the LPG cylinder on the front bumper was blocking air from flowing through the radiator. There was little we could do to rearrange the contents of the truck in any way that would help the problem, so we continued south in the rising heat with the propane cylinder on the bumper. I had learned from Sammy Díaz, at the bay, that traveling south along the central desert, cars always ran hotter than traveling north. The reason for this was that the prevailing wind was from the northwest and followed the car going with it. Thus, less air passed through the radiator going south. But we continued and I kept an eye on the gauges.

We passed the junction, turning onto the bay road. It was sixty-six kilometers of dirt driving to the bay. I was careful to not beat the refrigerator too badly with the rough road.

Two hours later we entered the village. We were so anxious to get the refrigerator working that we drove straight through the village without stopping. Six kilometers south we turned onto the road that led to the beach and our hut. I pulled the truck up, onto the dune where the hut was situated. The two of us pulled and pushed, getting the old and heavy refrigerator out of the back of the Land Cruiser. Finally it stood at the rear of the truck in the sand. I was hoping that we hadn't been so rough with it that we would need to burp it again.

It took the two of us the better part of an hour to move that box the twenty feet to its new location inside, against the back wall of the hut. This was the coolest, most protected place we could find in our little world on the beach. I worked the fuel tank off the bumper and rolled it behind the hut and fed the fuel lead through the wall of fronds and went inside to connect it. I opened the valve and lit the flame under the back of the heating box. Now was the hard part.

It was about four in the afternoon when I lit the flame that, with luck, would provide us with cool water and food preservation for the rest of the summer, at least. But we didn't know it would work. We opened the door every fifteen minutes and checked the tiny freezer for cold. Every time we were more and more disappointed. Did the fellow lie to us for the money? How could we have been so trusting? How long should it take before we could see that it was working? Was it too hot for it to work; was it overwhelmed? Finally we decided that it was too intense just sitting and waiting to see if it worked.

We changed clothes and sat in the damp sand on our beach, tired from driving eight hundred kilometers over dirt and badly paved roads in the last two days. We had been so excited about the refrigerator that we had forgotten how glad we were to be home.

The sun was setting behind us in a bank of clouds along the west coast and the pelicans were heading north for the night. The nightly rituals were falling into place. It was good to be back in our little home, surrounded with only known and friendly objects. We fixed a simple dinner and sat reading before it was completely dark, then lit the lantern and sat outside for a few minutes. I felt that this was as much a home as I had ever known. There was no way to compare it with other homes in the sense of a child in a house with his parents, or a supposed home later in life with children. I only knew that this place and its environment, including Mary Ann, was where I wanted to be right now. I had enjoyed our trip to town. And now we were home. It was *our* home. In fact, we owned our own home, north of L.A., but it could never be more our home than this little hut on a sand dune in Bahía de los Angeles.

Before we went to bed I checked the refrigerator. It had been several hours since we had opened the door, and when I did, looking at the freezer I could see the small fuzzy crystals of ice forming on the aluminum casing.

R & R

The days idled by, filled with blue water and sky and the sand and stones of our beach. The view from the hut included only those elements. There were so few things to consider among them that my mind slowly unwound from the years of living under the gun with one eye always on the clock and my nose to the grindstone. I had never been so relaxed. The knots were working their way out of my shoulders.

Living primitively, it took longer to perform the basic necessities than it did living in a more regular environment. But there was no schedule to meet. Cooking, bathing, washing clothes and dishes, and hut maintenance all became processes that we did leisurely and without thinking. We got up when we wanted; we went to sleep when we wanted, and we usually took siesta during the hottest part of the afternoon. Often we drove to the southern end of the bay, where there was a series of lagoons, and watched the egrets and herons working the shallows for food. The water in the lagoons was so still some evenings you could see the reflection of the Santa Ana and Bahía mountains and the sunset behind them. A few miles further south was the deserted Las Flores mine where Antero Díaz had worked for years before evolving into the patriarch of Bahía de los Angeles. The area around Las Flores was a cactus forest, sustained by the cooling mists of the night and the occasional *chubascos* that were captured in the bowl formed by the Calamajué range and Punta Colorado, the southern tip of the bay.

The early evening was our favorite time, when the colors became exaggerated with the golden hues and long shadows thrown by the sun. There was always some stretch of beach that we enjoyed, taking long walks, looking for shells or anything interesting that might have washed up. As the temperature dropped back into the double digits the animals regained their strength and slowly began their search for food. I'm certain that the lack of complexity in our surroundings caused us to become less complex too. I noticed in myself a rebirth of caring that had been missing for years. I paid attention to simple things and gained a new understanding of my environment and the ecology of the earth.

Returning to the hut after an evening walk, the tide was going out and we had been gone for quite a while. A murex, a Coue's spindle shell, about four inches long, lay in front of our hut. I picked it up to keep but noticed that it smelled. The snail inside the shell had died. I tossed it back on the beach and we finished the evening and went to bed. The next morning I got up and went out to fish. The shell was there on the sand. It was covered with sow bugs, eating the remnants of the snail. By the next day I noticed that the sow bugs were gone, but sand fleas were doing their work. Over the course of the next several days the tiny animals feeding off the remains became so small that I couldn't see them. In the end the shell was polished clean and had provided nutrition for a whole universe of small beach creatures. Nothing had gone to waste. I realized what a perfect order there was to life. I doubt that these animals lived in perfect harmony and I'm sure they all had their pecking order, but it had been worked out millions of years ago and the treaties were well understood. The environment I had been watching was about as efficient as it could get. Everyone got along, knew how to behave, and everything was used efficiently.

Once, as a young boy, I had been out in the desert with a friend and our .22-caliber rifles. We shot a rabbit, skinned it, disposed of the carcass without ado, took the skin home and dried it. Our parents didn't like this. On a later trip with my buddy, we were walking along a path in the same desert area and a small bird landed a few yards away in the branch of a tree. I took aim at the bird and fired without thought. The bird was struck and fell dead in the middle of the path. I was pleased with my shot. But before I could move to collect the dead bird another bird flew from the same bush and landed beside the one I had shot. The second bird hopped around his friend, turning his head from side to side trying to understand what had happened. I stood stunned, watching this. When I could move, I approached and the second bird flew away. Something in me snapped and I sat down and cried. Later I was reading the anthropologist and playwright Robert Ardrey who explained to me that birds mate for life. I never forgot the bird I killed for no reason. Turning a grain of sand in a river, I had changed the course of the world irrevocably.

In later years I re-read John Steinbeck's *Log from the Sea of Cortez*. In this book there is a passage that did well to sum up my understanding of our wild environment.

"That night" writes Steinbeck, "we intended to run across the Gulf and start for home. It was good to be running at night again, easier to sleep with the engine beating. Tiny at the wheel inveighed against the waste of fish by the Japanese [who, even in the 1930s and '40s, were abusing the gulf]. To him it was a waste complete, a loss of something. We discussed the widening and narrowing picture. To Tiny the fisherman, having as his function not only the catching of fish but the presumption that they would be eaten by humans, the Japanese were wasteful. And in that picture he was very correct. But all the fish actually were eaten; if any small parts were missed by the birds they were taken by the detritus-eaters, the worms and cucumbers. And what they missed was reduced by the bacteria. What was the fisherman's loss was a gain to another group. We tried to say that in the macrocosm nothing is wasted, the equation always balances. The elements which the fish elaborated into an individual physical organism, a microcosm, go back again into the undifferentiated macrocosm which is the great reservoir. There is not, nor can there be, any actual waste, but simply varying forms of energy. To each group, of course, their must be waste—the dead fish to man, the broken pieces to gulls, the bones to some and the scales to others—but to the whole there is no waste. The great organism, Life, takes it all and uses it all."

What I had learned from my recent shell observations on our beach was that nature has great efficiency in her distribution of resources, and we have no right to allow ourselves to be any less efficient. While this thought is not in disagreement with the quote above, it represents common thought sixty years after Steinbeck's (not so common) thought of things being more or less limited. The more I watched the animals with which we shared our world, the more I realized that anything that could be used, was. As a matter of necessity and also to vent my anger at the early morning intrusion into my life, I would pick up a sandal and swat as many flies as possible as they swarmed around my face in the dawning light. By the time I got up, I had managed to kill about thirty of these devils. They lay lifeless in the sand of our beds. One morning I lay in bed later than usual, tired or reading. As I lay there I saw ants carrying off the flies I had killed. Nothing went to waste.

We could see that there was no sense of sympathy or empathy among animals. Animals that had additional burdens, a broken limb, a deformation, just carried on with life as usual. We never sensed that they felt sorry for themselves, they just reacted to the fact of life and did the best they could. This commonly meant they were willing to take additional chances to get adequate food. After all, that is what most animals spend almost all their time doing in the wild. Wounded wildlife often would wander so close to the hut that they would have been in danger had we been hungry.

Between most animals, there were territorial wars and much fighting over food. When I cleaned my fish each morning the beach was filled with hundreds of brown pelicans and California gulls. The pelicans were voiceless but aggressive with their beaks, going after each scrap of fish I threw their way. The gulls were vocal to the point of being offensive. They stood on the beach or floated on the nearby water and squawked their indignation at their peers. The most assertive and longest winded won the contest.

These birds were hungry and on the lookout for a free meal. When I threw a piece of fish gut it almost never hit the water before it was caught by a flying beak.

The weaker birds were always willing to take risks that the more fit birds were not. Often those that came the closest had been previously injured. Occasionally a bird would be tangled with a piece of fishing line, or have a small lure caught in its beak. If I was fast enough I could catch the bird and undo a bit of damage. But their wings were strong and their beaks could draw blood easily if they weren't restrained. Through these episodes I found myself to be a good guy and a bad guy as well. No matter how conservative I was I could still do damage to the lives of these wild things. I tried to cause myself to think as they might, but this was a difficult objective.

The birds were accustomed to living with each other, within and across species boundaries, and while there was a lot of noise, there was seldom unnecessary or unwarranted aggression. What I might call sad things happened, but they were not usually without a reason.

It also seemed that these animals had a limited, if any, concept of time. By that I mean the passage of time, not the time of day. What is time? I wondered. We measure it by the occurrence of events, I think. But intermixed in these events is our concept, as humans, of death and of influence over our futures. I don't think less complex animals share these thoughts. When we left our dogs on the beach for a few minutes or for an afternoon, they were equally happy when we returned. I think they just noticed our absence at some point and didn't like that fact but then went about whatever they were doing until we returned, and were glad to see us again.

The life forms I could identify with the least were the fish I caught every morning for dog food. I regretted every life I poled from the shallow waters in front of the hut, watching the puckered face of every triggerfish, cabrilla, and puffer fish I caught and apologizing silently for my deeds. But I still thought of them as less refined life forms than the living things on or above the surface of the water.

I used octopus that we caught off the small decaying pier at La Gringa located at the north end of the bay for bait; it kept for several days in the heat without spoiling. How could I measure the intelligence and sensitivity of an octopus? The fish that snapped at the bait were so frenzied that they were fighting with others for the hook. How smart was that? I was confused by the concept of intelligence. I hadn't thought at that point that all of us come from a unique environment and we all have unique forms of intelligence and knowledge of how we might use it. Humans have chosen a measure of intelligence as the speed at which we learn, but we are only good at measuring our ability to learn with things we can understand and that we need to learn. I began to think that, to measure a fish's intelligence, I would have to live as a fish to determine their otherwise invisible and unknowable priorities of life and death.

The Local Atmosphere

The village of Bahía de los Angeles was only six kilometers north of our hut, but the road was so rough and our truck so old that the trip was difficult and took about half an hour to negotiate. We sometimes wanted some kind of social outlet or a meal from one of the two small cafés, so by late afternoon we would start the truck and head off for the village in a cloud of dust and smoke from the engine, winding our way from the beach to the road leading back into the village. The village road stayed near the water for a kilometer or so and then climbed into the steep foothills of Cerro Santa Ana and climbed behind Cerro Angelito, the hill which had years ago been mined. The narrow gauge tracks still followed us around the hill before we dropped back to the beach. In this area the entire beach was volcanic, rolling a good distance out into the water. It must have been an awesome sight when Volcán Santa Evita blew, throwing ash and molten lava far out into the Sea of Cortez and streaming down the steep sides of the mountains as they fell sharply into the sea. There would have been no chance of escape if natives had been living here at the time.

Along the road south of the village there were a few simple homes. These were weather beaten and covered with dust. Behind each house was an old car or truck. These homes belonged to families that flew private planes from the States for long weekends or vacations. Many were accompanied by small outbuildings containing electrical generators and water cisterns. The houses were mostly built from rock the same reddish color that was quarried in the nearby mountains. We passed Mike's home and stopped to say hello and then continued the last kilometer before the village.

We pulled up beside the Díaz ranch and waited for the dust to settle before climbing out of the truck and going up the steps onto the patio, an elevated area roughly thirty meters wide and forty meters long. In Mama's self-service store we took a strawberry soda and a Carta Blanca beer from a cooler. There was no one in the store, so I recorded our purchase in the nearby logbook under our name. We went outside to the patio's breezeway, where there was usually a breath of air moving between the store/restaurant and the Díaz house. Several fishermen were relaxing after their day's run. Acquainted by now with most of the townspeople in one way or another, we greeted the men and sat down beside them. The talk was, of course, where the fish were. Some men from this group were shark fishermen who regularly worked the coast south of our hut. In the 1970s there was abundant fishing in the bay and little conservation was practiced. There was little use for the meat of the shark. The value lay in the fins that the Japanese used for shark fin soup. The shark fins were hauled on a truck to Ensenada where they were shipped to Japan. Often our dogs would catch a scent from down the beach and rush down to roll and cover their own scent in huge mounds of shark guts and flesh. We often chased them off for a distance as they stank so badly.

We sat in the shade drinking our beer and soda and talking with the fishermen. Inside the kitchen of the restaurant the Díaz daughters and nieces were cooking dinner, gossiping and laughing. A couple of small children played on the patio, kicking a ball to each other and imagining they were famous soccer players. Several single engine airplanes were tethered behind the hotel rooms on the beach, having landed and taxied on the dirt strip right up to the rooms. Antero Díaz, known to all as Papa, was in his office, which was adjacent to the patio, talking to someone on his ship-to-shore radio. Papa was about fifty-five when we first met him in 1974, and was very much an alpha male. His wife, Cruz, whom everyone called Mama, passed from their house into the store and the kitchen to oversee the final preparation of the meal. She was a few years younger than Antero, and they had a number of children. Antero had spent years working the Las Flores mine, another five kilometers south of our hut. He had been somehow cheated by the mine and quit and came to the town and over the years become the patriarch of Bahía de los Angeles. He now operated a sport fishing concession for the tourists that flew in from the States. Cruz managed the store, the kitchen, and the several hotel rooms on the beach. Sammy, Mama and Papa's oldest son, was about thirty-two, married, and had his own children. He ran a *taller mecánico* shop behind the main compound where they all lived. Sammy's younger brother, Antero Jr. (known as Chubasco), helped out in the store and kitchen. They had a flock of sisters: the oldest was Rosita, then Elvira, Aurora, Prieta, Anita, and finally, María.

The Díaz family was known throughout the peninsula. Antero was the senior member of the village, pretty much the founder of the current collection of souls. He was respected by the locals since he was able to attract and entertain the Americans that drifted south from the *frontera*. His fishing boat, about fifty feet long, formed the principal vessel of his small fleet of *pangas*, a style of large outboard-engined skiff that was capable of handling the unpredictable gulf currents and conditions. Antero was confident, friendly and always busy, secure and in control of his environment, with a face that radiated from atop his large barrel-chested body. He shook hands firmly, like an American, whereas most Mexicans shook hands limply, as the firm handshake was outside the traditions of this small fishing village.

Mama was more reserved than her husband and appeared to be more serious. She was born in 1914. As we got to know her and became friends, she would often save for us some special tidbit she had in the kitchen or a special candy or fishing lures that someone had brought to the store. We shared talk about the happenings of the family and town and through her we felt connected to her family and the village.

We came from the hut into the village every few days for tortillas and the occasional vegetables that found their way down from the north. We would stop for a beer and soda at the Díazs'. There was always activity there and a friendly feeling; their wide patio was a magnet for the village and guests.

Antero had come to Baja from a mining community near Mexico City in 1935. He had originally worked in a mining community near El Arco, in Baja's central peninsula, south of the bay. After a number of trips back and forth across the Sea of Cortez, and through the births of their older children, he finally brought Cruz to the bay and they settled once and forever. When they first arrived, according to an oral family history, they slept for some time under a tree. No houses were there at that time, only a small fish camp on the beach.

If I reflect for only an instant on the scene surrounding the village; a palm oasis with fresh water, plentiful seafood, a climate that required minimal protection, it seems impossible to me that this site has not been inhabited continuously since the time of the first appearance of humans on the peninsula.

There were few buildings at the village when Antero arrived, but John Steinbeck reports in the *Log from the Sea of Cortez*, that on April 1, 1940 (or 1941), several substantial buildings were there, "screened and modern." Papa had been busy building a village while Mama had been building a family.

According to Samuel and Chubasco, in the mid-1950s an American named Harry Eslip somehow arrived on the scene at the village. He was penniless when he arrived. Papa gave him the equivalent of fifty dollars and enough gas, presumably airplane fuel, to get him back to the *frontera*. A year later Harry returned. With him, in the order of importance mentioned by the Díaz men, Harry brought as gifts for Antero: a .752-caliber Russian rifle, five hundred bullets, and information that his workers would be arriving shortly to construct a tin building for the village. This building was standing in fine, if dusty, condition in 1974, when Mary Ann and I first arrived on the scene. (It stands, in exactly the same condition, in 2005.)

According to the Díaz boys, Harry came back again in 1958 with two fishing boats for Antero. It can be assumed at this point that Harry was trying to set Antero up in the fishing business. In 1959 Harry sent three boats; the next year, four. Antero didn't need money — they were friends.

Between 1965 and 1968 Harry was continuously flying Antero between Hermosillo and the bay. Harry's magneto was always acting up and Antero, who apparently understood engines, continuously prompted Harry to fix the magneto. On a day when Antero was not on board, the engine failed and the aircraft fell to earth, killing Harry, his daughter-in-law, and her son, in Ontario, California.

Papa started a turtle business with his boats. He took Samuel at the age of six to Ensenada. Sammy was told he was "helping" his father. Sammy remembers sleeping the whole way. He laughs when he relates this.

Profits and Losses

The provisions available in the village were limited. Ice was only available when a truck arrived to haul fish to Ensenada. Other than the Díaz market there was only Dos Pinos, on a side street a few hundred meters from the Díaz ranch. Both stores carried the same basic goods: canned vegetables, tuna, and sardines; a few limp fruits and vegetables, usually a wilted cabbage; dusty boxes of crackers and cookies; a propane cooler that tried to cool the beer and sodas it housed; and canned evaporated milk. There was nothing truly fresh unless it was by accident. There was no meat, and no fresh milk. The nearest town that had even a small chance of offering a more optimistic collection of goods was Guerrero Negro, Black Warrior, several hours of hard driving to the south on the west coast.

Locating goods and services in the village was difficult; there were many offerings that we didn't know about. Advertising was done by word of mouth. In a collection of souls so small, why did they need any signs? Everyone who lived there, even in the most remote ranches and farms, knew where everything was in the village because that was where it had always been. The only signs I can remember from those days were signs painted by hand for tire repairs, *llantera*, for the gringos.

This need to have local knowledge was more endearing than the advertising I was used to. In the States we proudly announced the availability of all sorts of goods, creating a need and selling as much as possible. In this small Mexican village no one was interested in advertising anything for sale. If someone had a need, a solution could be found at an agreed price. In the States we were tied to corporate profits and business feasibility studies. In this isolated village in remote Mexico the people were occupied with the focus of living within their means and not encouraging unnecessary desires.

We were in town one evening as the day closed and the sun was setting over the mountains. During the day the Díaz family had slaughtered a steer from their ranch, a few kilometers south of our hut and carried the great beast's body in the bed of an open pickup into the village. There they had butchered the carcass. Antero had lit a mass of mesquite wood, gathered from the desert by salivating townsmen in anticipation of a feeding frenzy, in a fifty-five-gallon oil drum. A piece of expanded metal had been cut from scrap and placed on top of the drum.

Antero laid long thin strips of beef across the grill. The smell of searing beef and garlic was all-consuming. The aroma of barbecuing beef wafted throughout the village faster than a young man could run its length. Within minutes villagers gathered around the fire. No one had to be invited; they all knew a Díaz steer had been slaughtered. Everyone was welcome. The village was usually well fed, but the primary source of protein was fish and frijoles. The smell of blood and beef cooking over hot coals drew the entire village to the Díaz home.

Months of eating fish and feeling healthy were lost immediately. A number of primitive instincts were triggered. I wanted red meat. In my mind I could feel my hands moving toward my mouth with a torn chunk of meat, dripping fresh blood, my nostrils filled with the scent of iron and coagulants. I could feel my teeth sink into the flesh, tearing the fibers, pulling against the resistance, a primeval instinctive rush that caused adrenaline to course throughout my own flesh until I was one with the beast I had killed. Killing was an extraordinary act for a human. For an animal surviving in the wild it was instinctive and necessary; they must have felt very close to their prey as it lay dying in their clenched jaws.

As Antero carved and passed out the cooked steer to the men standing beside the barbecue and then to the rest of the audience, I felt he must be in his element. Men just like being heroes.

On an evening several weeks later we came to the village to celebrate Antero's fiftieth birthday. Once again it was a village-wide event. Many of the men were congregating around a punch bowl filled with margaritas and actual *ice* on the Díaz patio. An aging group of mariachis was playing wonderfully warm music on severely worn instruments on the patio and the party was well under way. The women were taking care of the families and other necessary details while the men talked and drank beer and margaritas. Plates of fish, rice, beans, beef, salad, and salsa circulated and we all visited, telling our stories and hearing other's stories of tragedies, marriages, childbirths, diseases, and other significant events. Mary Ann and I were not accustomed to being with so many people and I was drinking from the bottomless margarita bowl throughout the evening. Pleased to be included in this event, I felt that we had been accepted into the society of the village. I was so happy with this status that I drank from the watering hole way more than I should have. By sometime around ten at night I was maxed out and was getting humorously obnoxious, at least to myself. We decided it was time to make our departure and said good night to our friends. Our Land Cruiser was parked alongside the Díaz patio, which happened to be where everyone had collected. There was a minor storm, because the wind was blowing, gusting to about thirty knots off the westward mountains. Of course, I chose this moment to criticize Mary Ann for being too slow or something, and just as we were climbing into the truck I made some particularly nasty comment designed to provoke. In an action I had not experienced from her in our short relationship, she threw her well-aimed purse directly at my head. It was a very dark night; the moon had not yet risen. The only light was from the million stars twinkling overhead.

While I had been drinking, I was not oblivious to this speedy pro-jectile, incoming at warp speed. I ducked just in time and the purse sped by and fell lifelessly into the sand on my side of the truck. Al-though we didn't know it because we were still arguing, the purse had opened as it fell. Among its contents was the money to support the remainder of our trip. Nineteen one-hundred-dollar bills floated freely on the wind. We were in the midst of a hundred townsfolk, partying, some of whom had gathered around to tell us good-bye. There sudden-ly was much commotion, with people scattering, but it was difficult to comprehend it all with the tequila pulsing through my brain. I was looking frantically everywhere around me to see what was happening. People were gathering in what seemed to be small groups talking rap-idly and with animation. In the fog of my mind I couldn't put events together into a stream of images I could digest. Confused and nearly panicking, I closed my eyes for an instant, trying to clear my head. When I opened them Sammy was standing directly in front of me. With the wind-driven dust and margaritas fogging my vision and blowing his hair, Sammy held his hand out toward mine. I thought he had felt bad about our arguing and wanted to shake hands in understanding. As

I reached for his hand, still confused, his fingers relaxed a bit, his hand opening. His thumb, still firmly in place against his palm, secured sixteen one-hundred-dollar bills.

As my mind struggled to comprehend the past few seconds, I knew that when Mary Ann's purse hit the sand the people around us had immediately recognized that our money was blowing in the wind and had done whatever possible to capture it. The activity that had confused me seconds after was the crowd scrambling, looking frantically for the lost bills.

Each of us can count on a single hand the experiences of utmost importance in our lives—special events—births, deaths, marriages of children, a first lost love of your youngest child, and so on. I remember this moment at that level.

The money itself was significant, but the gift of integrity, honesty, and friendship was far more meaningful. Within an instant in time many people had wildly scrambled to gather money blowing across a beach in the dark and without a moment to think had all given it to one of their peers who had returned it to the person who had lost it. When I think about qualities of life in a society, the villagers of Bahía de los Angeles are a symbol to me.

We didn't insult their honesty with a monetary reward. But because it happened so quickly in an accidental, spontaneous situation, I knew that it was a reaction of the village as a whole—a collective gut reaction. They were a homogeneous element living in a threatening world. Yet they had protected us against an unknown. To treat it as exceptional was unacceptable, as it was their norm.

Mary Ann and I were more than thankful for such honest friends. We were still burdened though with the loss of three hundred dollars out of a budget of two thousand dollars to last us the year. When I went to bed that night the events of the evening were heavy on my mind.

When I woke up they were still there. How could we have lost three hundred dollars through such a stupid accident?

As I thought about it I realized that part of my problem was that I felt foolish, that I no longer fit in my surroundings: many of the people with whom we had celebrated Antero's birthday didn't *have* that much money to lose. How could I identify with them and they with me when our environment was so different? I was away on a vacation that would last a year when others couldn't take any vacation at all. I was basing my value of individuals on money or power rather than intrinsic worth. Character and values were emphasized in the environment in which I was raised. And so was money. My family had, for the most part, been financially secure, but I had grown up competing for money as one measure of my value. I tended to establish my self-worth on the amount of money I could earn, or my future earning potential. In Baja social time is valued over money. This is also true in much of Europe and parts of Asia, Africa, and the Middle East. Americans will do more for money than any other people, given that they are not starving. Americans work longer hours and take less vacation than just about every other relatively comfortable country.

But here we were, on a beach among a set of people that lived very different lives from ours. In many ways their standards were higher than mine. Their need for, and reliance on each other were high. They were a small village woven together through lifetimes of personal experiences. They had friends who had helped deliver their children and enemies who had stolen from them and lived down the earthen street. They had worked together, faced *ciclones* and *tormentas* and deaths and loves together. Yet they functioned as a single entity when it was necessary.

My contribution to the planet was to help send spacecraft racing through the universe. Someone else's job was to put fish on everyone's plate. How could our individual contributions to society be compared? My home village in the foothills north of Los Angeles was busy making and enforcing laws that encouraged us to work and contribute to the gods of the gross national product. We joined clubs and mixed with others like us and moved into the suburbs where society wore off all our rough edges like a rock tumbler. At the bay, the society was more tolerant of a person's rough edges. Living on the edge of a continent had given this small community a need to face challenges alone and not expect support from a larger entity. How easy it is, in U.S. society, to pretend to be whatever you wanted others to think you were. But here in the village what you were wasn't determined by a dream but what was collectively thought of you. There was no hiding the *actual* you. And the more others thought differently of you than you thought of yourself the greater the external pressure to align with that difference. This was social averaging in practice.

The next morning a man who worked as a fisherman for Sammy came by our hut. The sun had been up for an hour and I was done fishing for dog food and was cooking the results. His name was Margarito, I believe, but that was so many years ago and I was never sure of it even then. We knew him from saying hello and short conversations in the village. Margarito lived with his wife and teenage son and daughter in a house in the village. He was darkly tanned from spending many hours daily in a boat on the water. I had never been out in a boat fishing in those days so I knew little of the ways of that world. Margarito was sorry that we had lost money in the storm. I told him how grateful we were for everyone's help recovering the money and how unbelievable it was that, with the darkness and the wind, they had only allowed three bills to escape. Soon, Margarito got to the point that had brought him visiting—he could hire me to work with him and his son on his boat to help us recover the money we had lost.

I had just enough self-control to hold my mouth shut. But my heart wept. And I knew immediately that I had to respectfully decline the offer. The only fishing I had done at that point was from along the beach at Laguna, California, while I was stationed at Camp Pendleton. I would be a real danger in the boat with two experienced fishermen. I also knew that Margarito was trying to ease our concerns about lost money. This was his way of telling us everything would work out. But it was a most gracious act, a reminder that I integrated into my database of qualities, collected from humans of all types and from many locations.

Margarito's sentiment was echoed by many of our acquaintances in the village when we visited later that week. Rather than laughing at this comparatively rich gringo, they were supportive and kind, full of warmth and understanding.

Looking at our financial loss from the present, I am glad we lost that money. I came to realize that if we needed others more often we would find there are many wonderful people waiting in the wings to be supportive. When we live our lives completely controlled and without the possibility of need, we allow many positive things to pass us by.

A Family Visit

Somewhere in August, when it's so hot you can't get out of the ocean, my mother and brother arrived, unannounced, for a visit. We had no clue they were coming because they didn't know about the limited mail service. One lazy afternoon we were wallowing in the water trying to cool off when we heard a vehicle in the distance. Car sounds were always of interest to us because we were never busy and they were unusual. We climbed out of the water and walked toward the road to see who was passing.

As a Jeep neared the track leading to our hut, I thought it looked like my brother's, but that seemed impossible. It was moving slowly over the rocks and sand and brush in the road and I squinted, trying to see more clearly. Walking to a nearby sand dune that had better elevation we looked again. It *was* my brother's car and both he and my mother were in it. My mind raced to figure how they could have found us in this isolated place. I had written letters home, but I was not sure if they had reached their destinations. And the descriptions I had given of our location could not have been enough to locate us. Nevertheless, here they were, and we had about sixty seconds to get ready for our first American guests.

We ran out to the junction to greet them and show them the side road to our hut. They were hot and sweating in the heat and humidity, and exhausted from the drive. It was hard to imagine them driving over all the miles of dirt road to get here in a two-wheel-drive Jeep. They parked and we went through the greeting ritual. We helped them get their belongings from the car and into or around the hut, asking how they had ever located us and how long could they stay, and was anything wrong. They had found us by following vague directions we had provided to a friend, and they could stay only a few days. I couldn't imagine my mother sleeping on the sand, but that was a done deal, unless she slept in the car. We got them cool drinks from the refrigerator and sat in a circle talking about the adventures of their trip. Was there a family emergency? Had someone died? Were we at war? None of the above—they'd just come for a visit.

So visit we did. They told us all the events from southern California. They had talked to Mary Ann's family before they left, and carried messages for her. We had received only a single letter from them in the time we had been gone and were thirsty for any and all information. They heaped it on us and we were full of questions about the doings of our friends and haunts and JPL.

We talked and talked and before we knew it the light was softening and the pelicans were soaring north and it was evening. We were excited to fix our first meal for guests and, still talking, moved from the sand of the beach to the smooth stones of the kitchen, all of several meters square, and looked over our meager supplies to decide what we would feed our family.

Mom wanted to help fix dinner. I thought she wanted to experience what it would be like to work in a kitchen such as ours. The three of us were more than there was room for in the small space, so I went back outside and sat with my brother. It was nice to see him and to sit talking and hear feminine voices speaking English in the kitchen, doing things we were used to hearing them do. Our meal was simple and took little to prepare. At one point I heard Mary Ann and Mom talking and something struck me as awkward in the tone of their voices. I laughed to myself, thinking about men's concepts of two women in a small kitchen.

Dinner was ready about the time the sun fell over Santa Ana, spilling its orange rays down the mountain's slopes and into the Sea of Cortez. We lit the lantern, regardless of the bugs it would attract, and sat in the sand to eat. Mary Ann and I still had more questions of home, and Mom and Tony were interested in seeing and hearing about our happenings over the last months. It was fun to describe how we lived and filled our day-to-day needs, laundry, drinking water, bathing, etc. The lantern burned late into that night, throwing its warm golden light on the walls of our hut, the sand, the water and four people enjoying being together. When it came to an end I unrolled my mother's and brother's sleeping bags under our porch and got them settled for the night and we all lay in the sand and talked until we couldn't find another syllable worth uttering.

The next morning I was awake early and fishing before I heard anyone else move. Tony came down to the beach and I handed him the rod. The line was in the water and I told him to reel it in slowly. The fishing was so rich that almost every time I brought the lure in a fish would strike. Within a few seconds he had a good bite and was excited to haul the cabrilla up on the beach and toss it in the bucket. I showed him how to cast the line and he took the pole and brought it in again with another catch. Triggerfish were more fun because of their broad structure: they could fight better, throwing their flat body against the tug of the line lodged in their mouth. But my pleasure that day came from standing on a beach with my brother. I asked him quietly how Mom was doing. She had always had a problem with drinking too much; there were complications in their relationship. Tony told me that she was still hitting the sauce but that they were okay with each other. They had resolved their previous differences.

Before long Mary Ann and Mom were up and had coffee for us all. Tony and I had caught enough fish for the day and we joined them around our oilcloth-covered table. Mornings were the nicest time of day weather-wise. The air wasn't quite hot and there was moisture from the night.

Somewhere about this point, Mom broadsided us with the real reason for their visit. The next twenty-four hours were so stressful that I can't fully recreate how the day unraveled. The reason they had come on this great trek to see us was that they didn't think our marriage was in our best interest.

This didn't come out all at once but unfolded in layer after layer in the fabric of hidden agenda. It also didn't begin in the vindictive, hateful way it ended, but I was initially choking at this attack from my own family.

I had been raised by my mother; my father had died when I was less than a year old. She had not remarried until I was in my early teens and then I was often away at military and parochial boarding schools. My stepfather and mother had only been married three years, long enough to produce my brother while we were living in Cuernavaca, in the 1950s. My whole young life had been spent between boarding schools, living with grandparents and spending time on my own at home with some well-punctuated moments with my mother. She was a great teacher, very ethical and bohemian and artistic and freethinking and loving in her way, but her attention span didn't run long on young children. I resented her wild antics and social performances with her culturally rich friend-set. I never got a lot of attention. But my mother had married well in the financial, cultural, and social senses.

My father came from an old-wealth family out of Pasadena who had made money in a Missouri mill. My stepfather's family had even larger financial holdings and provided for my mother's future after her inevitable divorce from Tony's dad. Here were significant broken relationships, but I grew up listening to arias and marching to John Philip Sousa.

Mary Ann was born into a German family coming out of North Dakota. Her hardworking father was away from home many hours each day. Her mother was a housewife on an allowance who saved money for her Christmas gifts from her weekly stipend. Dad worked sixty hours a week and all holidays as the manager of a department store. Mom cooked pot roast, baked bread, and hated fish. Mary Ann was raised in a completely normal, middle class world. She had a brother and two sisters from the same marriage who could interact on an even keel over the course of their young lives, doing the thing siblings do best—biting, kicking, and lying to each other about meaningless annoyances. Mary Ann was raised in a constant and predictable and loving environment. She did the things a normal child did while living lovingly in a normal and average family. And her favorite music was popular.

My mother knew little of Mary Ann's family. I suspect she was disappointed by them, and found them base. On the other hand it was none of her damned business. *I* found them comfortable and caring. Both of Mary Ann's parents came from large sets of siblings and had learned the importance of integrating early in life. They all knew they had importance and just how limited it was. They formed a social set on their own. But the wants of a parent for a child's spouse must be always ambitious.

Whatever my family's issues were with our marriage, my mother and brother were crossing a dangerous line in questioning decisions Mary Ann and I had made about our lives and future. But my family was not to be cut short of a long and lengthy hearing. They had discussed this issue at length, feeding their own furies as they drove two days to get this off their chest, and weren't giving up. They called me aside and argued with me throughout the day and into the night, trying to get us to come home, to go back to work, to re-evaluate our marriage. I was about as mad as I could get. Who were these people to think they could come to our home and attack us like this? We went to bed that night in a completely different mood than we had the night before.

The next morning we went through our early morning routines quietly. Mom started in again and I exploded and told them that if ruining Mary Ann's and my relationship was the only reason they had come all this way that we didn't need them to stay longer. When they persist-ed, I told them to leave. I couldn't believe all this was happening. It was a bad dream.

Within an hour we had gathered their clothes and camping gear and loaded up their Jeep. They sat in the truck with great pouting. We told them to have a safe trip and that we would be seeing them when-ever we came back to the States.

Off they went away from the beach, up the road that just two days before we had been so surprised to see them come down. A lot can happen in two days.

It took us a few days to get back to our simplified lifestyle after so much disruption and antagonism. But the environment soothed us and presented its own reminders that we had not been paying full attention for the past couple of days. Repairs to the hut and car were needed and laundry was piling up. "Even in this romantic setting we are reduced to such base tasks," I thought, still upset and resentful.

We didn't write or talk to my family until about eight months later, when we were back stateside and stopped by unannounced one day to see my mother. Everything was fine. We never raised the issue again. When we next saw my brother, his visit to the bay was forgotten. The two of them had erased it from their history. I wished my mind were as cooperative and forgiving.

Their attempt to cause trouble in our relationship has been proved wrong many times, and especially now, when we looked at our sons, who are twenty-eight and twenty-six years old. The relationship between Mary Ann and me was a long way from perfect. But it was enduring.

Salt Water and Fresh

I built a fire in the fire pit and lugged bucketsful of seawater up from the beach so we could bathe and Mary Ann could do the laundry. We had a metal pail with a handle that held about two gallons and a larger, flatter bucket that held about twenty. We had built the fire pit so it supported the larger bucket and we filled it with the smaller one.

The simple process that had evolved for our bath and laundry days started with filling the larger bucket with seawater from the smaller and heating it on the fire pit. That was enough water for us both to shower and then wash clothes.

When we had finished bathing, the remainder of the hot water was used for washing clothes. Mary Ann washed the clothes in the large bucket and rinsed them in the sea. She hung them to dry on ropes we had run between the shower and the hut. It usually took only a short time to dry them in the heat, but on humid days it took longer.

For dishes and pans we kept the smaller bucket filled with seawater in the kitchen and deposited dishes and utensils in it after their use. Whenever the bucket got full we lugged the bucket to the shore and washed dishes with seawater and liquid soap. The sand of the shoreline was a great abrasive for the tougher cleaning jobs.

Getting fresh water was a chore and we learned to use it sparingly. There was a spring near the village, in a niche between the bases of Cerro Bahía de los Angeles and Cerro Santa Ana, which kept the population supplied with a manageable amount of water throughout the year. Villagers trekked to the spring daily, carrying their water jars and containers by hand or in the beds of rusty, dust-covered trucks. It was a harder trek for us than it was for the villagers, because of the distance, and we came to the spring usually in concert with other activities, to sit on the Díaz patio with a cold *cerveza* and talk with the fishermen, or to buy food.

The *tiendas* in the village had small supplies of water in one-gallon plastic bottles for sale. But when we had decided to stay for an extended period at the bay we decided we should get used to the spring water. I'd gotten mildly sick once from it but it was generally clean and didn't bother us.

Every few days, in the late afternoon, we would make a list of needs and load the empty five-gallon water jugs and head to the village. This short but rocky trip was always hard on the truck, which groaned under the load. One afternoon we were lumbering down the road and Tortuga, the old lady, was making more than her usual complaints. We stopped in the road and I climbed out and raised her hood. The engine had fallen off its mounts and was several inches below its normal position.

We had changed out the stock Toyota straight six for the Chevy engine, a standard adaptation, but of course it was done by the seat of our pants. Now the motor mounts were coming loose and the whole engine could fall out of the vehicle at any time. There was little I could do there, halfway to the village, so we crept into town and took the truck to Sammy and showed him the unbolted mounts.

He told me to pull the truck over his mechanic's pit and he would fix the problem. I stood with him in the pit while he grunted and sweated, trying to raise the engine until it aligned with the mounts and then re-secure it. Finally, with nothing I could do, I went to get the two of us a beer and tell Mary Ann, talking with Mama Díaz, what was happening.

I walked into the Díaz *tienda*, took two cool beers, and wrote the credit into my account in the small note tablet secured to one of the food racks. When I brought Sammy his beer, he was cursing at the truck, trying to raise the motor several inches with a pry bar. He had a long threaded tool for that purpose, which he placed under the engine and rested on the floor of his pit, then extended the bar by unscrewing it, raising the engine. While I was ineffectively "helping" Sammy, Mary Ann called me to help translate something Mama was saying. After that I walked with Mary Ann to Dos Pinos, where we bought several cans of vegetables. We idled some time away in the village and it was two hours before I remembered Sammy working on our truck.

I walked back to his garage as he was just finishing up the job. The engine was back in place and secure. He warned me that the original bolts had been lost; the ones he had used were the same diameter, but shorter. There was a chance they, too, would fall out, so I should keep an eye on them. I told him I kept an eye on the *entire* truck because it was so old and abused and under-maintained, then asked Sammy what I owed him. He wanted three dollars.

With transportation once again, we headed for the spring, the highest point in the village. Many palm trees surrounded the little oasis, a depression at the very base of the confluence of lava from the two mountains. The wild plants thrived in the moist environment and the early shade of the volcano as the sun set early behind it. I filled our tanks, standing in the shade and cooler air. The water trickled into the five-gallon cans slowly and gave my mind time to wander. I thought about Sammy working on my truck for several hours for three dollars. He could have charged me much more than that, and he knew I would have been happy to pay it. The job was *worth* more. But he had set the price in his mind at a value, which didn't include what the customer could afford. He didn't have *two prices* in mind—he had *one*.

Dinner at the Díaz Ranch

With the Toyota's engine remounted and our jugs filled with fresh water, we stopped at the Díaz ranch and had dinner with a number of fly-ins. The dining room was large and had many long tables around the room. Meals were typically reserved in advance, mostly by the groups of flyers, and were served family style. This not only simplified the work of the staff, it made the event more social. Guests were seated at the same table as other guests in the order they arrived. Everyone shared their day with those sitting around them and the conversation was loud in the tile hall with its windows wide open and the breeze billowing the curtains into the room. Platters of fish were placed every few feet along the tables and were followed with salad, flour tortillas, rice and beans. Whoever wanted drinks retrieved them from the coolers in the market. They would be counted at the end of the meal and added to each bill.

The fly-ins often had tales of their journeys and the problems they encountered in the air. None of them could understand why we would have driven to this place. I wondered how you could see what a place was like from the air; there would be so many details you would miss.

In the Marines, I had been shipped to the Far East during the Vietnam War on a troop carrier that took thirty days to cross the Pacific. There was no transition between the place I was leaving and the place where I arrived, no visual changes in that month except various conditions of the sea. Flying was to me the same as sailing over long distances. I wanted to feel the changes, to smell the air, to feel the heat, and to share the earth with those native to the area. One of our purposes in living this way was to share such experiences. If we'd wanted to make things more manageable, we would have taken a guided tour of Mexico.

But it was a pleasure to share a meal with this mixed and rumpled bag of guests. We talked through dinner and opened other bottles of wine and beer and drifted to the patio to join in with the village, which was beginning to gather for the evening ritual.

On the way home after dinner I was thinking about the differences between people—the air folks and the ground folks, the gringos and the Mexicans. We all had our points of view.

In society north of the border we were usually trained at some specific task. Almost always that task was *part* of the overall process rather than the *entire* process. In my first job at the Jet Propulsion Laboratory I delivered the massive piles of eleven-inch by seventeen-inch computer printouts that the IBM number-crunchers ground out in reams all night long in spittle-like streams from their high-speed printers.

The work involved several persons. Person *A* took decks of punched computer cards of varying-sized stacks from the science folks who dropped them by the computer room on their way home. Person *B* loaded them into a card hopper and pressed a start button where the cards were read into a giant machine and neatly stacked on the other side. Person *C* retrieved the newly stacked cards, rebundled them and placed them on a working surface. Person *D* ran a console where instructions were given to the computer in the event the instructions contained along with the data on the cards wasn't adequate. Person *E* removed the printed outputs from the high-speed printers and associated it with the input cards. Person *F* (me) would then come by periodically and distribute these inputs and outputs to the offices of the submitters, scattered throughout many buildings over hundreds of acres of the Laboratory. The point is that none of us could see the big picture. We were assigned only to the smallest portion of an entire process.

On the other hand, if I considered the daily activities of Margarito, my local friend, he got up in the morning, put his boat in the water and went out fishing. He would review in his mind the experiences that made up his history and choose a location from which to fish. If there were no fish at his first choice, he would make another selection. His mind would unconsciously process the sun, temperature, wind, humidity, tide, and sea swell conditions, integrate them into bird activity, gas availability, fish demand, and who knows how many other considerations, until he reached a decision *that he alone had made* and set off in pursuit of the results. With no choice but to be responsible in his undertakings and correct in his decisions, because his livelihood depended on his immediate judgment. The entire process was his to control. He knew the big picture because he lived it.

A Better Visit

Sometime in the very middle of summer, when it was an effort just to sit without sweat pouring down your face and torso, a small group of friends arrived. This visit we *had* been expecting. They had written us weeks in advance and we had actually received the letter. We were looking forward to the visit and had the hut organized and in good condition. I, being the great party animal, was really looking forward to our friends' time with us. I've always been very outgoing and had been waiting to hear what we'd missed and to relate what we had experienced in our months at the bay. As the day of their arrival got closer so did my pulse.

The group we were expecting was all male. Bill was my oldest and closest friend. We had been pals since we were five, at a small elementary school in Montrose, California; he started at JPL after getting his master's degree in mathematics and had gotten me started there. It was with Bill, sitting on a wall in a kindergarten playground in the 1940s, that I had first been told that there was no Santa. We were tight friends. He was a single dad, and a good-looking guy that attracted the ladies.

Nick was a close friend to both Bill and me since elementary school and was especially close to Mary Ann. Nick was very large, a trunk of a man, and stood at a height of six feet, three inches. Dryly humorous, he always kept us laughing, and when he laughed along, his whole body shook. Nick was an avid reader, chewing on everything he could get his hands on, and worked for the California Department of Transportation.

John was a guy I worked and shared office space with at JPL. Like Bill, John was a mathematician. He was slight with long curly hair and spouted dry quips from his classical academic background in English literature. We were good friends, spending many of our workdays on shared projects struggling to survive the pressures of the space business, and more than one too-long lunch when the pressure was off.

Pete was another JPL guy with a graduate degree from Cal-Tech. He was thin with flaming, curly unkempt bright red hair, fair skin and heavy freckles and wildly animated gestures. Pete was a real mental wizard, but I feared he might prove frail in the Baja sun.

All of these guys were smart, well educated, involved, and active, and they were among my closest friends.

Bill drove a Corvette. In a letter we received earlier in the summer he had asked how the roads were here. We knew he wanted to drive his car and told him not to bring it. I knew even then that if he came down he would drive his Corvette. The Baja transpeninsular highway was being graded and paved that year, and was almost completed. But there was still a lot of rough road left and sixty-six kilometers of pure dirt that wound from the turnoff through the dry desert dust to the village. We had told Bill to catch a ride with the other guys, that it was a bad idea to bring his Corvette. Being my close friend, of course he was obliged to ignore my advice. Many men share this problem.

Mary Ann and I went to the village early, on the afternoon of our friends' arrival. They had never been to the Baja interior, and were carrying supplies for us that would slow them down. I knew the trip would knock them for a loop in some ways, but I couldn't predict in what ways. At noon, sitting on the patio at Casa Díaz, beer and soda in hand, we waited for their appearance. En route to the village they'd be visible from miles away in a cloud of dust. At two in the afternoon we were still waiting in the heat, with no sign. At four we were worried. But with hundreds of miles between us and their departure point, there was nothing we could do, and no way to search for them. So we waited.

By six the shadows were starting to grow long and we knew that something was wrong and they were delayed. Since there was only one road into the village, we thought we should go at least some distance and look for dust. We jumped into Tortuga and told Chubasco and Mama that we were going to look for our friends.

Heading into the desert, we'd driven several miles when, crossing a high saddle, we could see dust in the distance. We stopped and turned off the engine and could hear at least two vehicles working along the road. So we restarted the truck and followed the road toward the sounds and the dust cloud. As we rounded a turn in the road, we saw Bill's blue Corvette being towed across a sandy riverbed by an old pickup truck.

The driver was a fellow we knew from the village. Bill was behind the wheel of his Corvette, riding the breaks to keep from ramming the truck when it slowed. Following his Corvette were John and Nick, in John's VW bug. The procession stopped; we were blocking the roadway. We all got out and started asking questions at once.

The truck driver had come on Bill and Pete in the riverbed in Bill's seriously injured car. Apparently, Bill had seen a sandy river bottom, about a hundred meters across and, worried about getting stuck, had revved his engine and let it rip, thinking he would have enough momentum to get through the loose sand. This was a good idea in the eyes of a gringo. A Mexican might take a less aggressive approach.

Lurking just under the sandy surface, waiting for centuries for its chance to vindicate all the mistreatment it had endured, was a rock of great dimensions and weighing many tons. As Bill's Corvette danced lithely across the sinking surface, the rock found the perfect moment and struck, grabbing for the lower extremities of the low-slung Corvette. It first snapped all the steering linkage, so the front wheels were no longer even talking to each other and headed in their own directions. Then the rock encountered the transmission and ripped it from the remainder of the power train. The car stopped immediately, bleeding oil and transmission fluid, and soon human sweat and tears, on the dry sands of the riverbed.

John and Nick were close behind Bill and Pete when this happened. They jumped from the VW and inspected the damage, which was clearly extensive and a very bad way to start so distant a visit. But there was nothing to do and so they waited in the heat wondering…And along came a Mexican in his truck with camper shell, a rusted metal god(dess), a savior in the desert.

Of course no one would pass by another in need.

Fair Pete, overexposed in the heat all day, was staggering as he climbed out of the damaged car. He stood, swaying and trying to make sense out of the happenings, and finally struggled over to the back of the truck, opened the tail gate and passed out in the bed. The other men looked him over. His breathing was even but his whole body was flushed and very hot, so they elevated his feet and left him as he was.

The truck driver told Bill that the only option was for him to tow Bill's Corvette to the village where the necessary repairs could be made. It is a very bad plan in Baja that includes abandoning a vehicle, even for the shortest time.

This was the state of our friends when Mary Ann and I happened upon their sorry lot.

As our friends brought Mary Ann and I up on the events and I introduced them to our Mexican pal, we saw Pete lying in the back of the pickup. His face was flushed and my first thought was heat stroke. He and Bill had decided it would be a better trip if they had the top off Bill's Corvette. About halfway through the trip down the peninsula Pete had started to feel bad. His condition had worsened up to the point where they got stuck, he'd almost passed out when along had come the pickup, headed toward the village. The bottom line was that Pete was not immediately threatened but had had way too much sun. John and Nick were okay but depressed by the problems. Bill was aggravated about his car and embarrassed about his misjudgment behind the wheel, but otherwise alright.

The pickup led our sad procession the dusty miles into the village. A weary legion of whipped soldiers, we arrived in front of the Díaz patio, thanked the pickup driver and unnecessarily rewarded his gracious act.

By now, it was evening and our friends were exhausted. Pete had partially recovered, the sight of cool beer played a part in this; we were all sitting in the shade on the patio and I was in the process of convincing Bill that repairs could be made here in the village. (He was resistant to this thought.) John and Nick now were in better spirits, but had lost a little enthusiasm with this trouble. We sat in the cooling evening air, with a small breeze from the north and a few beers, and friendship as deep as it gets. Soon we moved Bill's car to Sammy's repair shop behind the patio and store. Sammy gave Bill some good vibes about fixing the steering. However, the transmission would require parts from Ensenada, which would take some time.

With this done, we piled into their VW and our Land Cruiser and followed the long and winding road out of the south end of the village and headed for our hut. The time of our arrival couldn't have been better for our friends' first moments in our new world. Setting sun, water, sea life, wind and temperature were working in concert, playing rich chords to present the wonders of Baja for their pleasure.

The sun threw her last direct rays on the water. The porpoises, sea lions, and whales worked the bait on the surface not far offshore. The pelicans were the leaders into the night, and played the violins of wind toward the north end of the bay. Bait, leaping by the millions, were the cymbals, and the occasional breach of a gray whale was a base drum. Gulls trumpeted the end of a day as the sun fell below the rugged mountains. Soon, all within our view was at rest, but the sounds of our voices on the beach were the saxophones and harp late into the evening. When we slept, late in the night, it was the rest of small children, too long missing kindred spirits that were now rejoined.

The next day we lay in our beds on the sand and arose, each at our own pace, to fit with each other or reject company for the small pieces of time when we wanted something special to ourselves. We sat on the east-facing beach watching the sunrise or turned our backs on the light and closed our eyes for another few minutes. But the hunger of the day kept us from staying too long on the sand and we rallied around the American tradition, from both sides of the border: a cup of coffee.

La Gringa

Mary Ann and I spent the day showing off the south end of the bay, by the lagoon and the small thatched *palapa* where we could all sit out of the sun and shift our chairs every few minutes because the sheltering shade was the exact size of our group. Then we loaded ourselves into our vehicles and drove to the north end of the bay to La Gringa. Here was a long steep beach composed of smooth round stones that eased their way into a smaller bay, with a large, tidal lagoon behind. This lagoon was home to a number of blue heron and white egrets. When the tide was right, there were blue crabs that could be caught with a small net.

La Gringa Bay is a smaller protected bay within the larger Bahía de los Angeles. The calmness of the water at La Gringa is assured by the northern point, which stops the northwestward swells from the open Sea of Cortez. The sea gulls and pelicans love La Gringa because it is shallow enough to encourage the bait to the surface—fast food for the feathered predators.

Our group walked out toward the point at the northernmost part of the Bahía de los Angeles. We could see the outline of the village in the distance to the south, settled under the two towering mountains; the green of the spring at their base was disruptive against the barren browns and tans of the desert.

The smooth stone beach held uncountable varieties of small seashells, washed up in waves by the storms. The lines of shells ran parallel to the water's edge as far as we could see. As we walked, we gathered our personal favorites from a selection of murexes, helmets, small conches, augers, dove shells, trumpets, whelks, periwinkles, turbans, snails, cowries, olives, limpets, chitons, scallops, cockles, clams, mussels, oysters, sand dollars, and sea urchins. Mary Ann and I had come here often to collect the dove shells that we strung together with fishing line into necklaces that we wore over our tans.

Toward the north end of the lagoon, where the water was the calmest, there were butter clams lying on the stones at the ebbing water's edge. On a rocky point behind the lagoon at the beginning of a long stony spit, we saw the nest of a very large osprey. The breeze blew off the water, cooler and fresher as it traveled from the mainland across the gulf.

In the time it took us to reach the place where the bay becomes once again the open Sea of Cortez we had collected more shells than we wanted to carry. Nearing this remote point, a blending of the environments occurs. The rougher and cooler air and water of the open gulf meet with the calm and warmer waters of the bays of Los Angeles and La Gringa. Rounding the point into the deeper water the sea was wild and the wind whipped the ocean swells into whitecaps. In the distance gulls and pelicans were working the surface for bait. We watched them surfing the wind.

Between the point and the southern end of La Gringa Bay was a small pier located about midway on the stone beach. It had been used to load copper or some metal that was refined out of the green rocks from a mine in the depths of the hills behind La Gringa and carried fifteen kilometers to this beach where it was loaded into a no doubt small but sturdy vessel to be shipped who knows where. South of the pier, strung out on the beach like a strand of off-color pearls, were a number of green plywood huts. These housed ruddy local fishermen and sometimes their families. In front of several of the huts were old and worn *pangas*, looking exhausted and spent, like flotsam from a shipwreck.

Each hut was twelve feet square and had, of course, no electricity. A pipeline that was ten kilometers long, with a half-inch diameter, lay full in the desert sun and encouraged murky green water all the way from the village of Bahía de los Angeles to the doors of the fish camp huts.

In the midst of the camp was an open-air fish processing plant with a number of men and women cleaning and packing fish. There were two electric freezers, old and rusted, and an even older gas-powered electric generator driving the freezers to exhaustion. The workers called back and forth to each other as they filleted fish, all in good humor. Behind them were the green huts where they lived and the stones of the beach curving into the purest simplicity of blue sea and sky.

In this setting, with Mary Ann and our friends and a lonely wild stretch of beach, with Rochie and Dulcie running and playing at the edge of the lagoon behind us, I was completely comfortable; somehow I had become one with all of these things. After being by ourselves for so long it was great to be with our close friends. We walked from the fish camp back down the beach and sat for a while just absorbing the simple scene, so few encumbering items and things to ponder.

Back at the cars we deposited our collections of shells in various repositories and drove back to the hut. By the time we arrived it was close enough to evening to begin dinner preparations. The only thing we had in enough quantity to feed us all was fish. We had tortillas, some cabbage, a single tomato, and mayonnaise. With these ingredients we managed to construct a version of fish tacos. While our meal was a lot of work because of the number of people we were feeding, poached cabrilla in soft tortillas with cabbage and mayonnaise was not the meal of choice of our friends. Mary Ann and I endured great humorous harassment about the meal we fixed them, after our friends had driven all this way. In the end, the dogs got as much of the food as we did. But we laughed and opened another bottle of third-growth Bordeaux our pals had brought (the guys knew that Mary Ann and I had been reading about wines before we left the States, and had lugged an abundance of excellent bottles) and told stories and made jokes and whooped it up. After dinner we bathed in the ocean as the sun was setting and dried in the heated air on the beach.

At the hut that night a mellow and upbeat mood wrapped around us like a shoreline fishnet, drawing us into a small and intimate shared microcosm. We pulled the cork (actually, we pushed it because we had no corkscrew) on a bottle of 1966 Château Montrose, a tannic St. Estèphe served a few degrees too warm because the old refrigerator was overwhelmed with its new assignments. With cheap glasses we toasted our communal journey through life.

The heavy supply of wine our friends had brought meant we had serious work to do. We opened other bottles and raised our glasses again and again in celebration of many important happenings. We toasted Mary Ann's and my voyage into new lands, Mexico, the United States, the hut, sea life as we had never known it, and pelicans. We recognized our friends' hardships in trekking all this way to join with us. The evening grew late but we were not to be deterred. We were happy, by now silly, and we were together after months apart. We sang dumb songs on the beach and laughed and got drunk on the product of a country half a world away. The guys brought me up to date on JPL and the happenings in space flight projects and where I could get work when we came back.

We called in more toasts to the world in general, to our enduring friendships, to our parents, to our unborn children, to the calm of the sea providing us this tranquility, to the fish tacos we had for dinner, to hazelnuts and punchbowls and feathers in the wind...until we all were asleep, most of us out of our respective beds and on the open sand.

Bad Hangovers

In the morning we were well aware that we had been happily irresponsible the evening before. As we individually lay semi-awake with thunderous headaches, retching stomachs, dry and foul mouths and very bad attitudes we, one by one, struggled to stand and make it several yards to the water to rinse the sand off our bodies and clear our heads. Actually, salt water is a really good mouthwash.

Somehow, together, we made breakfast. More experienced gringos would have whipped up a pot of *menudo*, but we were green, both from lack of experience and from the wine, and so we fried up several cans of Spam and potatoes.

One of the items Bill had brought for us were a number of fifty-pound sacks of dog food, so there was no immediate need to fish early that morning. Thank God for that.

We choked down our greasy food and eased our way into thinking through the evening before. What a hell of a time. Several of us had fallen, causing a number of small but proud wounds, and we laughed at our stupidity as only guys can do. Somewhere during the wild night Bill had cut his thumb. We all examined the wound, which was fairly deep, running entirely across the top. Someone remembered that he had brought a hard salami and was trying to slice it when he hacked his opposable digit.

Nick had been the best behaved of us all during the partying. This morning he sat in the sand and poked fun at the rest of us, struggling with whatever we tried to do, with his great joyous outbursts and bouncing belly. Peter felt *bad*. Not one of us was a serious drinker, but being the slightest, Peter was most influenced by the alcohol, and still weak from his bad time in the desert on the way down. He was pale and suffering quietly to himself.

Bill, John, Mary Ann, and I sat in a huddle on the beach, recovering, going into the water, adjusting to the demands of and on our bodies, which were trying their very best to determine what it was we were set on doing to them. By midmorning we were recovered enough that we could function almost normally and we went for a walk on the beach toward the lagoon at the south end of the bay. The wind was from the north and even though it was hot, it wasn't unbearable.

Our friends were further into Mexico than they had ever been. They mentioned how impressed they were with the simplicity of the physical environment and the sincerity of the people.

Mary Ann and I talked of our experiences living with the locals. There were all kinds and types, just like anywhere else. But overall the people we had been experiencing while living at the bay were not just Mexicans, they were rural Mexicans. They were slower than their citified counterparts, more tolerant because they had more time, and willing to help with any problem you had. They were both trusting and trustworthy.

We talked about the nature of prejudice and we tried to understand what it was about Mexico and Mexicans that we *needed*. It was actually a need. I had felt the tugging for many years and could recognize it in my friends. There is a simplicity in Mexico and its people that is difficult to find in southern California. The U.S. is so full of itself and has so many rules. Mexico is wild and free, in a sense that the U.S. has lost. There are so many people in the States living in such close proximity that we need to have rules for that environment. But sometimes they are just too much. Sometimes I just need Mexico.

The land is so sparsely populated in Baja that there is far less need for structure. If there's no one to offend why would you need a rule? But even if there were more people here, the Mexican nature is very tolerant. There is strength to the Mexican spirit which must come from the genes shared with the Toltecs, Aztecs, and others who populated the region before the Spaniards arrived. This spirit, tempered by often living with less than enough, has been carried from generation to generation. Our neighbors were always willing to help anyone, regardless of their own condition.

Living most of our lives in southern California, we knew we had certain biases. We all thought of these as prejudices. The easiest to relate is this: if I meet ten people of a given race and eight are lazy, am I prejudiced if I assume that the next person I meet of that tribe will also be lazy? There are some obvious ways that this assumption is both right and wrong. I would be stupid to ignore valid statistics, but I would also be wrong to assume that all people of that same collection were identical.

Each of us, Mary Ann and I and our friends on the beach, had exposed ourselves openly to the variances of environments and peoples. We were all educated, open, receptive—we were not prejudiced. But what was prejudice? In the end, we agreed that it was a simple description: if we predicted the overall behavior of any individual from past acts of single others, that was prejudice. With this definition we could accept generalizations like *most Mexicans are kind* without applying it specifically to a Mexican I didn't know and accepting it before I had knowledge of that person's kindness.

The tide was coming in filling the lagoon behind us, as we sat on the beach at the south end. It was hot and the mountain on the southern point of the bay, Cerro José, blocked cooler air from the open Sea of Cortez. The beach is pure, light golden sand for miles; whereas, in front of our hut, we had a small patch of sand, but rocks surrounded it. In the southernmost cup of the bay the water was calmer and warmer. There were several small houses nested in the sand on the hills above the beach. The protected water was almost still and crystal clear.

Hundreds of small stingrays schooled up and down the length of beach where we were sitting or walking along the shallow shoreline. They scattered when one of us approached the water but returned as we retreated. We watched them settle to the bottom, onto the sand, flipping their wings to create an underwater nest. When they were buried we could still see an outline beneath the water, but it was soon gone with the ebb and flow. The small sandy beach surrounded by rocks in front of our hut was one of the reasons Mary Ann and I had chosen our location. The rocks discourage the rays from settling; we were in the water half of the day. If rays had been present we would have had to take some measure to drive them off before we went into the ocean.

A friend of ours had told us the typical damage that could be done, even by a small ray. He had been walking in shallow water at San Felipe up to his knees and barefoot, and had stepped on a ray about twelve inches long. The immediate pain was tremendous and he had stumbled from the beach, trying not to use his wounded foot, to his group camped on the nearby sand. They had gathered around to see what they could do. A member of the group had told him an old wives' tale he had heard: place a raw cut potato directly against the wound. No one knew if it was true but someone had seen a local fisherman doing it. When my friend rinsed his foot of the sand he gazed at a hole, a quarter inch in diameter, in his heel. Someone on the beach gave him a slice of raw potato and he had alternated leeching the wound with the potato and soaking his foot in hot fresh water. The severe pain had lasted for hours, but had diminished after the first two. He could not walk on his foot for several days. This story was enough to keep the shoes on our feet and our eyes on the water as we shuffled along the shallows of the shoreline.

At the south end of the bay we often found sand dollars, the type with five enlarged holes known in southern California as Iron Maidens. We collected a few of these to work into macramé strands of shells our friends wanted to make.

A sailboat was moored at the most protected part of the southern bay and a young couple moved around the boat, about a hundred meters offshore. They were the only other people within miles. (The houses on the hill behind the beach, thrown together from material cast off from construction jobs or surplus piles, belonged to Americans who occasionally flew small planes to the dirt airstrip just east of the southern lagoon; from there they'd walk to their homes, retrieve an old and rusting car or truck, and return to the plane to off-load their weekend gear.)

Watching the couple on the boat was warm and romantic. The good-sized sailboat was anchored in a protected bay, safe from the wind and rough water. It was a scene set in a tropical, albeit somewhat barren, setting on an isolated beach…a young man and woman in bathing suits, oiled and tanned, blond hair and rigging blowing in the slight wind. A picture-perfect backdrop of blue gulf and sky and the rusty hues of Punta Colorado formed the southern point of the bay. We struggled into the sun from the shade and started a long, slow walk back up the beach to the hut.

Later that afternoon I drove Bill in to the village to determine the fate of his car, which Sammy had been working on. The steering was fixed but the transmission case was definitely cracked and would need to be replaced. Bill decided a job that size was better done where parts were more readily available. We asked if he could leave the car with Sammy and come back in a few weeks with a flatbed trailer to retrieve it, and Sammy agreed. Bill and Pete would squeeze into the back seat of John's VW, a tough ride for such a long distance.

Mary Ann and I were not about to repeat the heavily lambasted performance of the previous night's dinner of fish tacos. Fortunately Bill had brought a pork roast. When we got back to the hut we put a pot of salt water on to boil and dropped the roast into the water. Two hours later we built a fire beneath our scavenged oven, perched over the small pit, and placed the overcooked roast into its mouth. We soon heard sizzling sounds and smelled the garlic and searing pork scent wafting through the air. A half hour later we pulled the roast from the metal box, tugged shreds of meat from the roast, wrapped them in Mari Elena's tortillas and ate. We sidled gently up to the remnants of the Bordeaux from the evening before. This evening was less ambitious and more relaxed, with little steam-blowing. As the blue sky faded into black we sat on the beach to watch the nightly performance by our aquatic friends. Soon, a moonless sky presented the stellar view that an IMAX theater would have killed for.

Above the islands, silhouetted against the Sea of Cortez, and the mountain peaks to the west, the sky was lit with millions of bright and distant points of light. John, a physicist and astronomer, filled in the details as we pointed to the more brightly colored and randomly associated stars and planets. It was impossible not to recognize our insignificance in the world order in this environment. We wondered how we could live so long in the same galaxy and know so little of the basics. But in busy and well-lit southern California there is little time or darkness to work with. It may be that people living always in a city are so little exposed to the massiveness of the universe, of the unendingness of our oceans and deserts, that they are unable to identify with elements larger than, for example, an office building or a neighborhood. What would the configurations of the southern hemisphere look like? I knew, looking at the overall pattern of the northern sky, it would just feel different—a somehow subtle but recognizable change that would be uncomfortable until you had pinned it down.

Night Moves

Late in the evening a new moon climbed over the eastern islands and increased the contrast between the sky and the earth. The sea was calm, with no swell whatsoever, as it so often was at night. The surface of the water was undisturbed by tide and air. But underneath the surface was another story.

Feeding or just entertaining themselves, the fish were frequently breaking the water-air barrier. Mullet, a fish of two or so pounds, dove into the air and landed broadside on our side of the surface, causing a gentle splash. Bait, chased by larger and hungry fish, launched by the thousands the instant the predator passed, arcing back into the water milliseconds apart in an audible fluid waterfall. The unseen bottle-nosed dolphin worked back and forth near the shore. The clue to their presence was the puff/swoop of their rising silently to the sea's surface to expel old air and inhale fresh.

Whales occasionally passed by in deeper water during the dark hours. Without night vision the primary way to identify them was by their breathing. But that was similar to the dolphins and you could not tell how far they were out in the water. The whales' breathing is deeper and longer between breaths. We sat on the beach and helped our friends learn to identify the uniqueness between these two aquatic mammals by only their sounds.

Another entertainment was to understand the differences between fish and birds hitting the water. Both were completely invisible and we had to rely only on our ears to determine an event and its participants. Over time the difference became detectable. A fish jumping makes only the sound of its body reentering the water. It makes no sound when it rises through the surface. A bird makes no sound as it spies bait or strikes its killing pose in the dark sky, but its entrance into the water is audible in the dead of night for several hundred meters. And it makes an additional sound when it surfaces: it shakes, vibrating its entire body to rid its feathers of as much water as possible. This shaking sound clearly identifies it as a bird.

We had learned to detect the types of birds that were diving in the night. There were basically two types of diving birds: gulls and boobies, and the brown pelicans. There were several types of gulls and boobies at the bay but they were all about the same size, two feet long with a wingspan of five feet. The weight of each of these birds might have been a pound. The pelicans were California browns and were a larger bird, with a wingspan and length longer than that of the gulls, and each weighed about five pounds.

When we couldn't see, it was at first difficult to determine their kind. Over time we learned that the gulls didn't vibrate in the same way when they surfaced. But the real clue was when they returned to the air. The gull had a distinct advantage in that it needed only a short airstrip for takeoff. The poor pelican required a relatively long runway. And as it cleared the surface there were those pesky small swells of the bay to pull it back into the water.

Mary Ann and I were proud of our simple knowledge and happy to have our friends share in the experiences of our time here. Testing each other with games of identification, we two had challenged each other in the way that only people who are entirely comfortable and unafraid with each other can do. We had always been this way together, but it was amplified by the uniqueness and looming threat of the remoteness of the environment. A storm could come at any moment. Since we were so remote and had no radio or other communication, we would not know. The potential danger caused us to unite in a way we had never done in the States. There was, we sensed, no society, no government, to protect us. But this was why we were here. We didn't want the smothering of protection.

This was a subject of our conversation: I hated the concept of a nation feeling responsible to and for me, personally, to print on the back of a can of peas the entire set of ingredients and issuing warnings for me to read. For me, and some of my friends did not agree, our north of the border society with all its rules and regulations was too tight. I liked less protections and greater room for movement. I found the vast restrictions of life north of the border were always stifling my creativity.

Years later, I was involved with a committee at JPL to study the use of institutional standards, common methods for performing institute-wide processes. We met as a small group weekly and tried to understand how we could help our peers work more effectively through standard processes. I eventually withdrew from the group, for the following reason: standards are most important when you are repeating processes, for example in manufacturing where you build thousands of the same part. In that example there is no room for creative thinking.

But in those days at the Lab, almost no process was repeated, all think-
ing was new and even if it wasn't new the people attracted to the space
environment wanted to use their creative nature. To these folks, a stan-
dard was a nasty concept. Since I understood their viewpoint, and agreed
with it, I quit the standards game.

Eventually that night, one of the guys broke out a bottle of tequila.
We boys on the beach passed the bottle slowly and pensively back and
forth up our row in the sand, contemplating the meaning of life. Mary
Ann made a cup of tea, sat in a sand chair behind us and harassed us
with the sole female opinion in our masculine midst. Bill and Nick
protected her from our extremes.

We sat in a tight collection, held together by previously sewn threads
and tightened by the bonds of Baja, listening to each other and our
obscure thoughts and the night moves from the sea and sky. On that
beach it was natural to feel oneness with all things. We were close as
humans, and we were close to the noises of nature. We could not avoid
the actions of the air, land or water.

It was rewarding that we had come to know a place so close to the
edges of our experience. From this place and time, we would individually continue our separate paths. We could launch a spacecraft, we could
lower another submersible to the ocean depths, we could build a house
and roads throughout our cities. We could create other lives for ourselves as we chose. But wherever we went from here I knew we would
never see the world in the same light again. I appreciated an opportunity to have our friends see a world that they had never seen and to come
to conclusions of their own that we could share and contemplate. And
Mary Ann and I learned from their observations of our world.

Our friendships were enriched forever because of those too short
days on the beach.

The next two days passed with Mary Ann and I introducing our
friends to other qualities of the bay and us absorbing as much of their
friendship as we could hold, to carry us through the coming time we
would be alone again. We had more leisurely walks on the beach, shore
fishing expeditions, philosophical talks, and warm remembrances of
times past. But too soon their visit was about to end. They were gearing up for the slow trip north, and we were preparing for resumed isolation, looking forward to our time alone and yet missing our friends.

The aspects of the coming parting held good and bad facets for all of us. Our friends would be threatened with the desert as they headed north and would be without us. We would be left to the tranquility of our remote beach but without their presence. But Mary Ann and I knew that we could now close our relationship once again and recreate our newfound security and stability between the two of us and Rochie and Dulcie.

On the day of their departure we followed our friends into the village where they said their good-byes to those they had met during their stay. Mary Ann snapped a photograph of the five of us guys on the patio of the 1970s Casa Díaz. Bill, John, Pete and I were seated on the patio with our legs swinging over the edge. Big Nick was standing next to us in the dirt beneath the patio. We were wearing cowboy hats and were all tanned from long hours outdoors. Our arms were around each other's backs and we were smiling and looking like five Sundance Kids as the shutter clicked.

We led them out into the desert to the road heading for the junction with the transpeninsular highway, our mutual hearts crying at leaving each other. At the road we stopped and wished each other a safe journey and proceeded with great handshakes, hugs, tears, and kisses. We would all write each other though there was no knowing that the mail would get through, and we would call them as soon as we got back to the States. And before we were ready to accept the fact that we were separating, they set off into the desert. Mary Ann and I stood watching their dust until the wind whipped it into the rising heated waves and it spread, thinning into the air. We set slowly off on our drive back through the village to the lonesome hut, the dusty road softened by the reflections of our time with our friends.

The remainder of the day was filled with small talk of what the visit had contained at our personal level. Our choice to deprive ourselves of the luxuries of southern California turned out to include social and intellectual, as well as physical, comforts. We had made a choice to come here for a good reason and that reason continued. We both missed our native environments, but they would be waiting for us. We clung to each other emotionally that evening. And eventually the day eased into night and we lay on the sand talking about our last few days until we fell asleep.

Flood!

Before we realized it, the hottest part of summer was bearing down. We stood on the beach looking over the gulf to see thin, sleek, and silky cirrus clouds forming over the islands. We learned to read the humidity from watching the volcano on Isla Coronado; when the wispy clouds began to form a cover over the volcano the humidity was over eighty-five percent. This happened over many weeks, as we lived our simple lives, washing, repairing, reading, bathing, cooking, and taking long walks on the beaches of the bay. The four of us had really settled in. Rochie and Dulcie might as well have been our children...

An increase in temperature seemed to cause an increase in humidity. Arguments between the elements in the white-hot midday sky were becoming more obvious. The frail and vaporish clouds were slowly turning into heavy cumulus, daily more laden with water, casting dark, heavy shadows that crawled along the earth, spilling into the arroyos and flowing toward the sea as they worked northward up the gulf.

On a day several weeks after our friends' departure, the sky was dark and threatening at sunrise; the humid air surrounded us. We felt isolated from the outside world. Visibility was down to about a kilometer. Everything outside the hut and inside was damp and dripping with condensation. We felt that when we breathed we inhaled more liquid than air. As the morning continued the sky grew darker still. The temperature hung around the hundred-degree mark and the humidity was over ninety-five. There was no air movement. There was something uncomfortable in the weather that we couldn't define.

Over the morning and into midday the clouds continued to move from the south along the open water of the gulf. The sky grew darker, impossibly, with each hour. It was hard to imagine rain, but it was looking more and more like we were in for a torrential storm of some kind. If I had known what was about to happen, I would have grabbed Mary Ann and the dogs and headed for the north end.

Within minutes the sky had turned black and was ready to burst. We didn't know what to expect, so my mind was working furiously on anything I could do to prepare for something I didn't understand. There was no radio in the hut and we hadn't been to the village for days. We had lived with the extreme heat for so long that it had never occurred to us that the weather, like the tide, could change so dramatically. But it did.

The bay is wide-mouthed, with low hills and deserts forming the north end, which is a low altitude passageway for weather changes between the west and east coasts of Baja. High mountains to the south and west contain the south end of the bay, ten kilometers distant from the north end. These mountains act as a catch basin for the storms that occasionally move up the gulf. Thunderheads lumbered into our normally cloudless sky and worked to climb the precipitous cliffs of the mountains to our west. The towering ridges of the Santa Ana and Bahía de los Angeles peaks were clawing at the blackened underbellies of the clouds, which were fighting to escape their peaks to drop their torrents on the parched desert. In my heart, standing and watching the dynamics of that moment, I knew what was about to happen. But I was too naïve to believe it. I knew who would win this battle, but I didn't have a clue of the results.

The clouds built and the sky darkened until it was purple, beyond black. Then we heard the pelts of engorged raindrops falling on the thatch of the hut's roof, smashing almost hail-like with their drive and intensity. Quickly flowing through the troughs of the fronds, the liquid carried mercurial dust down on our heads and shoulders. We gathered whatever we had that rain would damage, books, binoculars, bedding, dry goods, and put them in the truck. The onslaught thickened. We went into the hut, more as a formality than because it would offer protection: the roof was loosely woven ocotillo and thatch, only designed to offer shade and, under these circumstances, falling scorpions.

Suddenly, something disemboweled the underbelly of sky that passed over the entire south end of the bay. The clouds ruptured in a deluge that lasted half an hour and dumped many seasons worth of rain, long restrained, in minutes. We stood in the hut, soaked to the bone and paying full attention to weather, full in our face. Lightning and thunder erupted, accompanying the torrent. The wind blew sheets of water through the thin walls, knocking things about and shifting the hut back and forth. We realized our house of sticks was about to come down.

The clouds lowered, seemingly pressing us into the sodden earth, as if the clouds were merging with the sea, vapor into water. The deluge increased. It was aggressive. We huddled, Mary Ann, me, Rochie and Dulcie, inside the hut, afraid to go out and not sure how threatened we were. Between the deafening roar of the rain, the blinding white flashes of lightening and the thunderous roars just following the bolts we were terrified. But we knew it could not get much worse; there was no way it could rain harder that it was. It could get no darker or more threatening. Then it began to ease off, just a tiny bit at first, but it was an encouraging sign.

After about forty-five minutes the rain slowed to a point that we could at least see the ocean, twenty feet away. I went outside (an unusual concept, since we had been inside and were soaked as though we had been standing in the full force of the rain) to see what damage had been done. Without the cactus walls around me and with no rain pounding on thatch, I could hear a sound that had been inaudible in the hut. A low rumbling, only a deep vibration at first, expanded into a roar in less than a minute. The noise grew louder and louder and I couldn't think what was happening. The earth was vibrating. It started with a very low frequency, coming in large waves that I could feel as well as hear. My first reaction, coming from southern California, was to think *earthquake*. But something was different. Then I heard another deep noise coming from near the hut, to the north. I ran in that direction, only several meters, until the earth ended where there had been a sand dune before. I stopped short, looking down into a channel at least ten feet wide and six or eight feet deep, full of brown water, mud and huge boulders being washed down from the peaks and mountains west of us. We were in the midst of a flash flood. I froze, not at all certain what I was seeing. Before me was a bad dream. The earth ended no more that five yards north of our hut, just beyond where we had built our shower.

I looked down into the river of dark brown water, thick and rushing, twisting and gnarled, falling from the steep escarpment of the mountains behind us. The rainfall had collected quickly in the dry gullies and canyons flowing down the nearly vertical drop toward the two-mile-distant sea. The small cacti and plants, shallowly rooted there, were uprooted along with every other thing in the water's path, on its hot rush to the sea below. Our hut was on the edge of the water, in the way of the millions of gallons of water seeking the path of least resistance. Worse, we were the only man-made object between the mountains and the sea.

More roaring drew me to the other side of our dune. Another canyon was forming there. The noise we had heard and couldn't identify was the water rushing off the mountains toward us in a giant wave: a flash flood of major proportions. But as it encountered the earthen fan leading it to the gulf, the water slowed and confined itself to manageable tantrums, leading it to the lower-lying *barrancas* and gullies, carrying with it massive thick tangles of desert plants and boulders that it swept into the gulf. The attacking river had split in two, only yards before our home, otherwise it would have swept us to a fate we couldn't imagine.

Part of the overwhelming noise and vibration we had heard was the massive boulders the flood was moving in its path. As we watched from the dangerous and rapidly eroding banks of our twin rivers, rocks six feet in diameter rolled with the force of the water into the sea and disappeared. The entire south end of the bay was turning brown with the sediment carried from the tops of the mountains, down the steep slopes, across the plain and into the sea.

Once we identified the phenomenon it was clear that we were in the midst of it with no way out. West of us the flooding water parted just behind the dune on which we sat; to the immediate north and south were the new channels swirling with boulders and debris from the flood; to the east the southern bay was boiling with the turmoil of the down-flowing residual of the storm. Even over us the sky was filled with wind, rain, lightning, and thunder. We were completely insignificant. But when we understand the causes of our fears they are controllable —like the naming of a disease.

The rain was easing and the clouds were less threatening. The water was continuing to carve major excavations on both sides of our dune, but we could see that the worst had passed. The water flowing down these deep channels was no longer brimming as it worked out into the gulf. The rain, though not as heavy, continued to fall. I suddenly thought of how rewarded the plants must feel, after so many years with no moisture except the dew that was drawn hesitantly from the ocean on lucky nights. Now they were sucking up the life-giving liquid and a new set of life cycles were being set up for the next few years.

Nature quieted her anger and we looked around us at the devastation. It was difficult to think of a natural process as devastating; the terms were conflicting. Nature was perfect and *natural*. The activities of nature were *natural*. How could I think of the word *devastating*? The experience we had been through was a natural process. The world we were surrounded with was accustomed to the lack of water, the deluge, the floods; it was all a natural process. We were the unnatural elements. So devastating things could not happen to the elements surrounding us, only to us, the new kids on the block.

We were simply being indoctrinated. We were being fit into the process. Our instinct or perhaps an accident had picked a dune of the correct height and width to allow us to survive. A process of selection was at work. Twenty feet in any direction and we would have been de-selected as an evolutional entity. But having lived through the storm and seen its edges and limits, and recognizing there could be worse storms, we were part of the natural element.

For several days we were stranded in the desert. We probably could have gotten out if it had been critical, but Sammy would chastise me over the motor mounts and we were witnessing a rebirth of the land. Many cacti came into bloom within days of the storm. So we stayed put. The road was washed out in both directions. But the two local families that used the road poked and prodded at it until the rough edges and the rocks became buried under silt and sand and the less rugged vehicle could pass. Soon the kneading tires had decomposed the toughest rough transitions into and out of the drying streambeds.

After two or three days we needed to go to the village. It was rewarding when I turned the key in the old truck—it shuddered and the engine started after sitting idle for many days. But the road was virtually gone, particularly the part that climbed the escarpment, inland, to round Cerro los Angelitos, before dropping into the village. Major outcrops of rock made the track all but impassible even in four-wheel-drive. The water had taken the path of least resistance, which was often the roadbed.

Over the next few days we cleaned up and repaired our home, thrashed from the rain, flood, and wind. We rewove the arms of the cirio cacti that formed the basis of the hut and repositioned the palm fronds and scraps of other materials that were our roof and walls, until we had a rough replica of the original hut.

One day we drove south along the washed-out road for a few kilometers. The damage was less severe here. The mountains to the west were not as prominent and were further from the shore; their decline to the sea was less pronounced. The area between our hut and the village was the hardest hit. We drove to La Gringa, at the north end of the bay. No rain had fallen there at all, only a few kilometers to the north.

A few days after the flood Bill returned with his father in a pickup, arriving in the afternoon. We drove together to Sammy's house, where Bill's flashy metallic blue Corvette was sitting in the sun covered with dust. Sammy had finished the repair work on the steering and had been paid before Bill left for the U.S. Bill and his dad had rented a large flatbed trailer to haul Bill's car home. But because the road between the transpeninsular highway and the bay was not paved, they left the trailer at the junction. There was a loading ramp at the junction, just a slot cut into the ground, that they could use to get the car up onto the bed of the trailer. But they had no way to get the car out to the junction, sixty-six dirt kilometers away. Sammy solved this problem. He went to the home of one of the villagers who owned a truck large enough to carry Bill's car. They agreed on a price for carrying the car to the junction. The only thing left to do was to somehow get the Corvette into the truck.

There was no loading dock that we had seen in the village. But Sammy told us that the original purpose of their large patio on which the villagers enjoyed the evenings was as a loading dock. We got the assistance of several fishermen who were sitting in the shade of the patio and pushed Bill's car from Sammy's yard up to the patio. Sure enough, it all came together. There was a ramp at one end that was wide enough for us to push the car onto the patio. The driver backed his truck up to the east end of the patio and the bed of his truck aligned perfectly with the height of Bill's car. It had all been engineered so many years ago. We pushed the Corvette onto the bed of the truck and they were set for heading out the next morning.

It was evening and we all had dinner at the Díaz restaurant with a few pilots and their guests. Bill and his dad spent the night in one of their cottages; at first light they drove for the border. I found out months later that, after Bill had the transmission repaired on the Corvette, he had taken it to a wheel alignment specialist. The repairman had driven the car onto his new high tech alignment-measuring machine and run an analysis of what was needed to align the car. The answer was nothing. The Corvette was in perfect alignment. Sammy had bent and welded crude pieces of rod and metal that were available to him at the village, making a perfect repair without any measuring equipment. The final alignment was made with Mexican ingenuity. I can only guess at the tools Sammy used to align Bill's Corvette: a piece of chalk, a nail, and a length of string.

San Francisquito

Somewhere in the later summer we were tired of the daily routine and decided to take a short trip or two to explore the areas near the bay. Our map showed another bay about 120 kilometers down the coast and we decided to have a look.

We loaded up Rocinante and Dulcinea and our gear and went to the village where we bought supplies to last us a few days and headed down the road. A few kilometers south of our hut the road forked, with the east fork heading around the south end of the bay. We stayed on the southern road and continued past a small, dilapidated ranch and several broken corrals. As we passed, a grizzled hand was working on the railings and we stopped to ask if we were heading toward San Francisquito. The rancher was older and burned from working in the sun and dust and dung—the ranch was a working cattle ranch owned by the Díaz family. He said that we should stay on this road for twenty kilometers, where another joined it from the east. That was the road to Las Animas. We should stay to the west.

A few minutes after leaving the ranch the valley opened to both the east and west. The cacti grew larger and more abundant. Some of the taller cardón and cirio cacti had Spanish moss, *orchilla*, hanging from their upper masts. There were wildflowers and ground cover here and we speculated that the rainstorm had brought these to life. Yellow and purple flowers covered the desert floor and red and gold buds sprouted from many of the lush green cacti. It was clear that this valley got more that the average rainfall for central Baja, thanks to the tall mountains that had almost caused our demise.

In the midst of all this color we came upon an old abandoned town, spread across both sides of the roadbed. The adobe buildings had mostly melted, but there was a single building with two-foot-thick walls with holes that served as windows, with bars built into the old adobe. Our assumption was that this had been the jail for this village. On looking around it was obvious this had been a mining town. The map named it Las Flores and told us that the ore processed at this village had been brought down the steep slopes of the westward mountains from a mine, San Juan, not far from Mission San Borja. But regarding the jail, I read several accounts later. Some called this single thick-walled edifice the jail. One account, however, designated it as the vault that held the silver ore.

Across a dirt road that had once been the main street, an old and rusting narrow gauge locomotive sat in the sand, one or two ore cars trailing sadly behind. Guessing from the number of building remnants, we decided the town could never have housed more than a hundred people. It was easy to romanticize the lifestyle fifty years ago, which might have been like Alta California during the gold rush. I could see miners covered with the red of the earth, off work for the day, heading for the local cantina, drinking as hard as they worked in their hard lives, staggering to their adobe houses for dinner and falling into bed to rise before the sun six days a week. It had to be a hell of a town because the square footage of the jail was about a quarter of the square footage of the combined housing. A short distance from the old village a small graveyard was situated, giving the names and dates of birth and death of those buried there. People, we noticed, didn't live long in those days. Years later the tiny locomotive was trucked to Bahía de los Angeles and placed on display as a centerpiece to the village square.

While we were stopped we added oil, cleaned the sparkplugs, and cleaned out the carburetor. This well-rehearsed process took only a few minutes and we were back on the road to San Francisquito. From Las Flores we continued down a long wide valley through the continuing cactus forest. We climbed slightly and the road was flat and sandy. Where the rancher had told us to expect a road we did encounter one, so we followed his directions and kept going straight.

Soon we reached the southern end of the valley and came to an area that was similar to but gentler than the escarpment behind our hut, continuing for many kilometers. We climbed into and out of many dry washes that crossed the roadbed, and onto low, flat meadows rich with flowers and green ground cover. There had been rain here recently as well.

We passed no other vehicles during this entire trip. The road was not well traveled. No other tire prints were visible since it had rained last. Two of the deeper dry creeks we crossed led us west into the foothills of the mountains and here we found cattle ranches. In the deeper arroyos the water seeped slowly from the mountains, apparently with enough abundance to support the two ranch families and their cattle.

There were several small areas where the ranchers had grown patches of crops. I remembered reading about Sonoran and northern Baja Indians who had continuously over several human generations selected the seeds of vines for the next season's crops that had matured the fastest during the preceding season. Eventually they had reduced the time the crop came into fruition from twelve weeks to just five, and they prepared the soil well before the time they might experience even a single rainy day. When rain occurred they planted the rapidly maturing seeds immediately after, diverting any residual water over the plantings. I wondered if these remote survivors followed the same technique. I guessed they did. It's amazing what the mind can come up with when it has the time to think.

Today, the map calls these ranches Los Paredones and San Pedro. They were both lonely places but the families gathered at the sound of our approach and waved. We always asked if all was well with them and were we on the right course even though there were few possibilities for error.

In one of the arroyos a steer was lying dead beside the roadway. I wondered, with it so visible from the road, why the ranchers hadn't taken the carcass as food. They must have known it was sick or at least didn't know if it had died of some disease. Regardless, it was a lot of food that went to waste in one of the most barren places on earth. But, of course, there is no real waste here.

South from these ranches the desert became drier. We continued a number of kilometers and then dropped into a low arroyo. At the southern end of this we stopped and looked up as the road climbed straight up a cliff that was at least forty-five degrees from horizontal and about five hundred meters in length. I looked for other roads that took easier, less direct routes, but this was the only road. I shut off the engine and we walked around the area to see how others had bypassed this impossible climb. There was nothing.

The hill in front of us appeared to be the only way to San Francisquito. It was filled with ruts and holes eighteen inches deep and raw rocks jutting up at least that same distance. It was worse than anything we had ever encountered in the deserts of southern California, where we'd gone looking for bad roads. For its distance it was worse than anything on Baja's infamous east coast road. I stood back and examined it, analyzing the worst parts of the climb and how many inches I could maneuver one way or another to avoid an obstacle. The bottom line was that it was an impossible hill. To make matters worse, the west side fell sharply away, preventing any maneuvering as the driver climbed higher. It was hard to imagine a road that had carried us this far only to end in this situation. But I knew that not all people who traveled this road had four-wheel-drive. Either somewhere behind us there was another route that avoided this problem or they had just been better drivers than I was.

This last thought was the one that triggered my approach to solving the problem. I had many years behind the wheel of my truck and I knew how to drive it. So I made an assumption. Driving dirt and sand, a person is often met with conditions that can fool you. A few degrees change in temperature and humidity can make a bottomless pit into an easy drive-over. I thought about the time of day, our distance from the sea, the wind, the humidity, the glare, and the tire pressure and we decided that we were just going to have to tackle the hill.

The road at the base and all the way to the top was so rough that there was no way to take a run at it. It was low range, low gear the whole way. If we dropped beneath a certain slow speed there would be no more than tires spinning on rock. I shut off the engine and opened the hood. For the fifth time over the last eight hours I added a quart of oil to the engine. Climbing back into the truck we studied the road one last time through the glare of the windshield. I dropped the transfer case into low range and put the transmission into first gear. This is where we would stay until we reached the top, I expected. I released the clutch and fed gas to the carburetor and the truck inched forward. Feathering the clutch and throttle, we began our slow, gear-grinding, tire-spinning, rubber-burning, exhaust-spewing ascension.

We had to maintain as much momentum as possible; if we stopped for an obnoxious hole or rock we'd never get started again. Working the clutch and throttle I kept us moving, or at least rocking, so we were never completely stopped. The truck listed fifteen, twenty, thirty degrees and we knew we were going to roll over the edge and into the arroyo below. But we continued to climb, rock, dip, tilt, and then climb. The protruding rocks smashed and shook the undercarriage, sending strong vibrations throughout the frame of the truck. The dust flew in all directions and the smell of burning rubber filled the air.

Within thirty seconds we were at the halfway point and it began to look better. At one point the hill was so steep that we thought we'd roll over backwards. But we slowly continued climbing, and the angle dropped to thirty degrees and then to twenty and near the top of the hill the roadbed was less littered with holes and jutting rocks.

We hit the summit and pulled onto the surrounding plateau and turned off the engine. We got out and looked back down the hill and congratulated ourselves. Mary Ann got her towel and some water and we washed the dust from our faces and congratulated ourselves again. Sometimes our greatest recognitions of our selves are really not too complicated.

After a few moments out of the vehicle we resumed our endless trek. It was late in the afternoon and it seemed like the road was going on forever. We were expecting a route to approach ours from the east. This would be the San Francisquito road coming from El Arco. At that point we would still be more than ten kilometers away.

We pushed on for another hour and eventually we could see signs of more travel and a few side roads. Finally our road dead-ended into the San Francisquito-El Arco road, and we turned east, knowing we were no more than an hour from our destination. After a few kilometers a fence line with a closed gate blocked the road. The fence ran perpendicular to the road as far as we could see. This was really a remote area and we couldn't guess why there would be a fence. The gate was posted with a number of no trespassing and private property signs, but it was not locked. We were hesitant to open the gate and cross, but we had come a long way. We had heard that this was a resort and couldn't imagine it would be closed to the public. (What we hadn't known then was that everyone flies into San Francisquito on small private planes.) But here we were. Finally deciding to open the gate and close it behind us, we drove the remaining kilometers worried that we had broken some rural rule.

The last part of the drive to the coast was sandy and smooth. As we neared the water, many side roads wound off into the desert, mostly to the south. We stayed to the one most traveled, except where there was a sign for a ranch, El Barril, further south on the same point as San Francisquito. Eventually we arrived at a long, flat, dry lakebed near the beach. There were dirt airstrips in several directions, and on the beach were several small stone buildings.

The truck was barely running. The last few miles we had been battling a carburetor problem. When we pulled up near the buildings the engine was coughing and spitting and when I shut it off it backfired with pre-ignition several times. It was disruptive to the peacefulness of this remote place and we felt it. Before we looked around I spent a few moments field-stripping the carburetor. A man, American, came by on his way to the buildings and we asked if this was San Francisquito. He said that it was and asked what we were doing here. I said that we had come to stay for a night or two, if they had accommodations. He was very condescending, telling us that they catered to fly-ins and that people that arrived by land were not particularly encouraged. I explained that we had made a grueling all-day trip from Bahía de los Angeles and were planning on staying here regardless of whether we slept in rented facilities or on the beach.

It turned out we did both. This collection of buildings was home-spun by U.S. standards, huts on the beach. There was, first and fore-most, a place for everyone to congregate, a restaurant and separate bar with tables and chairs spread around under a roof of palm fronds and walls waist high that were of thick rock and concrete. From there to the roofline the walls consisted only of an occasional vertical four-by-four, every three feet or so, to support the frames of the thatched roofs, leaving the buildings secure from the sun but open to the views of the desert and ocean.

The beach at San Francisquito was long and sweeping, steeper that those of Bahía de los Angeles and more open to the gulf. The swells were big enough and the beach steep enough that the waves smashed on the sand, seeming to shake the whole length of beach. There were several square *palapas* scattered along the beach for shade and sleeping, constructed like the restaurant and bar. We rented one of these from the haughty American and made plans for dinner.

San Francisquito was more tourist-oriented than Bahía de los Angeles. There was no realistic way in or out except by private plane. It was habituated by a number of Flying Samaritans, U.S. doctors that flew missions into Baja to offer their services to the locals free of charge. There were a few guests and we met them all at dinner. I asked how they got their supplies. (Guerrero Negro was the closest town and it was a two- or three-day trip to get there and back by car.) Americans managed the place and most fresh food was flown in weekly from the States. It seemed mostly like a place that the same small set of gringos frequented, but there were few guests while we were there. This was fine with us as the first fellow we'd encountered, who turned out to be the manager, was such a putz.

After our first encounter the putz's attitude improved. After dinner we sat at the bar to see who would appear to entertain us. There were several fly-ins and we joined their group and shared comparisons of Baja from the land and air. So many pilots in those days brought friends to the remote beaches of Baja by air, and they seemed to think that air travel was the only way to get there. Putz was quite clear about his high-flying superiority over us road warriors. I wondered how flying to a remote place would encourage one to feel superior to those who drove there. Certainly the ground traveler experienced at least as much as the folks who flew. I guessed it was more a matter of a plane costing more than a car, thus those in cars were looked down on, both literally and figuratively. Oh well. The gentle folks of San Francisquito were mostly friendly and it was comfortable. Putz even condescended and bought me a drink as the evening wound to an end.

We spent two days lollygagging on the beach, enjoying being around Americans. I was surprised that the place was owned and operated by Americans and assumed it was somehow sponsored by a Mexican attorney. Putz acted like the owner and said he was. But his body language was too insecure to have any true authority or autonomy. He was one of those lovely folk who are so inadequate they can't show anyone what they're really made of for fear of criticism; they think they can keep you at bay with a blanket of false security. There is no room in Baja for arrogance.

We left San Francisquito on a rock-strewn, westward-bound road-bed when the doctors taxied north and lifted gently into a silky sky with a tail of runway dust. San Francisquito was deserted except for Putz and his crew. The good doctors had passed on the advice they had overheard from the local boy that provided overland supplies: go back to Bahía de los Angeles by the west coast route, through El Arco, a mining community about fifty kilometers away, and from there north to Black Warrior and then the junction with the Bahía road.

We listened to their advice and headed into the rising desert. The trip to El Arco was uneventful except for a steep grade that led to an unlocked gate. But we had experienced the steepest of grades and had also learned at San Francisquito that a gate with a private property sign, *propiedad privado*, does not always mean don't enter, it means that you should remember while on that property that it is not yours and be respectful.

The dusty haul to El Arco was about two hours. This town is spread over a number of low rolling hills. There were several small stores and many simple homes. We could see mines tunneling into the higher hills to the north where gold had been mined around the turn of our last century. The community was more comfortable than many, perhaps because they had once had a single focus.

Roads led from El Arco in several directions, but ours led toward the west coast. The transpeninsular highway was only twenty kilometers west from here, and the road was graded most of that way. We worked some of the stiff muscles out of the truck and made the new pavement by midafternoon. At the highway we turned north toward Guerrero Negro, the largest supply point in the central desert, where we had not been on this trip.

Planning to buy canned meats and a few fresh vegetables that would keep on the trip back to the bay, we arrived in Black Warrior about three in the afternoon. Siesta was in effect, but nearing its end. We had a soda and waited for the shops to open and then made our purchases and left. In the smaller villages of Baja the people may have taken siesta but it was discrete. This town completely shut down between one and three in the afternoon, except for the cafés.

The paved highway going north was smooth and black. (It was only recently completed and yet to fill with the potholes of the years that followed.) An hour and a half later we came to the turnoff and headed for the bay. Sixty-six bone-jarring and dusty kilometers later we passed through the village just in time to say hello and drive back to the hut before dark. We had had a good time but were glad to be back to rest position. Over the next few days we reconnected with the environment and relaxed around the hut, performing routine duties and falling back into a well-understood pattern of behavior.

San Borja

A few days later we took a shorter trip, to the Mission at San Borja, built in the 1760s with old money from Europe. We drove out the road that led to the transpeninsular highway, which the San Borja road encountered in the vicinity of kilometer forty-four from the turnoff near Punta Prieta. Rochie and Dulcie were probably wondering if this trip would be as uncomfortable as the last. The road to San Borja is reached by climbing into the central desert, west of the bay, and then turning south after we had passed Volcán Santa Evita. From here a rock-strewn and tilting road climbs slowly to an altitude of five hundred feet.

We spent many hours traveling over this very bad road with sharp volcanic shards and no sign of even a dry watercourse. By early afternoon I was wondering if we were on the right route but it was the *only* route. Many hours after the original junction we came to an area that was greener and where there were cattle and horse tracks on small trails in the midst of the few tire tracks from pickups or cars that had passed here recently. The road turned gradually back west and we entered a protected shallow valley, heavy with undergrowth and a number of ironwood or smoke trees and large broom baccharis stands. The trees were so large that we were driving underneath their branches and in the shade for short, shadowed moments. In the near distance we could see tall palms.

We exited the tall brush and dense trees to find San Borja.

Here was a basin of about fifty acres that was unlike any of the surrounding desert. A small stream flowed from somewhere east; a channel had been dug and maintained over many years, centuries perhaps, and used to irrigate the several acres under cultivation. This was the epitome of subsistence farming, but it was a wonderful green and almost lush oasis after the hours of throwing up dirt on a road that had seemingly lasted forever. Fresh water from a spring always causes the hair on my arms and neck to stand. My first thoughts are that here I am standing in a place that has had a natural attractiveness for as long as the water source has existed. Here, my mind informs me, have lived and passed by many people over the centuries. Here families have come forever to sip sweet water or fill small water baskets. Here the padres tried to raise crops enough to feed the Indians and themselves.

San Borja had an annual celebration that drew many locals from the hundreds of square miles of surrounding territory. Because of the water, the village had a colorful history. Let the peón live in the desert where there was no water, my mind said; the good life will be led here beside the sweet water from the earth.

Two or three families were living at San Borja. To our surprise there was a very simple store where sodas were offered at room temperature. At the temperature of this room it was lucky the caps hadn't blown off the bottles. A young boy, perhaps ten, was selling these drinks. He was shy but friendly and fun to talk with. It is always nice to spend time with people who are so bored that they're sorry to see you leave. I could talk all I wanted and no one seemed to mind.

The boy assumed correctly that we were here to visit the mission. He asked when he could show us the ruins. We said immediately, if he wanted. He did, anxious to show his knowledge of the mission's history and to establish his value as a tour guide.

The adobe mission was two stories tall, combining many rooms for living along with the church itself. Enough of the L-shaped building was intact that it was easy to capture the lives that had been spent there in the love of God and others and of labor. Our young guide, in dusty white pants and shirt and sandals, talked to us of the lives of the priests, Indians, and soldiers as if they were here with us.

I took a picture there that I've held in mind ever since that day; I'd have it in a frame somewhere if it hadn't been destroyed. Joining the first floor of the main church to the second, which was mostly decomposed, a spiral staircase rose, made of adobe and enclosed by circular walls. Each stair advanced upward in a tight spiral. The form of a single stair was somewhat like a keyhole in an old door, but about three feet long. These steps were individually formed from damp adobe, dried, and stacked, offset, and in ascending order, on top of each other. The circular part of the keyhole was not offset so that portion formed the center part of the spiral. Circumscribing these was the round exterior wall of the cylinder. We climbed this adobe staircase.

There was not much left of the second level except to look down upon the ground level of the church that was open to the roofline. I tried to imagine the lives that had been lived there; the priests so far from home and living in conditions so foreign. What had driven them to this dusty place? Were they bored or were they driven to save the souls of these people they couldn't understand? What would drive a man such a great distance from Europe—so far from his family?

To the Cochimí, who had wandered throughout this desert for centuries before the missionary's arrival, the priests and the church must have been confusing. The Indians were self-sufficient and content before the Europeans came here. But the Europeans had strong ideas and a strong God. It is always easy to follow people with strong commitments and voices. And guns. The padres built grand buildings and had complex rituals. The uncomplicated Cochimí must have held the Europeans in awe, at least at first. Respect must be carefully placed. Too many people suffered here and at other missions, as a simple people met with a complex people. It was a difficult time for both. But the Cochimí gently faded into extinction because of the things priests and soldiers brought in apparent good faith. The padres and their associates presumably came here to save the souls of the Indians. We cannot know whether they succeeded at this, but they certainly didn't do anything for their bodies. So many lives were sacrificed unnecessarily and so much history erased. Only a few cave paintings and sleeping mounds and high heaps of shells remain, at rest, with the degraded cliffs of remnants of other, earlier ages of prehistory. We will never know the whole story.

Our young escort led us to the site of the spring that provoked the padres to settle here two hundred years ago and that today still provided the irrigation for the meager crops of the moment. We walked amidst the small plantings of corn and chilies clustered together, each catching a bit of another's shade, under palms, following the water to the fields of thirsty, twisting furrows ploughed by hand. There was barely enough water to keep the sparse crops alive.

San Borja had been a *tinaja*, a watering hole, before it had been a mission. I suspect many missions were built where the Cochimí had congregated. The priests needed water more than the Indians as they were less acclimatized to the desert. But they also had another purpose. If they could raise crops they could feed the Indians and indenture them to the church.

The boy ran out of prepared and remembered words upon our arrival back at our truck. We complimented and tipped him and thanked him for a truly educational and animated introduction to the mission. We asked him what was the easiest way back to Bahía de los Angeles.

He said the shortest way was the way we had come. But the fastest way was to go to Rosarito, twenty kilometers west, which was near the transpeninsular highway and then go north to the Bahía junction, like we had done returning from San Francisquito. We approached his family, telling them of the qualities of the boy as a tour guide. They were comfortable and at rest in this peaceful setting. In the few moments we spent there we were introduced to the entire family. Talking with them, we found that they were Jehovah's Witnesses. It was curious that people devoted to one religion were taking care of the objects of another.

Leaving San Borja, once again we headed west, and it took us several hours to get home. And, once again, we were glad to get back to the hut, where we spent the next few weeks falling back into our routine.

Black Warrior

By the end of the hottest part of summer we were ready for another adventure, which, it turned out, was the best of our trip. One evening, after dinner, sitting with the gas lamp lit and fighting the bugs, we opened the map on the outdoor scrap of washed-up plywood that served as a table. We wanted to be gone no more than a week. Even though we had no front door to close and lock and we had never had a visitor except our guests, we didn't want to be gone long enough that it appeared the hut was deserted.

Looking at the map we couldn't decide where to go. We had been the length of the peninsula many times and knew many of the ways and byways, but nothing grabbed at us for a visit. We decided that we would start by crossing to Guerrero Negro and just see what happened.

For the third time in a month we loaded up our gear and the dogs, checked the oil and motor mounts in the truck and took off. We bounced through the accustomed dust and heat to the highway and drove south toward the division between the northern and southern Baja states at the 28th parallel. We had been through this area on our trips to San Francisquito and San Borja recently. Once the road passes south of the village of El Rosarito it crosses the arid northern Vizcaíno Desert. It is very bleak, attractive only to the most dedicated desert lover. Many dusty tracks issue west into the flat desert with no indication of a destination or rendezvous.

It was midmorning by the time we reached the states' division. We were enjoying the ease of driving the paved road when suddenly the engine began making a heavy metallic banging that shook the whole truck. I pulled off the road, shut the engine off and got out to investigate. There was nothing unusual to see under the hood but I knew we had a serious problem. Some major internal parts were obviously loose or broken, and based on the severe noise, I guessed it was a piston rod.

We were about fifteen kilometers from Guerrero Negro. It was too far to walk comfortably or otherwise in the sun. I didn't want to leave Mary Ann alone and try to get to town myself on foot, but we didn't have too many options. I tried the engine and it started, acting like it was good for one more revolution. We pulled onto the highway and drove at five miles an hour into town. How fortunate there was little traffic on the only Baja highway!

We made the junction and turned, driving past a long kilometer of trash before we saw the first buildings. I stopped at the Pemex station at the bend in the road and asked where I could find a mechanic. The three attendants all pointed across the street to a string of simple houses and said that a good mechanic lived in the blue one. I walked across the street and knocked on the door. A woman answered and I asked about a mechanic. A man came out the screen door. I was introduced to an Asian-Mexican by the name of Genaro Kim. The relationship that formed as we shook hands lasted for many years and carried us each deep into both sides of the border.

Genaro agreed to look at my truck, so I drove it from across the street, and before I had shut off the motor he had formed the opinion that I needed to swap engines. I knew we were having serious problems but had assumed that my current engine could be fixed. "Not so easy," said Genaro, "in this outpost. This is Arabia." It was much easier to just buy another engine, he told us. When I asked him how to approach this task, he pointed to a passing Chevy and said to just buy an older car and swap engines. After that he would have the work done in a few days. It was beyond my imagination how all this could get done with so few supplies and equipment out of the clapboard partial building that was his garage, with the few small hand tools I could see. But we had no choice and he was a confident, no-nonsense fellow, so we agreed.

As he lived on the town's main street, we stood there watching the cars and trucks go slowly by, avoiding the washes and potholes, until he saw a car that had the engine model we wanted. We waved to the driver who stopped and, when asked, quickly told us he didn't want to sell his car. After two or three similar experiences we stopped a man who asked how much we would pay. I looked at Genaro and he said one hundred dollars. The man got out of the car and said that was good. I handed him five twenty-dollar bills, and he left—no muss, no fuss. He didn't have a single item to remove from the vehicle.

Mary Ann and I gathered the gear we would need from the truck and walked the distance to the part of town that housed the salt company. Knowing we needed a place to stay for about a week, we walked through the quadrants of stores, workplaces, and houses, eventually finding a small Mexican hotel with six or seven rooms, all at ground level, and each about eight feet square. The rate was three dollars a night. The bathroom was down the hall. Each room squeezed in a double-sized bed, a single chair, and a bare light bulb hanging from the ceiling by the eighteen gauge wire that trickled electricity to the dim and pulsating bulb.

We took the room and sat on the bed wondering what we would do for a week in Black Warrior.

Before we could begin to answer that quandary, I ventured to take a shower, in the single room that served as a bath and a toilet for all. The room was five feet square and housed three items: a toilet, a large bucket, and a small bucket. The toilet had no running water as input. There was, in fact, absolutely no plumbing anywhere to be seen. There was, though, an oil drum, full of water, immediately outside the door to the room. The drum was positioned to catch any condensation or runoff from any rain that should fall on the roof of the hotel. All was in perfect harmony.

After analyzing the surroundings, a process became evident to the whole operation. In order to flush the toilet, you would fill the small bucket from the oil drum and dump that into the toilet bowl. It turned out that the toilet output was plumbed, in the dirt. In order to bathe, you would fill the small bucket, stand in the larger bucket, dump water over yourself, soap up, rinse, dry, and then empty the larger bucket into a drain in the floor. I was sure that this gray water of the drain supported a garden of thirsty plants somewhere outside. I didn't want to think about where the water from the toilet went.

So I completed this simple task and went down the breezeway to our room. I told Mary Ann how things worked and she repeated the process.

Nothing very extraordinary happened during our stay at Black Warrior. Without a vehicle we had lots of time to kill, walking around town and sitting in small restaurants, talking or reading over coffee. I had always kept a log and that filled my time. Mary Ann read romance novels, which made me jealous.

One day, out of boredom, I decided it would be nice to have a bottle of red wine. I had no idea where to find one or even if there was a liquor store in the town. Leaving Mary Ann in our room reading her book, I walked down the side streets to the main thoroughfare into and out of the town, a wide dirt road. In the center of town was a single, dust covered taxi. I asked the driver if he knew of a store that sold wine and liquor. He certainly did and immediately gestured for me to get into the cab. I told him I was fine to walk, but he said it was too far to walk. He was animated and quick and insistent that I sit in his cab and be escorted to this store. Seeing no simple alternative, I sat and we took off, east.

We passed through the salt company part of town, continued through the eastern part, and drove through the dump and straight out of town under my constant questions and his strong assurances that he knew exactly what I needed. We drove to the junction of the transpeninsular highway and, where the road forked for the northern and southern routes, we went straight.

We drove several kilometers into the desert. I would have been concerned, but my host was so carefree and casual. Three or four kilometers from the highway I could see a cluster of buildings in the distance. We entered the odd assemblage of fifteen or twenty one-story and several two-story structures spread across both sides of the road. There were men and women crossing the street and coming from and going into the buildings. Many of the buildings had large signs advertising the availability of beer, music, and dancing.

The driver stopped in front of one of these and jumped out and opened my door and with a bow and outstretched arm ushered me inside a dingy cantina. I was thinking maybe they sell wines and liquors to go also. There was no such luck.

We entered a large, dark, windowless room with a bar and a number of tables. A number of men and two women stood at the bar, drinks scattered around. More men and women were sitting around the tables, some playing cards and dice. Rowdy recorded Mexican ranchero music radiated from a dusty, battered record player in a corner of the room.

Several couples were dancing. Many of the men were drunk. A sign on the wall told me that I could buy a dance for a peso, about a dime. I could judge from the scene that I could buy more than a dance for little more than a peso. This was a scene out of the early American west. I realized when this thought struck me that this actually *was* the early American west. It was just on another side of a border. *Early* is, in fact, immeasurable, and relative.

The place was a grimy dive and I was stuck with my friendly driver whose feelings I didn't want to hurt. But I was disgusted by the sorry sight of this roomful of dusty cowboys and oily overweight prostitutes. We went to the bar and I ordered two beers, one for my driver and one for me. I told him that my mediocre Spanish had perhaps conveyed the wrong message and that I really did just want a bottle of wine. I said that we should enjoy our beer and get back to town because people would be worried about me. We watched the women, loud mouthed and loudly dressed, sidling with their men around the dance floor, their bodies close and suggestive and rocking with the music. I assumed that the second floors of the buildings were bedrooms. I was happy for these people that this place existed. But I was ready to leave before we entered.

We finished our beer and I convinced a red-eyed semiconscious fellow beside us that I really couldn't, at the moment, enjoy the services they had to offer, whatever they were, and that I didn't know how to dance, thank you. We left, got back to the car and returned to town with my apologies to the driver. I have looked occasionally since at the various maps of Baja we have encountered and have never seen this town identified. I assumed that it was one more benefit that the salt company provided to keep the lonely workers at this remote outpost happy, or at least content.

One afternoon the rains came. We were walking around town when the thunderheads built darkly to the west and floated over town. The color of the landscape changed and the sky was ominous, so we walked back to the hotel. Within a few minutes it began to rain and soon was pouring heavily. The undrained dirt streets quickly flooded and water ran to the paths of least resistance. One of these paths was the breezeway connecting the rooms of our hotel and, as our room was on the street side, it flowed into our room. I fetched a broom from the hallway and tried to sweep the water away. All the grime from the street was filling our small cubical. In the midst of this we heard loud bursts of thunder. A sudden flash seemed to come from right out our single window, from the center of the street our room faced. It was accompanied immediately by a deafening roar. We stood in our room afraid to leave, but getting deeper and deeper in the runoff rainwater.

The storm moved on quickly and left us with muddy quarters but no other damage. We were sure the lightning had struck in the center of the street right outside our room, but it was over and no one was hurt.

We spent a lot of time at Genaro's garage every day, helping him if we could, and hoping for his quick success. By the fifth day he had taken the engine out of the Chevy we had bought, removed the engine from my truck, and had secured the new engine in the Land Cruiser. He bought new sparkplugs from a small auto parts store and changed these, adding oil and other particulars. After he fiddled and tweaked for another hour he was ready to start the engine. We waited, half expecting the new engine to blow up, but it started and idled nicely and we were relieved. We left Genaro to continue tuning the engine. The next morning we paid our hotel bill, fifteen dollars for five days, and went to get the truck and pay Genaro. I was worried about his charges. We had very limited resources and he had worked on the truck for four days, plus he had purchased some additional parts. The truck was sitting in front of his house, newly dusted and ready. I asked him what we owed and he said thirty-two dollars in labor plus seven dollars in parts. I had to keep myself from whooping. This was much, much less than I had expected. I had also assumed that, since we had not agreed on a price ahead of time, I would get stung—but this was not so. Like Sammy, Genaro had an hourly wage that applied to his work. He had worked eight hours a day for four days at a dollar an hour.

I paid Genaro, adding a few dollars for his speedy work, and I thanked him, telling him that all our mid-peninsular repairs were forever his and we drove off from Black Warrior toward San Ignacio. Luckily, unlike my original peninsular friend, Epifanio, I saw and had dealings with Genaro Kim many more times over the years.

Return to Bahía de los Angeles

The drive back to Bahía de los Angeles was tiring, but passing through the village, we felt we were coming home. A *chubasco* had gone through a few days before, we were told.

Back at the beach, we found that the hut had settled at an angle of forty-five degrees and our belongings were thrown about over a wide area. The winds must have blown nearly a hundred miles an hour to do that kind of damage.

With both of us trying to salvage as many of our storm-damaged things as possible, cleaning up took several days, but they were slow days filled with the magic and tranquility of the bay. After our work was done each day, which was limited to a few hours in the early morning due to the extreme heat, we filled time reading in the shadows of the hut, swimming, going through the usual chores in our environment. The four of us took our long evening walks again, toward the soft golden sands of Rincón. Rochie and Dulcie running ahead, checking back occasionally to be certain we were following their lead. Flocks of birds worked the offshore bait, standing, feathers working with the wind, in the shallows of the lagoon. Magnificent frigate birds hovered far above, looking prehistoric with their angular black silhouettes of bent wings and split tails.

We drove to La Gringa and sat beneath the old pier there, shadowed from the morning sun, digging through the worn stones, collecting tiny shells that we could take home with us for purposes undefined. After a meal at the Díaz ranch we checked the public mail slot in Antero's office. Nothing was waiting for us there.

An old band of burros from the Díaz ranch wandered through camp looking for water one afternoon. One was so old that it could hardly navigate; perhaps the waves of heat off the desert were all that kept him standing. The five beasts were semidomesticated—they gravitated toward our camp but never came too close. Coyotes were constantly on the prowl but were never confrontational to either the dogs or us. Snakes and scorpions had become routine and we were forever on subconscious guard. We never saw a single tarantula, but that was just fine with us. In truth, the only single thing that we had felt threatened by was the weather, and we had survived that by luck or happenstance.

By this point, we had exhausted the supply of dog food that Bill had brought to us on the fenders of his Corvette, so I was back to fishing every morning for our beasts. Cleaning the fish in front of the hut was always an adventure. I had a small board that I placed on the rocks near the edge of the water to gut the triggerfish that Rochie and Dulcie loved. As always, the instant the first fish was pulled from the water, the gulls and pelicans hovered a few meters offshore or paddled almost within touching distance. They were leery but hungry and wanted a tasty morsel.

One morning a small pelican was nearly on top of me as I gutted a fish. He would almost eat out of my hand, but not quite. Checking him out, I spotted a piece of fishing line wound around his legs. Spontaneously grabbing him by the neck, I pulled him toward me. He could get me with his wings, dangerous enough in themselves but not as bad as his beak. Somehow I wrapped my arm around him and secured his wings to his body, grabbing his beak with my other hand. Quickly untangling the line from his feet, I threw him into the air to give him a head start as far away from me as possible. The rest of the birds scattered but were soon back, begging for the remaining scraps. The closer a wild animal is willing to come to a human, the greater his need.

Over the last few days we decamped slowly. When we finished with an item we thought we might use on future trips, we stowed it. Many items we had collected and most of our canned and dry goods we would give to the locals in the village. The refrigerator was the biggest item. We discussed that with Mama and she told us her niece could use it; on our next trip to the village it was loaded in Tortuga and brought to her.

Packing was sad, as we reflected on the last few months. This was a new beginning for us. We had been introduced to an environment that we had absorbed and adopted. It was now *within us*. This quiet time spent in this place, *our* place, had been enough time—not to own it but to have it own *us*. Sleeping one last night together on the sand, we listened to the small splashing, rinsing sound of the wavelets just feet from our bodies and to the rush of wind through the thatch of our hut, a symphony of natural frequencies pulling at the strings of our hearts. These were things we knew would be missed. We were weighted by our looming departure, knowing we were turning north, returning to the culture we had replaced for a period of time. This place of

isolated beach and sky was one we could return to frequently, for reju-
venation, and we would remember Baja often amongst our heady meetings and petty scratchings, looking for seeds of another kind.

And many lessons I could take with me.

Forever I would be the dolphin, sweeping before us, into and above
the water, teaching their young an art that was their own; forever I
would be the cawing, obnoxious gull, sea-chicken, on the beach, arguing over bits of fish flesh while heading into the windy gusts; forever I would be the mother whale sidling the shore in fifty feet of water,
counting the heartbeats until it was instinctively time to rise to the surface, blow, suck and dive again, teaching my newborn the navigational
tricks of our trade; forever I would be the magnificent frigate bird floating far above the water in the azure sky; forever the sea lion chasing
my fish over the rocks as a line drew the fish toward the fisherman
onshore.

Forever I would be each lesson I had learned here.

I would be the sand, the water, the air, an empty shell, a small
creature living in an inherited place. I would be the heat and the
dust.

I would be the pelican floating in the air, wingtips skimming the
waters, catching an updraft to climb a few feet and drop again. I would
sweep toward the hot cliff and catch the rising air and soar quickly
above the more and more distant water, until the waves were ripples.
Spotting a small school of fish, I would slowly and gently, in a comfortable way I had done for thousands of generations, tuck my wings
along the length of my body, stretching, stretching until I could touch
my wingtips to my backward-pointed legs and feet. I would form my
clumsy body into the perfect arrow and glide, aware of even the smallest change of air flow and density, gathering speed through hundreds
of feet of open sky toward the water and my fish. I would smoothly
penetrate the velvety surface, open my extended beak, fill my pouch
and swallow, rise to the surface, shake the water from my body, and
calculate the calories I would burn in lifting from the surface at various
angles with respect to my friends and adversaries, the wind and the
water. I would repeat the process.

And, early on some morning, I would fly low over Mike and Mary
Ann's hut. There was no purpose for this except that they are there and
I am here. We have shared this environment for a while now and I am
mildly curious.

The Slow Road to Another Home

Though we were sad, we knew we would be back many times in our lives. Members of our families were here, in a sense. The last night I sat getting drunk on cheap rum and crying on the beach. I did not want to leave the things we had learned to love. A new universe was here, and now that we had gained access, there was so much more to know. I knew we were returning to the fast-paced, ignore-as-much-as-possible environment of southern California. My heart was here in Baja and at the Bahía de los Angeles. In my country we had little use for the sensitivities that we had cultivated here. I was surprised to hear myself call my country my country. But that is the way it is. It's difficult to discard one, but easy to adopt another.

We gathered our last belongings from the beach and the hut and said our transient good-byes in the village and gave Mama a kiss and thanked Antero, Sammy, and Chubasco for the many times they had offered us all their help. We shook hands all around and slapped backs. And we didn't cry tears because that is not a Mexican trait. But our hearts were crying with the moment.

The long drive to the *frontera* was uneventful, and we passed through customs with no interference.

Back in southern California, we spent a few days with Mary Ann's mother and father. I had picked up a case of amoebic dysentery in the last short time and we took time for me to recover. After a week of rest I was ready, even anxious, to go to work. I found in my wallet a note from Bill. He had told me that a job was waiting whenever I was ready. *Was* I ready for emersion into a culture that I had tried to improve on? Of course—it was mine. There is only one of those. But this was a limited engagement. We were continuing our understanding of our individual lives and of our life together. We were planning to work nine months and then take a three-month trip through Western Europe. That plan would keep us focused.

And had we achieved our most important objectives? We had faced challenges, and survived together a set of unique experiences. We had worked together efficiently as a team. Separately we were individuals and together we were a couple. There had been time to get to know each other apart from the hubbub of our society and we would go on from here to meet the next problem. Our challenges were numerous: we wanted children, but couldn't agree on the number—one or two. Would Mary Ann work after we had kids? Would we be able to provide an adequate income to build a family as we imagined? Would our affection for each other be enduring? There were many questions to be answered.

And to get us through the excitement and stress of the space business and the Jet Propulsion Laboratory, the endless meetings, the egos, the correct and incorrect, the winners of arguments, and the losers, we had our memories and lessons of this time in Baja.

Through the battles we would have as our guide the pelican. Our focus would be feathered and sleek and slick, falling noiselessly through the brilliant, cloudless sky. We would become a grain of sand on a remote beach. We would become the smooth round stones of our beach at La Gringa.

An Interlude

After our time at Bahía de los Angeles Mary Ann and I knew we would have to work and rebuild the meager but necessary fund required to continue our adventures. Both of us found jobs immediately, thanks to our reputations and our friends.

Our house was still leased so we lived in a little motel in Montrose, California. Our rooms, called a "suite," were all of two hundred square feet—a tiny living room, tinier kitchen and bedroom, and a bathroom. During the six months we lived there we spent all of our away-from-work hours discussing our travel plans. By the end of that time we knew we'd need more than the original year we had scheduled.

The agenda we ended up with, which evolved rather than being born as a single plan, was to spend three months touring Western Europe, followed by another year at the Laboratory to replenish resources, then three months traveling throughout the United Kingdom. In 1977, our first son Michael was born, and the three of us lived in southern Spain for six months, touring North Africa, the Canary Islands, and other destinations in between.

During these years we still found time to revisit Baja California every year. Kevin was born in 1979 and we spent vacation time with the boys in Bahía de los Angeles that summer. Over time the bay was as well known to the boys as it was to Mary Ann and me. Every year we'd plan and pack and the boys would grow more and more excited as the departure date for even a short vacation drew near.

These periodic Baja trips were fine and well and were enough to keep the boys content, but both Mary Ann and I knew the boys were entering perhaps their most impressionable years. And I was consumed by the need for a serious freeze-frame of life inside our family.

Early in 1985 we decided to pave the way at JPL for another extended absence. We both completed our assignments and started gathering the gear we'd need for a second hut, hopefully somewhat nicer than the last. After all there were four of us now.

Part 2

A Family Drops Out

Plans

In 1985 our business was doing well and was as healthy as I wanted it to be. Mary Ann and I were in the midst of raising a family and ready for a change from the endless round of T-ball and soccer circuits and school and work. While we four had never spent an entire summer at Bahía de los Angeles, it was already like a second home to the boys from all the visits we'd made. One night, on the way to the bedroom we asked Michael and Kevin if they would like to spend the whole summer at the bay. They were ecstatic, wanting to leave immediately.

"Yeah, let's leave right *now*, right *now*." Michael shouted.

"Me too! I wanna go *too*!" Kevin echoed.

The boys were at a perfect age to learn the many lessons of our favorite peninsula—Kevin was six and Michael was eight—so we began our planning process.

After dropping the boys at school every morning, Mary Ann did her morning walk with friends through the hills of Glendale and I attended to work. I was luckier than many parents because I worked at home and could be there for the boys more than I otherwise would have been. But I still felt my life didn't have the desired familial focus. Work was too demanding to allow me to settle in with my family to the depth I wanted. Mary Ann and I both knew that these next few years would fly by and suddenly Michael and Kevin would be grown. We wanted to stop time for a while and spend a summer with just the four of us, making a memory to last a lifetime. And the uncluttered lifestyle of Baja California, especially the Bahía de los Angeles, would be just the place. We made plans to leave the day the boys' school got out.

Mary Ann and I realized that some of the risks we had experienced on previous trips to Baja, while worthwhile, were not chances we wanted to take with young children for an extended stay. For one thing, the location of our first hut was less than ideal, which we had learned from the flash flood. Secondly, we needed a sturdier and better-organized hut. Another consideration was that both the boys had light blond hair with fair young skin and needed much more protection from the sun.

Hours were spent designing and engineering the hut, analyzing the dimensions and materials that we would need to build our home for the summer. We would need something bigger than the original hut we built for just Mary Ann and me, and decided on a length of sixteen feet and a width of eight feet. This would give us 128 square feet in which to cook, eat, and sleep. I measured the cook stove, kerosene lanterns, plates, and other cooking and eating utensils and made scaled-down drawings with proposals for shelf space, fruit-box cupboards, under-counter storage of ice chests, and mouse-proof food stores.

Stackable cots we'd purchased would be made into bunk beds for the boys to conserve floor space. Wooden fruit crates scavenged from the back of our local supermarkets would serve as bookcases and clothing storage. We collected empty five-, ten-, and fifteen-gallon bottles for fresh water and gasoline, knowing these supplies were still hard to come by at the bay; ice was more available though, by 1985, and we gave up the idea of another cumbersome gas refrigerator.

Calculating the number and sizes of wood beams we would need, I bought four-by-fours for the uprights and two-by-fours for the horizontal supports. We were careful to plan an environmentally correct hut as much as possible—everything we had brought would have to be removed after our months on the beach. So, rather than pour concrete to support the uprights, we would bury them again in the sand. For the walls we needed protection from the sun and a surface that permitted as much air to flow as possible. The availability of palm fronds was limited in southern California and I didn't want to wait until we got to the bay and trust we'd be able to scavenge enough; the boys would need immediate protection until their fair skin was tanned. Numerous rolls of split bamboo sunshades were bought, which could be raised when not needed and lowered for the night or to avoid early morning or late afternoon sun. If we were lucky enough to get a breeze, they would allow it to pass through.

I cut half-inch plywood into the rough shapes planned by my scaled drawings to serve as shelves and tabletops. We purchased and packed boxes of nails, hundreds of feet of several types of rope, cans of white gas for the stove and kerosene for the lanterns, plus a portable radio/tape deck and cartons of batteries. We bought one store out of every SPF numbered suntan lotion. We packed shorts, sandals, and boots or the boys, a single long-sleeved shirt for each of us to avoid the sun during the first days, and hats. The list of clothing we didn't need was longer than the clothing we did.

Aside from these simple items, we were beginning to realize that this trip was more complex than our last. We finally had to limit what we each took just from the standpoint of available space. The old and tired Land Cruiser of prior trips had been sadly replaced with a 1984 Cruiser Land Wagon. Behind that, to give us shade until we had finished the hut, we would tow a small tent trailer. All the building supplies would be stored, out of sight of Mexican customs, inside the trailer.

Mary Ann met with Michael and Kevin's teachers and we made trip after trip to the bookstore, buying cases of books, educational and fun and fiction children's books for the boys, and an assorted case each for Mary Ann and me. This was going to be what the doctor ordered: a lot of time to relax and let our natural lives float back to the surface.

During this time, filled with my thoughts of our coming summer, I was more at peace with myself, more focused on our family.

There are too few years in the life of a family where a parent knows the absolute perfection of affection from a small child. A child's life is filled with emerging trauma—in an instant outside the parents' eyes, he is hurt and falls, full on his chest. His consciousness fades for a moment and then he realizes he is alive, but breathless. He gasps, filling his tiny lungs full of air and then lunges for his father and burrows into the familiar folds of clothing and flesh, hiding his face to deter the fear that he has faced. The beating heart, his father's blood, pulses along the circuitous routes surrounding him, through his parent's arms, torso, neck. The child smells the familiar odors and the roughness of cheek and salty breath that makes a dad—*his* dad.

Father is the ultimate protector for only a brief time during which there is no distinction between physical, emotional, and intellectual to the child. There is no question of right or wrong. There is just how father does it. These are the years where the man that is father lives what he has fought for in his life. His fate is that of a salmon fighting upstream, but the spawning is over. This is the father's time to pass on to the child what he believes. He does this by example rather than words. He is right. He is correct. The father has the need to tell his son everything he believes; the son will bypass the intellectual processes that will encumber him in older years to accept anything said and acted out by the father to be that of truth.

Those years quickly pass. The father is unaware how vacant his life will be without the boy. The boy grows to become independent and self-sufficient. The father grows to become old and insufficient and dependent on the son. The father reflects on the moments of cuddling warmth with the youth, but that time is gone and cannot be called back except in his mind. The father fills his world with other undertakings, but none can ever rival the weight of the love for and admiration of his children.

Every father dies with the knowledge that he desperately gave whatever it took to bring his boy all the love and knowledge and hope that will be required to thread the child through life's rapids. And every father, when he's fading, knows he has done the best within him, has experienced the great love for and of his sons from the first moments of their lives and knows that they love him and will appreciate him later in their lives. The father knows that it is a mistake to want or expect words of appreciation or recognition. It will be half a lifetime before the boy begins to realize the validity of the father's words. But age is wisdom and the father knew this before he was gone. He knew that, although the son was not in tune with his words at the time, they will be of value sooner or later.

Finding Las Cuevitas

In the spring Mary Ann and I took a short trip to the bay to scout out the site for our hut. Four old friends, Barsam and Marlene and John and Laura, joined us. A location for an entire summer was different than one for a week or two; on a short stay we enjoyed being around a few other campers. But for an extended period we needed something like the beach of our 1974 trip, far enough from town to be isolated but near enough to make an occasional run for supplies or a visit with the villagers.

On this exploratory run, we covered the entire coastline of Bahía de los Angeles, from the extreme south end of the bay up to La Gringa at the northern tip. Nothing was isolated enough. We were getting discouraged when we found a road that climbed inland from La Gringa. This wound through hills less than a mile from the coast, going generally north. About two kilometers from its origin, the road forked in several directions. We spent the better part of the day exploring the area. Just before dusk we took a particularly bad branch that passed through deep sand of a dry creekbed, wound tightly through a steeply walled canyon and ended abruptly on a small alluvial fan coasting gently to the Sea of Cortez a few miles north of the protected waters of La Gringa.

The small fan here was fifty meters deep, about one hundred meters wide, and ended in small but steep hills. The south side led around a rise to another, smaller, more protected area. To the north, rising sharply from the water's edge, was a large elevated plateau which extended five hundred meters before it descended into another small beach. Also, 180 degrees of the view here was of the Sea of Cortez and the offshore islands, mostly Isla Coronado and its volcano; the other view was 180 degrees of barren desert hills and plateaus. No sign of man disturbed our environment for as far as we could see. Other than the difficult road entering the area, this was a perfect place. It was somewhat protected from the wind and had no major mountains behind to cause flooding. The beach had sand along the high and low tide lines but smooth pebbles further out. This would protect us from the stingrays that surfed the smaller swells looking for a sandy place to bury themselves.

It was unanimous—we all thought it was the site for our hut. We walked back up the rough road evaluating each rocky spike jutting into the trek, each turn, each overhanging tree, the depth of the sand. The final collective analysis was that the road was okay for the Land Cruiser, but it would be trouble for anything larger. There was one corner that consisted of two opposing sharp ninety-degree twists forcing the vehicles over an outcropping of sharp lava in the roadbed half a meter high. The walls of the arroyo climbed straight to a height of ten feet; their once molten layers were like Almond Roca candy sliced through and exposed in waves of dark and light nougat. But we needed to consider what the demands on the road might be. Like the last trip to the bay, it was possible we would have a visitor or two. I knew we could maneuver cars past this obstacle with no serious difficulties. Any vehicle with a longer wheelbase might be a problem.

Even with this sharp corner this was the place for our summer. The boys liked the deep beach, and Mary Ann and I liked the open area as a deterrent to rattlesnakes which were always a concern. The surf, rolling in from the open gulf, met an east-facing beach and broke down from its normal one-foot swells to knead gently on the shore. Rewarded after all our scouting with a good find, we returned to southern California and our preparations for the looming departure date.

We definitely needed a boat. On our first summer at the bay we didn't have one and in those days we didn't miss it. But in the years between 1974 and 1985 we had gone back every year, meeting our friends from New Jersey, Jimmy and Carol. Jimmy was a great fisherman and always towed a small outboard across the country. I had learned what little I knew about fishing from Jimmy.

But fishing was not what made having a boat essential. The Sea of Cortez, particularly in the vicinity of the Bahía de los Angeles, is packed with life, a living sea stew. This area of the gulf, known as the midriff—the narrowest part of the Sea of Cortez—is a bottleneck for the tides that constantly ebb and flow along its depths. The midriff is also home to the two largest islands in the gulf. These and numerous smaller islands interrupt the fast-moving tidal waters. In the deep channels, the water is forced under great pressures through the midriff. From the ocean floor to the surface the restricted water churns, disturbing the ocean's base, stirring up nutrient-rich foods. This insures that the area is filled with small fish, the bottom of the food chain for many of the larger fish, mammals, and fowl that inhabit the midriff in great abundance. Much of this is not visible from the shore but with a boat you can get into the midst of it.

In Alta California we shopped for and bought a Gregor fourteen-foot, deep-hulled, long-transom, three-bench, lightweight aluminum boat and a Johnson fifteen-horse outboard motor. We could carry the boat upside down on the tent trailer and fit the motor, along with vast quantities of other gear, into the back of the Land Cruiser.

As our departure neared, we finished packing the truck and trailer and arranged for our housekeeper and her family, friends from Peru, to stay in our home for the summer. With the building materials on board, the trailer was bottomed out on its springs. Land Cruisers are notorious for weak rear leaf springs and I knew we would have problems with it, so I had another set of leaves inserted, giving us better clearance while not throwing off the center of gravity. But both the truck and trailer were filled to beyond their spatial and weight tolerances.

"Are we ready yet?" eight-year-old Michael asked at dinner one night.

"*Almotht!*" six-year-old Kevin responded.

And within a few days we were.

The Trek South

On the day we were to leave, we called to Lassie, our Border collie pup (Rochie and Dulcie had left us behind at a comfortable old age), drove to school and picked the boys up after classes were out. The truck and trailer labored under the weight of everything we could imagine we would need. Looking like a one-vehicle band of gypsies with stuff piled high and jammed into every open space in the truck, we left southern California in the afternoon on a sunny day in early June— Mary Ann and I, Michael and Kevin, and Lassie the wonder puppy. The plan was to return in mid-September.

The trip to San Diego and the American side of the border was without incident. But as we passed through the Mexican side we were told to change lanes, pull over and be inspected. Understandably, the Mexicans didn't want us to bring building materials and other goods into Mexico that we could buy there.

Since I hadn't thought through this problem, I panicked. I had put hundreds of dollars worth of building materials in the tent trailer with only the most remote thought of import duties. But now, without time to think, I was afraid they wouldn't let us pass without a serious fine.

As we pulled up in front of the inspection point, I jumped out of the truck and told the guards that I had to return to where we had been issued our tourist cards, that I had left our passports there. I was in a panic, but for different reasons than I portrayed. Neither my family nor the guards suspected anything less than the truth. The guards happily obliged my return to the checkpoint, which was completely across the many lanes of traffic on the highway that passes through the border. The two guards, whistles blowing and arms waving, halted the entire incoming stream of traffic entering Mexico. Pulling our overweight assemblage in front of the irritated thousands, I parked in front of the visa checkpoint, rushed into the guard station, grabbed several blank tourist applications, and rushed back out the door and into the running truck. Acting like I was greatly relieved, I pulled out into the restarted flow of traffic, ignoring the checkpoint at which we had been halted for inspection. They were busy with other incoming tourists and didn't notice as we merged into the river of cars, busses, and trucks passing slowly through the congested *frontera*. We slipped quietly south, uninspected.

After the traffic and pedestrian sluggishness of Tijuana and the toll road to Ensenada, we ate in a small and familiar *restaurante* and continued through Santo Tomás, San Vicente, Colonet, and Camalú. Ten miles south of San Quintín, at a south-facing beach, we pulled into the Cielito Lindo campground. Removing the minimum gear, we set the tent trailer up and went to sleep, anxious to get to our destination still five or six hours away.

In the morning I was up early grumbling at Mary Ann and the boys to move their behinds and let's get on the road. The boys dressed groggily without washing their faces or brushing their teeth and went outside to play in the sand. Mary Ann and I finished the abbreviated packing, wedging everything into a tight, interconnected jigsaw of summer stores, supplies, and equipment. In short order we were on the road and I settled in behind the wheel. We passed through El Rosario, the last outpost before the barren central desert, before nine. Soon, we had cleared the El Castillo peak and climbed into the Cañada de Aguajito, ravine of the little water, and were into the red earth of the mountains before we dropped onto the floor of the central desert an hour later. Every turn of the road was known, every village recognized. We were in our comfort zone.

When I first came to Baja California I thought of her as barren and bleak. Now, after many trips, I had been given the opportunity to get to know her. She had grown on me and I grew also with everything I had learned about and from her. Every ranch was a place where I had eaten a meal, drunk a beer or had a tire patched. Several rancheros had kept a guarded eye on my broken truck while I hitchhiked to the *otro lado* to bring back replacement parts.

Passing through Cataviña, we stopped at Rancho Santa Inés for the sake of tradition and lunch. Mary Ann and I sat at the single table outside the kitchen while the boys chased wild burros that had settled on the airstrip behind the ranch house.

By two we were at the junction with the road to the bay, near Punta Prieta, and an hour later we pulled into the village. We stopped at the Díaz ranch to check in with Mama and to see how everyone had been since our last trip. Michael and Kevin knew many of the village children and quickly began the ritual through which young boys grow comfortable together. Mary Ann and I left them playing and visited the two stores to buy a few of the fresh vegetables that were available.

When we returned to gather up the boys, we told Mama where we were planning on staying. She told us the name of the area we'd chosen was Las Cuevitas, the little caves, named after the small caverns in the coastal volcanic rock created by the erosion of the sea. These flows formed points to the north and south of our beach three hundred meters apart.

The road between the village and La Gringa in those days was a single-vehicle-wide dirt track that roughly followed the shoreline most of the ten kilometers. The roadbed was a blend of dirt and sand which combined into a relatively smooth surface. The dry washes formed by the rare and often rambunctious rains that fell at the north end of the bay carved dips and loose curves into the road as it wound between the cacti and mesquite. This was a good road for having fun, as there were no other cars and we could get up a good head of steam, falling into the gentle turns and dips. Ever since the boys had been old enough to remember, we had named this Rocking Horse Road.

The glare and heat of the day faded and our rising dust left a wind-blown trail behind us. In front of us a skinny rabbit, tail bouncing in retreat, ducked into a small bush. We chased the sun into La Gringa, just shy of evening and our final destination.

Las Cuevitas Again

At La Gringa we made a pass through the deserted fish camp and down the strand between the lagoon and the protected bay. The herons and egrets were there, as well as the crabs and clams and small shells strewn along the beach of smooth round stones. There were also the overflowing memories we had collectively formed across the many summer months at the northern extremes of the bay. It seemed there were always three herons. They must somehow measure the real estate.

Nothing was changed on the beach; it was all there in front of us in its simple, natural majesty. We had many family remembrances of the old green huts, of families living there in the early years, of the fish processing plant and the Japanese family that struggled to harvest sea urchins for shipment east to their homeland, of the many moments in time we had lived and learned there in the magic of a kingdom off on its own—we had all missed it badly.

Driving back to the small side road, we traveled inland, heading westward then north across the several kilometers of sand and rock and down the rugged volcanic path to our new home. We parked along the beach above the high tide line on smooth round stones.

It was nearly evening so we opened the tent trailer and stacked the myriad supplies and gear outside. It was about ninety degrees, but the sun was in its dying arc. Michael and Kevin, glad to have the two-day drive behind them, shook off the boredom by running up and down the beach and into the shallow water, chasing sea gulls and pelicans with Lassie on their heels. We fixed a simple dinner, opened the camp chairs, and watched the magic the sun created on the cumulous clouds to the east, as it set over the hills to the west.

When it grew dark that first night, we lit a kerosene lantern and settled inside the tent trailer with the screens to protect us from the bugs attracted to the light. Before long the boys were slowing down, lying on their shared bed, reading. Mary Ann and I talked about building the hut.

I put on an album of low-key Spanish guitar and we listened to the small waves lapping at the stones. We were here now, arrived at the place we would spend our summer and lock a lifetime into a few months before I was too old to share the sensitivities of youth. By 9:30 we were all ready to turn the lamp off.

The first night on the beach at Las Cuevitas I knew we had selected a good location for our summer. The swells from the open gulf were slightly larger than at either the south end of the bay or at La Gringa; still inside the bay, but the change added a degree of freshness. The water here was more open, more free of encumbrances. Cliffs to our immediate north and south, defining the ends of our little beach, were roosting places for pelicans that came from the south end where they spent much of their day. During the night we could hear them occasionally diving for bait. Our beach was protected from the west by the hills of the plateau and by the northern and southern volcanic points and felt secure. A breeze stirred through the mosquito netting of the trailer, and we slept.

The Hut

I was up at first light and, still in work mode, I was ready to get at it. I walked around the beach looking for the best and safest place for a hut. There was one logical choice a few feet above the high tide line in an area that was covered with the smooth round stones we knew were preferable over sand. Sand was great for a beach, but in a house it got into everything, especially when the wind blew.

I went back to the trailer. Michael and Kevin were sound asleep in their bed, but Mary Ann was awake and up. We discussed the location and agreed on the site. I moved enough of the lumber to begin setting the uprights and organized my tools and equipment. The pile of materials didn't look large enough to build a house. When the boys got up and wanted to help, we had them carry the lumber, one board at a time, with one of them on each end across the short distance of beach to where I was working.

Measuring out where the upright beams would go, I drew lines to indicate the orientation of the hut with respect to the beach. The front of the hut would face the water, the volcano on Isla Coronado, and the sunrise. We scooped out holes in the sand to a depth of eighteen inches. If the eight-foot posts were buried at this depth, we would still have plenty of height, six and one-half feet. Once each beam was in place, we buried it in sand. One of us would scoop the loose sand out of the hole as quickly as possible and the other would plant and hold the post upright while the other filled the hole in with sand and stones. We repeated this for each upright, with the boys thinking it was great fun to have a reason to dig in the sand. Soon all the beams were in place and I started nailing the cross members to the vertical beams. The boys lost interest and Mary Ann took them back to the trailer to inflate beach balls and inner tubes. By midday, even though I was working slowly and taking breaks to cool off in the water, the framing for the basic structure was complete.

After lunch the boys enjoyed the water while Mary Ann sat on the beach watching them play. I started hanging the double-layered roll-up bamboo screens onto the framework as walls and roof. This went quickly and by early afternoon we had an eight-foot by sixteen-foot hut that gave us protection from the sun of day and the unknowns of night. We all started filling the structure with the food and gear, putting sleeping gear into the north end and kitchen goods into the south end. I still had to construct the kitchen counters and hang the fruit crates that would serve as cabinets, but that could wait. At least we had a basic structure. In midafternoon we moved our four cots into the shade of the hut and rested, reading. But there was still work to do and I couldn't relax.

Assembling the pre-cut plywood countertops, I nailed them into place, and hung the fruit crate cabinets from the higher horizontal beams. Mary Ann put self-adhesive lining paper over the raw plywood and we positioned the camp stove and canned food on the counter. We put the dry goods in an otherwise empty ice chest to protect them from the mice and kangaroo rats. Lengths of wire bent to form small hooks were hung from the ceiling in the kitchen and from these we suspended our pots and pans. The plates and cups were arranged in the cupboards, and silverware put into a partitioned storage case. I mounted other fruit crates onto the walls of the bedroom and Mary Ann put up foldable clothing and hung shirts from the roof there. Every open space was used efficiently without seeming cluttered or claustrophobic.

By evening I stood back and looked at our accomplishments of a single day and thought, voilà—instant hut. That night we spent our first in our new home.

As the sun's light faded, we made dinner and then lit the lanterns and fussed over the final arrangements of our collected stuff. Michael and Kevin decided which wooden crates were for their toys and which for clothes and arranged and rearranged and started over again.

Mary Ann and I walked outside to examine our handiwork. The golden lantern light from inside seeped through the split bamboo shades spilling onto the sand and stones of the beach. We could see through into the inside just enough to see the small bodies of our children as they moved around, discussing what went here and what went there. It was a wonderful and tender moment. This sight, coupled with the sounds of the sea and air, the absolute openness of the beach and the knowledge that we were here completely on our own, filled me with a feeling of accomplishment and completion. I knew this would be the summer of our lives.

We stood outside for a few minutes thinking about the additions we could make to improve our home. Another room, we decided, the same dimensions as the first, could be added to the beach side and left completely open to the water. Half of this area could be used as a library and eating area, the other half could be used for storage and we could add another small piece of plywood on a box as a coffee table. But those were efforts for another day.

By the time we walked back into the hut, the boys were asleep on their cots. We pulled the sheets around them and opened our chairs, sitting where the library would be. I found the tape player and put on a John Williams Spanish guitar album. This was the perfect end to a great day. We were looking forward to watching the boys slow down from the rush of everyday life in southern California. It would take some time, but we knew it would happen. It would happen to us as well.

A breeze came up and kept the insects to a minimum. With the guitar playing in the background, we sat reading by a dim light until we were tired. As I turned off the music, the night noises of Las Cuevitas took its place and we fell into sleep listening to new sounds.

Slowing the Pace

There was still work to do, and I was up early organizing materials and making plans in my head about finishing the hut. I had hung two layers of the split bamboo, one over the other, to ensure that a minimum of sunlight filtered through. There were several rolls left and a number of lengths of lumber. Based on our ideas from the night before, I laid out the framework for the additional porch which would run the full length of the existing quarters. This would give us a sixteen-foot by sixteen-foot square structure, 256 square feet in all. Half of this was completely protected except for the doorway (we had no door, nor did we need or want one). The other half of the hut was closed on three sides and the roof but was completely open facing the ocean just a few feet away. On the side of this addition, adjacent to the entry to the sleeping and cooking quarters, I built the remainder of the fruit crates into storage for our boxes of books, a lantern, our meteorological station, writing materials, and a small square table about thirty inches high for dining. At the other end of the porch, I positioned a low packing box we had emptied and partially filled it with stones to keep it from blowing away in the winds I knew would come, and put a two-foot by four-foot sheet of plywood on top. This was our coffee table.

All this took a couple of hours, causing grief to Mary Ann, Michael, and Kevin who were still trying to sleep. But, with the commotion of my work, they were soon out of bed and, before long, they were helping. We arranged simple deck chairs into positions likely for their best use and stowed books into the cases in the dining room-library.

Mary Ann and I had known we couldn't plan how our four lives would blend and evolve in this environment. We had wanted only for us all to be open to change and acceptance and integration with nature, each in our own way—knowing we would automatically slow down as we merged with natural processes. Reading played a major roll in being able to entertain a slowing mind.

We had brought a wide variety of books. For the boys we had schoolbooks for the grades they would be entering upon our return, but they had picked out many dozens of books of their own interests (sometimes not Mary Ann's or mine). They had coloring books, simple readers, choose-your-own-path books, and the fantasy books that Michael loved. For herself, Mary Ann had brought a variety, from romance and historical novels to biographies. I had brought mostly fiction, including many of my old favorites of the nineteenth and mid-twentieth centuries: Hardy, Hawthorne, and Conrad; Hemingway, Fitzgerald, and Maugham. For our mutual benefit we had reference books on the desert flora and fauna, on seashells and marine mammals and fishes, on Mexico and, in particular, on Baja California and the Sea of Cortez. Stowing these into the too-few crates, we constructed other places to stash them in this library that was just built but already overcrowded.

Also in the crates were the types of gear we would need to get us through the handling of the boat, maintaining the hut during and after storms, repairing truck problems, fishing, cleaning the hut, fixing fishing reels, repairing small items, performing first aid (there was sometimes a doctor in Bahía de los Angeles, but that was fifteen kilometers distant over bad roads), and dealing with the potential problems of rattlesnakes, sunburn, intestinal disorders, heat prostration, and who knew what other threats.

By the time we had filled the crates and hung maintenance materials from the walls and ceiling of the hut in every imaginable place, it looked like we had lived there for years. But we were pretty well organized and everything was secure. I was confident that we would lose nothing when the first wind came. With the major part of the work over on that second day, we ate and went into the water to cool down. Typically we wore only shorts or bathing suits all day long. There was no effort required to enter or leave the water: no changing clothes before or drying off afterward. We just walked into the water, cooled off, and returned to whatever we were doing before. During these first few days we were careful to limit the amount of sun we all got and to keep the boys covered with sunblock.

Walking back to the finished hut, I was impressed. It looked just like what I had envisioned in both my romantic and functional conceptualizations. Hanging suspended everywhere from the roof of our covered library and sitting area and inside the kitchen and bedroom were hundreds of feet of various kinds of rope, larger tools, come-alongs, saws, hoses of various diameters and lengths, pots and pans, kitchen towels and pot holders, buckets, and clothing. The fruit crate cabinets were crammed with a semi-organized array of foods, utensils, boxes, shaving kits, toilet articles, books, lanterns, binoculars, the weather station, dishes, clothes and all the supplies that we would need.

While this collection and its functional organization and appearance were important to me, they were not of the greatest importance. I not only wanted to be ready for any of the circumstances I knew we would face in these months, but I wanted a hut that looked and felt busy and was warm and inviting. The final result felt and looked like a hut you might happen onto in some foreign, remote place. *It was just that*. It felt connected and authentic, and it belonged here in our private place.

Snake!

Since our arrival we had been focused on completing the construction of our summer home. Now that the basics were in place, I felt like I could slow down. We took a break during the heat of the afternoon and sat in the shade as the sun passed behind the hut. The boys were in inner tubes in the shallow water, pushing and shoving and trying to drown each other in great flurries of splashing and shouting. The waves, constrained by our immediate north and south points, were safe for the boys' small sizes but still large enough that they presented some challenge if they got a few yards offshore where the water was a foot or two deep.

Las Cuevitas is a small bay facing Isla Coronado, or Smith's Island. There is a thousand-foot volcano on Coronado's north end. Forming our little bay were two rocky points, one north and one south, which jut into the Sea of Cortez and prevent the larger waves from hitting our shore except during the wildest storms. We didn't feel that we had to stay with the boys when they were in the water because we were only a few feet away and never out of sight. Even in the hut we could see through the walls of bamboo. Lassie was always with them. There were no other people for miles around and the risks were well known to all four of us from prior trips.

Over time, the boys were given great latitude of freedoms. During the first few days, we were all hyper and bored from our rush coming out of southern California. But, as the days passed, we slowly settled into a routine. The boys got better at inventing their entertainment. They played with their small toy cars, building tunnels into the sand and claylike earth. We cautioned them to always push a stick into the holes after they had been away to be sure no snakes or scorpions were hiding in them.

"Ooooohhh, yuck!" they screamed.

In the afternoon of the second day, Mary Ann was in the tiny kitchen and I was fishing from the shore. The boys had left the water and were digging in the dirt behind the hut. We had brought cowboy boots for them and had, from the beginning, a firm rule that they wore these whenever they wanted to go hiking. I heard them come in for their boots and then wander a few meters up the road that led back to La Gringa.

"We're going 'venturing." Michael called.

"Yeah!" echoed Kevin. "We're 'sploring!" We watched them walking up the road.

"Kevin! Come turn this rock over!"

"Ha! It's a bug!" Kevin shouted. "But Mikie, here's a path! Come and see!"

And off they went. They instinctively stayed within a safe distance. They disappeared over a slight rise along a path and were out of sight for several minutes, but we could hear them slapping their sticks against rocks and the dirt and running and laughing with Lassie at their side.

For a moment there was no sound and Mary Ann and I were both alerted. We stopped what we were doing and stood looking in their direction. Suddenly they both came barreling over a rise, dust swirling, sticks flying akimbo, calling to us excitedly. They ran straight back to the hut.

"Snake! Dad...Mom...*snake*!"

Snake! Alarms went off in both our heads. This was a situation I had known we would face before the end of our stay, but this was sooner than expected.

"Where is it? Where is it???" we called, running toward the boys. They grabbed our hands and tugged us in the direction of an ironwood tree along the side of the road. I snatched a stick we had for snakes and the four of us ran off to the tree with the boys yelling wildly.

They pointed to the underbrush that had collected at the base of the tree and told us that the snake was *there*, Dad, *right there*! I moved the brush around and we heard it rattle and I pulled the brush away and, sure enough, there was a medium-sized rattler, brown and tan and coiled with its forked tongue sensing the temperature. I pulled the spooky beast out of its cover with the stick and smashed its head with a rock.

I've never been a hunter and I don't like to kill animals for any reason, but I convinced myself that it was necessary to destroy a snake (whose territory I had recently invaded) that had the ability to possibly take a human life. Especially a child, *our* child. I didn't need this slinky thing living next door and constantly presenting a threat. I knew that the longer we lived in this place the greater the threat would be.

The four of us took the dead snake back to the hut and cut off and buried its head. We noticed that the snake had several protrusions along its tubular body, and we were curious, so we cut it open lengthwise and extracted three partially digested mice from its gut.

This was a good lesson for Michael and Kevin, not because we had chosen to kill an animal living in its own environment, but that care must be taken. We were surrounded with potential problems that, if not avoided, could become serious: scorpions, tarantulas, and snakes; two-inch black wasps; coyotes and foxes; eels, sharks, and killer whales; the water itself; the wind, rain, and lightning. In this environment any of these mostly unthreatening animals or elements could turn bad. Caution should always reign when there is no nearby cure.

The boys took the lesson in stride and went on to their next adventure. Mary Ann and I sat down and discussed a few rules and then called Michael and Kevin for a family meeting. After presenting a few ideas, we made sure we all understood and agreed with each. They should always wear their boots when playing outside our area. They should always let us know where they were going and for how long. They should go no further than the hills behind our camp and should come home whenever they heard us blow a whistle we had bought for that purpose.

Other rules developed formally over time, but these few were understood from the outset and almost always obeyed.

Black Warrior Chickens

With the hut built, we settled into the Baja routine. The boys were awake with the sun, about six, unable to sleep because of the flies. They read and played in the shade behind the hut while their mom made breakfast and dad fished for dog food. Before lunch there was swimming, looking for shells on the sand, and exploring for sea creatures trapped in the rocks as the tide went out. There were midday snacks and naps, and afternoon swimming, followed by short hikes in the hills, known as the Three Brothers, behind the hut. In the evenings we read and the boys drew or sometimes painted smooth round stones with watercolors. We ate an early dinner, read some more, and occasionally listened to a dim radio station floating south from Utah and broadcasting old *Whistler* mysteries. We'd get the boys ready for bed, play some quiet music for a while, and then drift off to sleep under the magical influences of Las Cuevitas.

It was a wonderfully warming experience to become this close to each other again, to rely on ourselves not just for a ride to school or to take care of elbow scrapes or to provide a warm hug when the need arose, but to actually participate on a moment to moment basis in each other's lives. We had all the privacy we needed individually and collectively, but, isolated as we were, we began to find other needs. Simple things were missing from our environment. The business and bustle was gone, friends were gone, television was gone. These were major adjustments. But we took them together in stride. Reading was the order of the day. Music was the dominant nighttime medium. The four of us shared the time and the space equally.

After the hut was complete, I was looking for simple, short-range tasks that would give me an objective each morning until I had adjusted enough to need no assignments. I decided that our beach would be improved with a set of stairs going down the several steep meters to the water. Presently we were stumbling through the smooth beach stones which were slippery and awkward.

On an exploratory trip into the local hills I had noticed an outcropping of flagstone. Early one morning I took the Land Cruiser back to this place and loaded twenty or thirty large flat rocks, about fifty pounds apiece, into the back. I drove back to camp and dumped these onto the smaller stones in front of the hut. Before it was too hot, I had worked them into stairs, steady enough to walk on. For several mornings I repeated this process. We soon had a rock staircase five meters wide leading down the short slope to the sea. The rocks were large and heavy enough that the small waves didn't disturb them. By the time we needed to do laundry we had built a large fire pit to one side of the stairs and could carry seawater easily to the large bucket used for heating it for showers and clothes washing.

It had been eleven years since Mary Ann and I had last lived at the bay. During this time the village had expanded considerably. Ice was almost always available. Electricity was generated by the Díaz family and available to the rest of the town. A second generator was about to be installed and would supply power during the day to as much of the village as wanted it. The hours of operation for the generator were from six in the morning until ten at night. Ice was usually trucked in from Ensenada, but it was off-loaded into smaller refrigerated local storage and sold to the locals from there. Every few days we would take the ice chests to the village and fill them. They would sit under the counter in the kitchen chilling sodas, Kool-Aid, juices and beer and whatever fresh food we had. When the ice melted it was drained off to give to Lassie to drink or to rinse ourselves with after our baths in salt water.

By the time we had been there a week, Michael and Kevin were bored again and having trouble settling down. They were used to TV and computers and school and friends and always having something to do. Looking back, I wondered if all the computer games we let them play back home had been a good idea; they were too used to being entertained constantly.

A trip to Guerrero Negro for supplies would take a full day, there and back, through the desert and across the peninsula. Leaving early one morning, arriving there three hours later, we made our purchases just before the stores and shops closed for siesta. We asked several locals where we might buy live hens because eggs were hard to come by in the village at Bahía.

There was a lady who sold chickens in Laguna Manuela, twenty kilometers north and on the way home, we were told. When we passed through Laguna on the way back, we found her house. She had a number of chickens for sale and we agreed on two dollars each. She spent half an hour chasing hens around her sizable property with a hooked stick to grab them by the leg. Soon the boys were racing after the hens and several local dogs got involved. By the time we had the chickens, they were not too happy. We put them into a large cardboard box with a cover and tried to find a corner of the Land Cruiser that was out of the sun for their ride home. By the time we made the two-hour drive back to the hut, the poor birds were exhausted from the heat. We opened the box and they wandered in a daze around the beach for a moment, and then scampered for the nearest shade. That afternoon we built a small roost that we could close them into during the nights. The five hens and single rooster, Hot Stuff, made themselves at home. That evening, well before sunset, they all found the roost and wandered in on their own. Chickens may or may not be smart, but they are certainly programmed.

After they adjusted to the climate (we had relocated them from the west coast, where the weather is relatively cool and damp during the nights, to the east coast where it seldom drops below eighty in the summer and is relatively dry) the five hens produced an average of four eggs per day. We were all entertained by the foraging they did on the beach in the small piles of seaweed that accumulated along the tide lines. Lassie chased them at first but never tried to hurt them and soon grew bored with them. Like we had with each other over our adventure, we soon integrated with these animals too.

Billy and Burlap

One afternoon we went to the village for a visit and for tortillas from the tortilla-maker, Mari Elena, at her house from which she supplied the village with her homemade product. She told us about a ranch, well out into the desert on the road to San Francisquito, where they raised goats. Occasionally they brought several into the village to sell. She suggested that we should get a goat, that they were hearty desert animals and would be fun for the boys. A few days later we talked about it and decided to make the trip to see what there was to see. We stopped by Mari Elena's to let her know our plans and, coincidentally, one of the men who lived at the goat ranch needed a ride. He could show us the way and we could return the favor by taking him home.

This ranch, San Pedro, is many kilometers south of the village, enough that it was a drive of at least two hours and into a very remote part of the desert. The roads were almost impassible in anything other than a high-clearance two-wheel-drive truck and easier work in four-wheel-drive, with much of it in low range. The boys were tired of riding and banging their heads on the sides and roof of the truck long before we got there. We hadn't told them we were going there to look for a goat. This was the same road Mary Ann and I had taken on our first stay and it led 120 kilometers down the peninsula to San Francisquito.

Several kilometers after the turnoff for Bahía de las Animas, an hour out of the village, a small track joined ours from the west, and we took this. Many kilometers later, at the head of a ravine where it encountered the sierra, we found the ranch sitting atop a hillock and well out of the dry riverbed. The house itself was a randomly hammered collection of short boards and twisted pieces of ironwood and cottonwood that had collected from time to time in the creekbed after a storm. There was a small artesian well that provided enough water for the three ranchers, two men and a woman, two children about Michael and Kevin's ages, and numerous cattle. Behind the house was a small corral containing a few goats. Our boys were excited and went immediately to the corral and were joined by the other children.

The ranchers, when asked if they had any goats for sale, said that we could buy any we wanted. We walked with the men back to the corral and asked the boys if they would like to get a goat to take back to

Las Cuevitas; of course, they would. Mary Ann and I negotiated with the ranchers over the purchase while Michael and Kevin ran off to play. We settled on a price of about twenty-five dollars and called to the boys to come and pick out which goat we would take.

"Mom. Dad! Come see what *we* found!" They called from across the property. We all walked to the other side of the house, where the ranchers had a donkey tied to a tree. This animal was smaller than any donkey I had ever seen. It was gray-brown with a silver cross running along its back and down both sides of its chest. The ranchers told us it was a Messiah donkey and would grow no larger than it was presently. The boys were already in love with the tiny animal and Mary Ann and I, too, found it hard to resist. I asked how much they wanted for it and we settled the deal at twenty dollars immediately. Curiously, they wanted more for the goat than the burro. But, when I thought about it, they would eat the goat, but not the donkey.

Now the problem was getting our new pets back the many kilometers and hours to Las Cuevitas.

I rearranged the supplies in the back of the Land Cruiser. We could get the young goat, a Nubian, in easily, but the burro was another matter. We lifted him up and he balked at climbing into the back of a covered utility vehicle. When we persisted, pulling him with his rope from the back seat and pushing him from behind, he grew so confused and uncomfortable that he resigned himself to settling in the rear of the truck. He could not quite stand, so he tucked his hooves under his chest and lay down. This was our first understanding of the intelligence of donkeys.

We bumped and bounced our way over the long, dusty track back toward the bay and then through the village where we stopped to show Mari Elena our new pets and to buy a bale of hay, and went on to Las Cuevitas and our hut. It had already been a long day for us all, including the animals.

It was late afternoon by the time we got there, so we spent the daylight we had left modifying the chicken coop to include room for a burro and a goat. The bale of hay was put in one corner where they could graze whenever they wanted. The chickens seemed confused at first, confronted with such large animals, but soon adjusted and climbed into their roosts where the goat and donkey didn't care about them. Somehow we arrived at the names of Billy the goat and Burlap the burro.

The next day Billy and Burlap wanted out of the pen as soon as they heard us stirring. Billy brayed until we let them loose, and we were confronted with deciding how to keep them from wandering off into the desert. This was not a problem with fowl; it turned out that once they settled in an area they would forage and scratch all day but always return to the safety of their roost at night, particularly since that was where we fed them. But we knew nothing about the habits of goats and donkeys.

We decided to keep them tied up behind the hut for a few days and then see what they did when we let them loose. They didn't like the ropes around their necks, but they tolerated them, and every day we gave them a greater length. After the third or fourth day we left the ropes tied to their necks but untied them at the other end, leaving a long length trailing behind them in the dirt. They wandered, but never far, and we could tell where they were from their hoof prints and rope tracks. Soon we found that it was Burlap that made the decisions as to where they went; Billy always followed behind. Now we released Burlap's rope, leaving Billy with the burden which he seemed to have adapted to anyway.

Our homestead was growing and so were our responsibilities. We had to feed the chickens daily but that was simply a matter of making sure they had water and throwing out mash and grain once a day. We dug a small shallow hole a distance behind the hut into which we put our garbage. The chickens kept this clean for us. Billy and Burlap could go to their pen whenever they wanted alfalfa and they wandered the nearby hills, foraging, every day.

Before we went into the hut for the last time at night, we closed the corral gate and dropped a piece of plywood across the hut doorway that kept Lassie from getting out during the night. We hadn't had problems with mountain lions, foxes, wolves or coyotes, but we knew they were around—we heard coyotes calling from nearby on many nights. Though we weren't expecting trouble, there was no point in taking chances. I kept a twelve-gauge shotgun loaded with birdshot (with a trigger guard locked in place) under my bed.

A few days after the first snake incident, we had decided it would be a good idea to clear the area behind the hut of the small brush and rocks to discourage small animals from crossing the cleared area and entering our hut. I spent an hour or so each morning clearing the land, before it was too hot. This was hard but rewarding work. I was still waiting to settle into Baja mode so I didn't mind the daily objective and I was, in those days, still used to living in the city, with a city lot and grass right up to the cement in an organized arrangement and no place for weeds. So I started raking at the several hundred square meters beside and behind our hut. This was an effort that occupied me for several days. When that was done, I was on a roll and arranged the larger of the rocks I had removed from the area into a line that defined it. I'm not sure who I was defining it to, but I did it.

By somewhere around the end of our second week at Las Cuevitas, we had built the hut, bought the half dozen chickens for eggs and built them a roost, brought Billy and Burlap from the desert ranch, extended the roost into a corral, cleaned up the area around the hut and built a large staircase down to the sea. I felt like we had accomplished a lot. The worker in me declared a vacation. Besides, there was nothing left that needed doing.

The Routine

For a number of weeks we fell back into the easy routine which Mary Ann and I had become accustomed to years ago on our summer at the south end of the bay. Our days were gently filled with fishing, cooking, washing, maintaining the hut, reading, swimming, and napping. We taught Michael and Kevin how to fish from the shore by casting with a conventional reel. The trick to this was to ride your thumb gently on the spool after you had cast to prevent the spool from backlashing. This technique took them some time to learn, but, within a few days, they were casting hundreds of feet into the water and bringing in cabrilla and triggerfish which we could feed to the animals or eat ourselves. Michael wanted nothing to do with eating anything that came from the sea. Kevin loved everything. But they both loved to catch fish. There was an ongoing contest to see which of the boys could cast farther. As far as I know, this is still undetermined.

When they grew bored with casting competitions, they evolved to rock skipping. When that got old they invented a game that included placing a small beach stone inside the hand-held end of a length of PVC pipe they had found on the beach, and slinging the pipe as though they were casting a rod out over the water. At maximum velocity the stone released itself from the pipe and flew a great distance.

The early morning became something to enjoy. I was usually up first and working on some small chore or reading. By the time the sun had risen, between six and seven, everyone else was up. The boys or Mary Ann would open the pen for Billy and Burlap. The goat and the burro would trot from the makeshift corral to the front of the hut to say good morning to the rest of us. Lassie loved Burlap and would greet him by licking his muzzle furiously. Burlap stood still while this was ongoing, for a minute or so, and then he would lead Billy around the area, galloping and kicking, pleased to see another day.

If we joined the animals behind the hut to watch their antics, Burlap would playfully try to ram us. Even though he was small, he still weighed 150 pounds and was charging you at about twenty miles an hour. We would dodge away as if he were a bull in a fight.

After their morning warm-up they would head for the nearby hills. Lassie would stay with them until she heard the boys getting ready for their morning swim. Then she would come back to camp to watch and join with them. Never was one of the boys in the water that Lassie wasn't there too. She clearly thought it was her job to protect them.

Evening was always my favorite time in Baja. The trials were over for the moment and the heat easing. There were few evenings that didn't present a spectacular sunset. During the heat of the afternoon, the animals all found shade and limited their activity, but when the shadows began to lengthen and the air cooled just a little, they came out and would begin to play.

Once again I had to ask myself if that made any sense. What is it to play? The dictionary says "to occupy oneself in amusement, sport or other recreation." How do you apply that to other animals? I watched this burro, goat, and dog on the beach and they were clearly playing. They were familiar with each other; they were not threatened by each other. They were filling time by performing some activity that they chose and it gave them pleasure. They were constantly challenging each other with some talent of their own. The burro would charge the goat or dog, the goat would rear up on hind legs or feign butting the burro, and the dog would nip at the heels of both. It was difficult to believe what I'd read. This was not something that happened occasionally but every morning and every late afternoon.

On the other hand I would have certainly agreed, by common observation, that chickens had absolutely zero sense of humor. They were only occupied with their constant pecking order and grubbing for food even when they had more than they wanted. They were the most productive of our animals (eggs), but least enjoyable even though we grew to know each personally by sight and behavior.

We always fixed dinner early in the evenings and well before it grew dark, avoiding gas lanterns while cooking because the bright light attracted bugs. Through the slats of bamboo the fading golden light of evening turned the hut into a magical place. We were alone, the four of us, each in our own world and yet together, closer now than ever. The boys and Lassie were typically in the water before dinner, laughing between the small waves that fell just outside. The chickens had gone to roost and were silent. The goat and burro hovered between the water and the hut, silhouetted against the calm cove. The arc of the sun through our visible heavens was nearing completion of its daily cycle from our minuscule vantage point; we were mentally preparing for night and darkness and a period of rest.

This time of day was often cause for a walk along our lonely shore. The volcano on Isla Coronado was almost directly across from our site and usually caught the final rays of the sun for the day. The twin blues of sky and water reflected the occasional clouds that collected their random reds, oranges and yellows. The pelicans nightly migrated from the south end of Bahía de los Angeles to the craggy peaks of our Las Cuevitas. Here, both north and south of our tiny bay, the cliffs rose directly from the beach toward the sky and enabled seabirds to launch into the weather from well above the water.

Small sea creatures collected along the shore in just inches of water. Tiny crabs, a baby octopus, a sea urchin, clams. As the darkness settled, we could light a kerosene or gas lantern and set it beside the water and watch the small beasts come toward the shore. Something attracted them to the light. We could position sand chairs there and just join in the show, as we were much too large for the small creatures to conceive of, let alone fear. And we were not out to disturb them, rather to observe, learn, and respect their ways.

Once the sun's energy had lost its influence over our day, the moon, if her cycles were correct, would introduce herself first as a dim glow above the now-silhouetted Isla Coronado and just a few minutes later as a golden orb pushing into the night's sky over the saddle, mid-island. A narrowing line of light, a reflection, pointed over the water to the moon when she was full enough, awakening in us a knowledge of our lack of importance in this universe and an understanding of the relative inconsequence of humanity in the bigger picture of things.

At Las Cuevitas there was only the peace and tranquility of nature and our interest in understanding it. The pressures of work and school schedules, meetings, unsolicited impositions, and myriad other activities were things of the past and the future. This moment was ours as long as we would make it last.

By Sea

We hadn't taken the boat out except to tie it up fifty meters offshore. There it had ridden out restless days and nights, rolling, bow tied to the partial chassis of an old car frame we had worked hard to get onto the boat and haul out into ten meters of water to drop overboard with several nylon ropes tied to it. Once it was resting on the floor of the bay, we had fastened an empty plastic gallon milk bottle to the surface end of the rope, tied the boat to it, and swam for shore.

On an afternoon when it was too hot even to sit in the shade on the beach, I swam out and pulled the boat ashore. Mary Ann and the boys climbed aboard and we headed out of our small bay and into the gulf. We soon left the protection of the Bahía de los Angeles and headed north, hugging the peninsula. The shoreline was rugged with many small bays and rocky points falling into the sea and reappearing as protrusions through the surface of the water. Winding slowly through these small coves and protected landings, we watched the surface for rocks, peering into the depths of the water. After we'd gone a kilometer or so, the boys found one bay that was so tranquil and clear we could see the fish circling the bottom twenty or thirty feet below. We stopped for a few moments and watched the slow-motion movements of the fish and the seaweed far under the small boat. Then we turned east and headed across the channel.

Isla Coronado is the nearest island to Las Cuevitas. It is the largest island near the bay, ten kilometers long. On its north end is a volcano. On humid days a corona of clouds covers its peak. From Las Cuevitas to the closest part of Isla Coronado is about four kilometers; it took us about fifteen minutes to get there in our small boat and outboard. The open sea in this channel is usually no more than small swells, one to two feet high. In the early mornings it can be dead calm. The wind was often from the east as it was on this day and the spray and spume was soaking but salty and cooling in the heat. We bored ahead, the light boat bouncing in a forward spin on the corrugated water, taking wet feathers of spume over the bow. The boys were shrieking and begging me to slow down when they were afraid or to go faster as soon as they were secure.

In calm weather the boys would take the handle of the outboard and drive. Their composure changed from happy and laughing to serious and focused as they did an adult's job. They acted responsibly, knowing that it was permissible for an experienced hand to get us wet and play around but not the novice. Soon, they were better at maneuvering and pulling onto the beach than I was.

The channels between Coronado and the Baja mainland and between Coronado and Angel de la Guarda are called Canales de las Ballenas, Channels of the Whales. The water rushing between landmasses and the chum it churned up attracted many forms of sea life, some of which were food for the massive but tranquil beasts. There is no other feeling like pushing through the water in a fourteen-foot boat when a forty-foot whale surfaces gently alongside to see what you're up to. A black mass of an arched back floats through the surface, moving parallel to the boat and in the same direction, at a gently higher speed. As it passes through the water it appears, from the perspective of the boat, to be stationary. But then a dorsal fin moves by, then a narrowing body and then a tail ten feet across. He slows and you gain on him and a giant eye rises near and then above the surface and looks directly at you. He blows, exhaling a hollow, tubular, gooselike ringing breath of air and spume, steaming and shooting into the blue sky. The spray falls across the boat.

A few times, we could almost reach out and touch their dorsal fins as they went silently past. It is an ethereal, unearthly feeling that something so large could come that close and be unthreatening, even curious about *you*. Often there were several whales, moving together, a hundred meters apart, diving and surfacing, blowing and diving again in unison and then separately.

When there were many whales over an extended area, the dolphins would pass through, seeming to use the whales to help herd the tuna—dolphin are, to me, the cowboys of the sea. With bait by the millions breaking the surface, the birds were coming from miles away and from all directions. They got so thick that the sun was shaded by a sky full of falling pelicans, gulls, boobies; the frigate birds hovered haughtily aloft. The surface of the water boiled and we could almost walk on the solid backs of fish. If we had brought a fishing pole we would have a week's worth of food in two minutes.

On this day, a pod of five-hundred-pound dolphins passed through our location across miles of open sea, circling, searching for food. On the horizon we saw a white crest of water moving toward us and heard their high-pitched chirps, so we turned off the motor and waited. They neared the boat, and passed, by the thousands. Some of them swam in pairs; the older appeared to be teaching the younger the techniques of maneuvering in the water. When they neared the boat, they would deviate just slightly and often leap over the bow, several at a time. We restarted the motor and stayed amongst them for as long as we wanted. They were not bothered by our presence; in fact, they seemed to enjoy it. Their tails, like hydraulic plungers, forcefully pumped them constantly forward, each pair traveling many meters under the water and than surfacing for air, often jumping, then diving again to just under the boat, to surface again a few meters on. They were the colors of the water and sleek and smooth and you wanted to dive in and be with them, to share their space.

Breaking reluctantly from this great celebration of life we turned east to north and motored along the inside shore of Coronado. About two-thirds of the way up the inboard side of the island, there is a large but shallow bay and several small off-islands that you cannot recognize as such from a distance. We motored between the small islets and Coronado into an area with a clear deep bottom and many jagged rocks shooting upward from the darkness to jut sharply out of the water. The tide was out and the water quickly shallowed in places. Michael and Kevin stood in the bow looking into the clear depths for rocks I should have seen. In an area near the shores in this small channel, we turned the motor off and the silence was deafening. There was no sound except the lessening passage of water under the boat. The water was deep and clear with shards of sunlight passing down, angled, illuminating its depths. We could see fish near the bottom. In their environment, fins and tails working, moving forward and backward, their eyes constantly on the lookout for food and danger, they seemed very vulnerable.

The boat drifted near a set of large rocks projecting from the surface of the water. Michael and Kevin climbed out of the boat and onto the rocks and dove into the water and climbed back onto the rocks.

They splashed us and dared us to jump in, but their splashing was enough to cool us off.

Further north along the same shore is a small lagoon, shallow enough that we had to pull the engine up and row in. Here there were thousands of stingrays and other flat fish. When we touched them gently on the back with an oar they would scamper away in a wake of bottom sand to bury themselves, flapping their fins and creating a dip in the floor at a place not far away. There was a small hut at a point of this lagoon that had been deserted for many years; the locals hunting sea turtles had once used it. The turtles were protected now.

I was often of the impression, in Baja, that issues of conservation and the environment were largely up for grabs to the highest bidder. During the early years I fished there, there was a great abundance of so many species of fish. But during the 1970s and 1980s the word was that the Mexican government had been bought off to allow the Japanese long-liners in to drag the bottom for miles at a pass destroying all life in their sweep.

I don't know the truth with respect to the political processes. I do know that the first time I fished from the shore in the bay, in 1974, I caught sixteen-inch cabrilla with almost every cast. In 1976 I trolled for the first time around the off-islands and caught yellowtail in a number of places. In 1985 we learned to fish our local part of the bay gradually and, as we became more knowledgeable, we caught more fish. Then, somewhere in the mid-1980s, I encountered a Japanese boat. There were more and more of these during those years. They were recognized to be illegal, but subtly permitted, through bribery, by the Mexican government. There was even a report that approximately one hundred Japanese fishing vessels had been rounded up, all with the same hull identifications, and all fishing off the permit for a single vessel. By the mid-1980s the fishing was not as good. The entire marine environment was reduced to a small fraction of its original proportions during the 1970s and 1980s.

We motored north up the inside of Coronado to the Isla Coronadito at the north end, a bird rock separated from the main island by fifty meters. Here the tide poured through the narrow, deep channel with a rush that tugged at our boat. As we rounded the northern limit of Coronado, we could see Isla Angel de la Guarda twenty kilometers across the open gulf. In front of us a giant ray, three meters across, broke through the surface and did a complete flip, hit the water and repeated his performance twice more, landing, finally, in a tremendous splash, before returning to the depths.

We skimmed around the northern end of the island and turned east along the kilometer or so of barren decomposing lava jutting almost straight up a kilometer into the sky. Landslides of red sand and gravel poured down from the heights stopping only at the edge of the sea where the small waves turned them even redder. Rounding the north point we turned south down the outer shore following this along the bays and inlets of the coastline to the southern end of the island. Along the outside of Coronado the water was much rougher. The sheer power of the tides was evident in the way the boat handled in the masses of water rising from the ocean floor. Occasionally we would pass a seal lion, typically a sole female. She would raise her head above the surface as we passed sometimes barking a greeting, sometimes diving until we had passed.

From the southern end we turned west toward our camp, about twenty minutes away. Halfway there was seal island, Isla Calaveras, and we pulled to the south end on this small craggy and tall islet to watch the seal lion colonies that habituated the rocky shoreline. A single male and his harem of fifteen females were curious about us at first but, as we drew closer, within several meters, even though we turned off the motor and rowed in, they grew nervous and more aggressive. They were not threatening but they were quick to let you know that you were too close. We backed off and sat watching their antics and listening to the male roar his defensive attacks at us.

Rounding the point we could hear and see another group of sea lions at the other end of the islet. We left them to their own attentions and headed for the hut. From halfway across the channel we could see our lonely patch of beach, the hut, and the steps. Farther north we could see the mesa. As we closed on the beach our summer became a reality. We were living out a dream.

Ten minutes later I dropped Mary Ann and the boys on the beach and tied the boat up and swam to shore. This was the first day we had been out in the boat. I had known that it would add a dimension to our trip—and this was a great beginning.

Perspectives

Thin shards of light, launched from a solar surface so many millions of miles distant, come to rest at last inside the western wall of our hut. It's truly not a wall, but only a thin edge between an *in* and an *out*. It's a boundary line between a place where my young children and my wife and I feel safe, and a place where we feel at risk.

I watch in the first few moments of my coming-awakeness as the slices of light march across the tatters of thatch and bamboo that form our walls allowing light and air to pass freely. I feel the small breezes caress my face, arms, and chest, now out of the sheets that have warmed me during the night and that are too much for the early morning temperature, quickly rising. Our bed is made of smooth round stones from the adjacent beach, stones worn by the decades of permanence in concert with each other and the water lapping there. Light continues marching. A squadron of flies circles the center of the single room. Our home. Occasionally they almost touch and spiral downward to regain their individual distances. Are they playing or fighting? Is ego involved? Is sex?

From the pen full of animals behind our hut I hear stirrings. At first light the chickens are restless. The rooster crows, a sound that is now white noise, invisible and lost, drowning in the small waves of Las Cuevitas. Through the thatch I catch vague and shadowed images of our burro and goat eying the gate to the simple small corral we have fashioned from pallets and cacti. They sense that someone is awake and want out of confinement, their prison.

I slip out of sheets and into shorts and sandals. I face the open portal of the hut, bordered against the early sun by gently moving tips of palm fronds, looking east into the Bahía de los Angeles sunrise. Las Cuevitas is a sheltered cove. Rocky points form the northern and southern rims of my closer periphery. Further distant is Isla Coronado, Smith's Island, her mysterious volcano to the north, her isthmus to the south. Even more distant in my view is the source of the rays of light on my walls, now behind me. The sun has magically arced an azimuth just over the saddle of Smith's and attracted the few billowy clouds it could find, bound them together and thrown some quiet pastels upon them, gentle hues of rose and peach, all for my sole pleasure. There is a God.

I exit the hut quietly, careful not to disturb the sleeping, soundless torsos of Michael, Kevin, and Mary Ann still absorbing night. For an instant I watch each of their deep breathing, their relaxed postures on the mats over the stones. Then my feet crunch gently amongst those stones, and the stones mesh and merge, shifting to accommodate, to not disturb. They have been together for millennia. They belong together, work together. They are a universe, a whole. I stand for a moment taking in the scene and realize that this may be the only peace I find in my harried life—this instant in time—this summer with my wife and two small sons. Tomorrow I may well be dead. Then I remember the burro and goat and turn to the corral.

Burlap and Billy are happily released and follow me, crunching through stones to the front of the hut. The small wavelets are lapping, the birds working, the clouds churning. Lassie greets Burlap with great licking of whiskers and quiet nuzzling. Burlap and Billy rollick, kicking up their heels at the facing of a new day. The air is cool and the sun is at a small angle and not yet intense. The rooster heads the brood off, pecking through the clusters of seaweed that have collected on our stones during the night.

I walk silently down to the beach on the massive stairway constructed from crude flagstones I have harvested from the desert and arranged on our beach. A monument to man that will surely survive, in my mind, beyond my shallow existence here.

At the magical place where sea meets land, I stand and watch the tiny ripples through which swim even tinier fish, minnows far from the protection of their mother, helpless in a world of snapping life and flashing death-in-an-instant. I marvel at the complexities of life and am pleased, thankful, that I am here. Is there actually a God? I'll never know this answer, but I'm thankful, regardless, even if only to Earth, a god of unfamiliar form.

A small sky cry drops from above. My attention is diverted yet further upward into the clustered billows and colors there and to a pair of frigate birds circling high above the quiet waters. They have spotted some bit of floating flotsam. Their split tails and bent wings are out of date and yet fill the sky with the moment. The scene is only complete with them there in air far over water.

A new day has broken at Las Cuevitas. Soon the heat will damage the freshness of morning and drag it toward noon meanness. Soon a halo will slowly form over the volcano heralding the rise to ninety-five degrees and high percentages of humidity. Soon the quiet personal moments of reflection will be lost to the discomforts and threats of the day. How fortunate I am, I reflect off the still waters of Las Cuevitas, to have stumbled upon this Eden. How could I progress (is that the right word, I wonder?) further through life without this depth-sounding heart to secure me throughout?

Evenings

The evenings were always a release from the heat of the day. There was usually a slight breeze and we could light the lanterns and all sit at the table or the boys would lie on their beds reading or talking. After the sun set it was difficult to read on still nights because of the bugs. They changed with the weather and we didn't have a bug book or know their names, but some of them were special. There was one that always got our attention.

This large black fellow weighed at least an ounce and was about three inches long. He was a flying insect. When we lit a lamp, he could see it from a great distance and wanted the light for a purpose known only to him. We called these great beasts "Four Milers" because we could hear them coming toward the light while they were far away from the hut. Their excitement was reflected in the high frequency hum of their wings. Their vision must have been farsighted because, while they could see the light from afar, they couldn't see the hut from anear. They worked up a terrific speed coming at us but didn't know when they'd arrived. We'd be sitting and quietly reading with only minimal other natural sounds and could hear this big bug zeroing in and we waited for the crash. And it would come within seconds as he hit the bamboo siding of the hut at some high rate of speed, fell to the stones and wandered dizzily around for a moment before flying off to try again. They didn't bite or sting and we were never otherwise bothered by them—only entertained.

The moths were also large, about three inches long with an even wider wingspan, but they were not as pesky. They would surprise you at first because they were so quiet and threw such a large shadow. But they would flutter silently about, throwing ghostly apparitions on the walls and ceiling, only to land somewhere for a moment or two, then fly off. The boys tried to catch them but they were evasive and stayed high on the walls. They were dark browns and grays with delicate patterns on their wings.

The kitchen was a lively place in the evenings. The mice and kangaroo rats, fragile, tiny rodents no more than two inches long at most, would come to clean the scraps we had dropped during cooking. They scampered around the ground and the lower storage crates. Early on we had stored all our dry foods in an old ice chest and kept it latched to keep these hungry little guys out. But they would inevitably find some morsel and make just enough noise to alert us. They were desperate for food and hard to discourage. We would often just reach down and pick one up by its tail and put it on the ground outside the hut. At the time we naïvely thought they were no problem and pretty much left them alone.

An occasional scorpion would be found in the sand when we moved something protecting it, but the variety here were not seriously threatening and their sting was only slightly worse than a bee sting. We showed the boys what they looked like and told them to keep their distance. We saw tarantulas twice but they never came near our living area.

One evening we had gone to the village for dinner and came home just at dusk. Mary Ann and I went to find Billy and Burlap and put them up for the night. The boys went into the hut and came running out screaming that a snake was inside. We both rushed to see where and what kind of snake they had seen. Michael said it was a rattler, that they had heard it. It was on the ground between or behind the ice chests in the kitchen. I reached down to move the largest of the chests and Michael yelled at me to stop, as that was where he was hearing the rattling. Neither Mary Ann nor I could hear it. I got a tool and pulled the chest away and behind it were two small rattlers, each about twenty inches long. We killed them, regretfully, and cut off and buried their heads and threw their bodies in the garbage pit for the chickens.

We evaluated the situation and why they had come into the hut. It was an easy analysis: we dropped food during cooking that attracted mice. Snakes eat mice. Something had to be done to keep the mice away from the kitchen. If there were no mice, there would be no snakes. From here on we were more careful to avoid spillage and to keep the stones food-free. We were aware that hidden dangers could be anywhere. It was a fact of nature; it didn't make life less pleasant, it just meant that you are more aware of your surroundings.

It's interesting how much we learn without even being aware of it. Many years after this snake event I was in our Glendale home cooking dinner. I was chopping some vegetables and a small piece fell from the chopping block to the floor. I watched it fall and come to rest under the kick space of the cabinets, but reaching to pick it up, I stopped instinctively in midmotion. I wasn't going to put my hand into a place where I couldn't see, a lesson unconsciously learned from numerous snake incidents. Also I was standing curiously away from the kick space, not putting my bare feet there either. This caused an uncomfortable angle for my body to work with the knife and block, but it was the way I had worked in the kitchen ever since our trip.

On nights that the bugs kept us from reading we often listened to an old-time radio show that came at 8:30 all the way from Montana. The station played the half-hour dramas I had listened to in the 1940s on an old Motorola radio. *The Whistler* was our favorite and it caused you to realize the ways television has changed our society, and society around the world. I have thought, since traveling to Europe and the Far East, that the U.S. had two things the rest of the world really wanted: cigarettes and entertainment. Many people around the world would do almost anything for an American smoke, film or television show or musical performance. I often thought that it wasn't too important what the diplomats and politicians did or said; the world saw it like it was, sort of, on American TV and film. We listened to the old shows until the boys' heads were nodding and tucked them in for the night. It was a nice feeling to be so far away and yet be able to reach for a small piece of familiarity during a dark night on a remote and quiet beach.

Don the Geologist

About the end of the first month we were sitting on the beach one afternoon and heard voices carrying over the wind. We'd never had visitors to our hut or the area surrounding it and wondered where the voices were coming from. I walked up onto the mesa behind us where I could get a better view of the surroundings, but I couldn't see anyone. Still, we heard people talking off and on for several hours. We watched the nearby beach, but saw no one.

By evening we thought we had been alone too long and were hearing things. Then Mary Ann spotted a man on the beach on the north side of the plateau. With the binoculars we focused on him as he was wandering amongst the rocks at the water's edge. There was no sign of anyone else. With whom he had been talking? That was the extent of our contact that day, but it was unusual to be so far in the outback and have a stranger unannounced and so close.

The next morning we had not seen any further activity so I hiked up to the mesa again to see whatever I could. About five hundred meters from our camp, in the center of the mesa, was a small open camp trailer; it looked like it was filled with travel and camping gear. There was no car or truck and there were no people anywhere that I could see. I walked back to the hut wondering if someone was in trouble.

Late in the afternoon we saw the same fellow on the other beach again, but we couldn't tell if he knew of our presence or not. If he was in trouble, would he be able to see us? Our hut hugged the shoreline, behind which were hills and the mesa preventing our silhouette from showing against the sky and making us all but invisible from his angle. He had now been there by himself for two days, had no fire we could see or smell, and cooked no food. We knew he had originally come with at least one other person because his trailer was there on the mesa. Whatever had towed it there was gone. And we had heard the voices.

By early evening we decided that I would go see if everything was all right. I climbed up the side of the mesa with the intent of going to the beach where we had seen him, but when I got to the top, he was standing near the trailer. I hollered to him from a distance to avoid startling him, and he looked at me for a moment, then waved. Walking toward the trailer I could see that he was about my age, mid-forties, and a gringo. He was a slight and studious, bookish-looking fellow that presented no threat. I asked if he was having trouble.

Don introduced himself and explained that he had come to Baja with a couple of new friends. They were two cousins from San Francisco who had planned to be gone several weeks. Don was a geologist and a professor at one of the California State University campuses, and was going to a new job at the Scripps Institute after his trip.

The three of them had car trouble coming down the peninsula and it had gotten worse just as they had come to the mesa. The students, both about twenty, had taken his car into the village to see about repairs. They had now been gone two days and he had not heard from them. I felt he knew more than he was telling. I told him we were living just over the lip of the mesa and asked if he would like to come and sit in our sparse shade and do some thinking.

I introduced Don to Mary Ann, Michael, and Kevin and we sat on the patio beneath the bamboo. I asked if he had expected his friends before now; he said that they told him they would be back by the previous evening. He didn't know where they were. The whole thing didn't set right. I asked him how well he knew them and if there was a chance they wouldn't return. I asked him what would he do if they didn't come back for him. He was clearly without a plan and it wasn't easy for me to understand how an adult could get this stranded. But matters got even worse.

When his friends had taken the car, it had his identification and wallet in it. On top of that, Don told us he was a diabetic and most of his insulin was in the car. Regardless of the sad circumstances that had left him stranded in this remote place, we could only identify somewhat with his predicament. He was a fragile, naïve guy, educated academically but not in the ways of an often rough-and-tumble world. I remembered the fish we had seen swimming in the depths of the channel off Isla Coronado, constantly on the watch for threats, a custom necessary for their survival. Don needed a little of that instinct too.

We asked how often he needed insulin and how long could he go without it. He had a couple of doses on his person, he said, and after that he was good for a day or two at the most before he was in more serious trouble. His life could be threatened.

Inviting him to stay for dinner (where else would he have gone?), we tried to sort out the situation and help him make plans. He had all the camping gear he needed for the night. His trailer was full of equipment and supplies. Together we decided that he should spend another night at his trailer and the next morning we would take him into the village to look for his car and friends. I was convinced they had deserted him but kept my thoughts to myself. We finished off the day and he went back to the mesa. Mary Ann and I put some Spanish guitar music on and we read and the boys went to sleep reading their books and listening to the tranquilizing sounds of waves lapping gently on a soft-shouldered shore in concert with John Williams plucking gut strings.

In the morning Don climbed down from the plateau and we took him to the village. His car was nowhere. We stopped by the Díaz ranch and I described the car and asked Sammy if he had seen either it or the men and he had not. There was only one other mechanic in the village and he hadn't seen them either. The grinding in my stomach grew worse. I knew Don's friends had stolen his car and his money. They had threatened his life by taking his insulin. When we asked what he thought was best, Don said he wanted to go back to the mesa and wait another day; he couldn't believe they would do this to him. I thought that they didn't care if he was alive or dead, but I kept quiet. Don was a nice, educated fellow and was enjoyable to talk with, and his business was his business. He just needed to learn how to choose his friends.

After lunch we all sat on the porch the better part of the afternoon. Don had come here to research the geology and the microclimate that had provided an updraft from the gulf around the bay that carried moisture into the desert surrounding the west side of the Sea of Cortez. He told us of the mysterious influences that drew the water from the coast to supply the cactus forest inland. Indeed, there was an explosion of cacti and elephant trees, and of Spanish moss growing from some of the taller cirios in the desert as it rose to the west of the bay. This forest was known throughout Baja. We all listened to Don's dramatic stories of the evolution of this part of the peninsula, of the formation of the mountains in a flurry of creative volcanic activity, of the decomposition of the lava into fertile soil over the centuries, millennia, and of the flora that had clutched tenaciously to the earth in the barren and rainless desert. He told us about the palm trees, some types of which were brought by the Jesuits in the 1700s, and taught us which plants and cacti grew nowhere else on earth. He was a wealth of information, a truly knowledgeable and interesting guy.

We were glad to have a visitor after so long on the beach with just the four of us. But we knew he was soon going to have to face the fact that his friends, for whatever reason, were not coming back. All of us went swimming; Don was beginning to look unhealthy with no insulin.

I couldn't understand how he could operate under these conditions with no plan, and assumed his mental processes were deteriorating as well as his physical appearance. Finally I told him what I thought we should do. In the village we could find out what time the daily bus to Ensenada passed by the turnoff with Highway 1. He had to get on that bus and get to the border—a trip of about fifteen hours—since he had family in San Diego and could rely on them to help him. He looked at me somewhat confused. I wrote it off to lack of insulin and continued with the plan. I asked if he could rely on his family to later help him retrieve his trailer. He could.

So I went into the village for information on the bus. It had already passed for the day but it went by the turnoff every day at the same time. I went back to camp. Don decided that he would be safe if he got insulin once he crossed the border late the next night. We moved his trailer down off the plateau and near our hut, and helped him pack. He would send someone for the trailer after the details had been worked out. I would take him to the highway the next morning. Mary Ann fixed dinner and opened a bottle of wine and we were surprised when Don joined us in a glass. Sitting through another sunset we swapped Baja stories. His were geographical and historic. Mine were about travel and friendly encounters along dusty roads.

It's funny how easy it is to connect with others when there is so little to interrupt you. For many reasons we had enjoyed his visit and wished him well and would be sad when he was gone. When we left camp the next morning for the junction, the boys and Mary Ann waved him good-bye and bon voyage. We had swapped telephone numbers and addresses; he would call us when we got home in the fall.

We arrived at the turnoff well before the bus, which was behind schedule. I couldn't even imagine the concept of a schedule over these roads. Don was looking pale and unhealthy, but the bus arrived and we got him on board and his gear stowed. I waved and the bus engine roared as it blew dust and diesel smoke across the road and was off for the north.

Several weeks later Don's mother and another member of his family came back for the trailer we had been "watching" (there was no one around to protect it from). They told us that Don had passed out in the bus before it had reached Tijuana, had been taken to the hospital there and transported across to another hospital in San Diego. He had spent a week there and had fully recovered. Then he had gone to his new job at Scripps. They told us that he had almost died on the bus, from the shock that a diabetic falls into without insulin.

Months later, back in the States, we got a letter from Don's mother. She thanked us for saving her son's life. He had come home for a few weeks after his recovery, and was now working at Scripps. We were pleased to help and it was too bad his trip had been such a flop. We had enjoyed his visit and missed him when he was gone. But I still had to wonder what the full story was. I grabbed another opportunity to remind myself: we are all smart about some things and dumb about others; we all have unique senses and viewpoints that we put to work. Sometimes they work, sometimes they don't. Occasionally we can see deeply into the murky waters and sometimes we can't see anything at all.

The Village

Every few days we went to the village just for a change. It was a half-hour drive along the dusty byways of Baja to get there. On the outskirts we passed a few randomly situated small clapboard or cinder-block homes and several small stores. There was a two-story building with a restaurant, La Enramada, on the top floor up the escarpment from the beach. It was high enough to catch a stray afternoon breeze. The owner had fastened hammocks to the second-floor arches that led to the roof. The boys could rock themselves precariously from this perch over the ground fifteen feet below. We would go late in the afternoon and sit on the balcony overlooking the bay and have cold beer and sodas. From this vantage point, we could see around the entire village. The men of the town and the soldiers from a small detachment of the Mexican army stationed there had built a soccer field near the beach. We could see them playing in the dust and heat and sweat.

In the hot and humid air, crows and buzzards sat in the tallest trees with their wings away from their bodies to shed the heat, their beaks ajar as if trying to catch breath. The water of the bay shimmered in the late afternoon sun and the islands looked less dry and barren in the fading light. On an earlier trip, we had watched a single-engine Cessna taxi to the Pemex station at the Díaz ranch, fill with aviation fuel, and then move on to the dirt strip. The pilot got out and executed his outback-abbreviated preflight checklist, manually moving flaps, struts and whatever. He reboarded the craft, revved up the engines, moved forward, quickly built speed down the strip and lifted gently into the shockingly blue and cloudless sky leaving behind a cloud of runway dust. Circling the town once, buzzing the house and friends he was leaving, he turned gracefully north toward the border and a different world. My eyes shifted downward where vees of pelicans slid smoothly just over the surface of the water. How calming and silent they were in contrast to the aircraft. We ate dinner on the balcony as the sun faded and the lights were turned on throughout the village. What a miracle it must seem to have electricity after forever having none.

Many of us take so much for granted: refrigeration, power, heat, natural gas, running potable water. In the bay, in the early days, the only refrigeration was for food and it was powered by bottled LPG. In order to refill an empty tank, you shipped it north to Ensenada. A week later you got it back, filled. In the early years electrical power was provided by the Díaz family to the village families who could afford it. Then another generator was added, operated by the town. Power still was not available between ten p.m. and early the next morning. Running water was available to a very few who had plumbed their houses to draw water, driven by gravity only, directly from the spring above the village. Most water was provided by individual *pilas*, filled periodically by oil drums. I don't know anyone who had or wanted air conditioning except in the simple hotels for tourists. These machines seldom worked and then only during the times when power was provided. You didn't come here for the finery. You came here for a rare form of the truth.

On the beach, the late afternoon fishermen folded or repaired their nets and hauled their *pangas* higher up the sand, away from the late night high tide, leaving deep grooves etched in the beach. They moved their catch in large ice chests to the common fish-cleaning platform and began filleting. The Cruz Roja truck, still living, careened across town, as ever in search of an official function where there were few. The driver's side door was now missing. The village children began to collect around the Díaz patio. Evening approached.

We called to the boys, downstairs playing with friends, paid the check and went to Mari Elena's for tortillas. She had many children, all of whom were good-looking and healthy. Her youngest son, Carlos, was just older than Michael and the three boys played together whenever we were in the village. Carlos sometimes came out to our camp and spent days and nights hanging out with Michael and Kevin.

We often tried to understand the differences between childhoods spent exclusively in the village versus in southern California. Carlos told us that the public school system in the village took him through the sixth grade. I believe this was the average for most of Baja California (I don't think it is for all Mexico; Baja is very rural and remote by comparison). Carlos had learned to be happy with simple pleasures and to entertain himself. Michael and Kevin had computer games and electronic toys and transformers and television and a swimming pool; they were not allowed to get bored. But, in later life, who would be the better adjusted? Would my children have problems focusing on some task that did not fully entertain them? Would Carlos be better able to maintain an interest in his work later in life if he only found menial work? Would his mind get stuck on simple problems, while Michael and Kevin went on to solve greater challenges? Would my children be more likely to develop attention deficit disorder because of the hype they'd grown up with? We are each so buried in our own lifestyles that we can't see things from the other side.

At the Díaz patio we stopped to say hello. Antero was gone by then but Mama and Sammy and Chubasco and their families were there. Mama was aging and her health was less than perfect, but she still had her spark and dry sense of humor. She would shortchange us in an instant, only to make it into a joke and give the boys some surprise worth ten times the value of the few stray centavos she had snitched. It was all a game.

For the villagers, it must have been rewarding to sit most of the year in the warm nights on a large patio with your grown children around you, your grandchildren playing nearby. In the outer ring of this circle of life were the townsfolk, those you had spent your entire life with; you knew who was to be trusted and who was not, and in what ways those not trusted could not be trusted and in what ways they could. No one was all bad or all good.

In the earth, a short walk from the home where you had raised your family, your husband was resting. Every night you visited him and thanked God for the time you had with each other and the time you would be together again soon. Life here was an unending thread of integrated births and deaths and events, significant and insignificant, strung together by the close and tolerant and flexible bonds of family.

Where would my boys be when I was old? Our typical North American families are often torn apart, or drift away from each other in search of jobs and income. Many of my friends at JPL had left home in their late teens for a quality education. From university they had gone where the work was. By the time they were thirty, they hardly had a thought of home. It was simply an obligation that they kept every other year for Christmas. Their folks were so old they were a burden. I would soon be old and I didn't want to lose my value with age. I knew that I could always have value to my children if I found a way to truly belong in their lives for as long as I lived. I didn't at all like the idea of seeing them for a few days every year or so. They were only six and eight at the time and we were already worried about them moving away on their own. Our relationship included four people, not just two. These villagers had what I wanted and what I held most important in life.

There are no simple answers when it comes to raising children or relationships and the things that influence them. I felt that this village had more of what I would want as an old man than my own society did. I knew I would keep looking south from my office at the Laboratory.

We spent too few minutes with the villagers on the patio and then Mary Ann and I walked up the street to the Dos Pinos market where Miguel sat at the back of the store, *cerveza* in hand, with a couple of pals. We bought some onions and potatoes and Miguel asked if we had been fishing and where. I said that we hadn't gone out yet. I was becoming aware that we had been here several weeks and only been out in the boat once. Walking slowly back down the dirt street to Casa Díaz, we collected Michael and Kevin. The air was cooling to hot from intolerable.

We said good night to everyone and drove back to La Cuevitas to put Billy and Burlap into the corral. I put James Galway on the tape player and we listened to Michael and Kevin's favorite song, "Piper, Piper Sing Your Song," before the boys settled down and went to sleep. Later, so as to not wake them, I moved my chair to the edge of the water and turned the music up. How could I have improved my life? No castle, no grand estate could have been better than this basic hut. It was so simple here and so pure with Mary Ann, and Kevin and Michael. I poured a rum and coke, snatched a handful of ice from the chest, put Pavarotti in the tape player and sat playing with the moon and its silver ribbon, tying that golden orb to me and the hut and my family, snuggled against the small swells swirling gently amongst stones on the edge of the Gulf of California.

Wily Coyote

One morning I noticed one of our water jugs had fallen over and drained into the sand. I didn't think any more about it than to realize we had lost water that was important to us. The village never had an abundance of water during the long summers and I didn't want to waste what was dear to them. We used three fifteen-gallon tanks to haul water from the well in the village; from these I filled a number of five-gallon tanks. One of these went on the roof to provide hot running water to the kitchen. We also kept a number of one-gallon plastic bottles for other uses, but we used it sparingly, bathing and washing clothes and dishes in seawater.

The next morning I noticed that another bottle had been spilled between the hut and the coop/corral. This time there were tooth marks on the top of the one-gallon bottle, and Lassie had been shut in the hut with us after we had gone to bed. Maybe we were getting coyotes in camp during the night. This was a worry because the chicken coop was not designed to keep midsized animals in or out; it was just a place for the chickens to roost and to secure Billy and Burlap.

That night I raked down the area between the hut and the coop and put a gallon bottle full of water with the top screwed on tight in the center of the area. I vowed to listen during the night for noises. Of course I fell asleep and didn't hear a sound. The next morning, though, the cap was removed and the bottle was turned over. I looked at the dirt and saw prints that looked like dog tracks about the size of Lassie's, but thinner. So we now knew at least one coyote was coming into camp during the night to drink our water. This was surprising because there were only several meters between the hut and the coop. Coyotes normally don't like close quarters.

This problem occurred several nights in a row. Though concerned with the loss of water, we were more worried about varmints becoming too familiar with our area and threatening us. It was a surprise that our chickens hadn't been killed already. That day I cut a small hole in the bamboo siding on the backside of the hut alongside where I slept. When we went to bed that night, I told myself that every sound I heard I was going to sit up and peek through the hole to see what was making the noise. From the hole I could see the coop and the entire surrounding area.

Several times over the next few nights I heard noises and quietly sat up to peek through the cutout. I never saw anything, but a water jug was spilled almost every night. This went on for a week and I had no clue how the coyote was getting to our water without my hearing. I was anxious to go back to sleeping the night through instead of getting up several times toward no end. One night I positioned the truck so that I could sleep in the bed with the rear doors opened toward the water jugs. I was sure the interior of the truck would be so dark that no animal would know I was there, but I would be able to see it from the light of the moon. Wrong again. No coyote ever came while I was waiting in the truck.

Deciding to rig a trap that would make noise when the coyote turned the bottle over, I balanced a series of tin cans on top of the bottle. I heard nothing during the night. The next morning the cans were all laid on the ground, the cap chewed off and the bottle dry. Finally, I gave up on the idea of scaring the coyotes away. But I put the twelve-gauge through the cutout at the rear of the hut aimed at the water bottle location every night. I vowed that if I heard any noise I would look through the hole to sight the shotgun and, when I had a clear sighting, shoot the coyote.

Our hut looked north and east. On the hillsides above the fan on the other side of the plateau where we had first seen Don, there were many small paths, with one passing through each saddle in the hills to the north. Clearly animals frequently used these paths, as they were always free of plant life. We assumed coyotes, mountain lions, and foxes, but when you almost never see an animal it's difficult to believe in its existence. One day we were sitting outside the hut and, scanning the horizon, saw a sole coyote, in full daylight, trot down one of the paths and onto the beach. She went straight to the ocean. Through the binoculars we could see her lapping up salt water. This was an indication of how desperate they must get during the days of summer heat.

For several nights I slept without hearing a sound. But each morning more water was missing. Then one night I awoke to the sound of water bubbling from the bottle and jumped silently to the peephole, saw the coyote, sighted the shotgun, and jerked off a round before I could get fully behind the gun. The recoil knocked me completely off my cot and onto Mary Ann's. The deafening blast caused an immediate uproar from the chickens and Billy and Burlap. Michael and Kevin jumped up in alarm. This situation with the coyotes had gone on for so long that they had lost interest and forgotten about it. I calmed everyone down and went outside to check out what I was sure was a dead coyote.

The bottle was on its side, water still running slowly from the neck onto the ground. The beam of my flashlight flicked over the area with no sign of the coyote. The boys came out to help me find the animal. I didn't want a wounded animal, suffering, and tracked the area in widening circles around our hut and coop, looking for drops of blood or other signs. We searched for fifteen minutes and found nothing, going back to bed disappointed and tired.

The next morning we got up and made breakfast and made a final inspection in the daylight. I was looking at the area where the bottle had been, and the tracks in the dust. The boys came back to help and one of them pointed to one of the outboard gas tanks located adjacent to the area where we kept the water. I looked at the can from a distance and something was wrong, but couldn't tell what. I walked over and picked it up to see that the blast from the shotgun had struck dead center broadside. So there was no dead coyote. My aim had been off by a number of meters at that short distance. We all got a laugh, and they started calling me "Deadeye." I relocated the water on top of the coop where the coyotes couldn't get it and I put the shotgun back under the cot. Let the coyotes win that round.

Desert Educations

Two colleges local to southern California held classes out of rough barracks in the village. Several dozen hearty students from the States braved the trip each summer and were introduced to the wonders of the Sea of Cortez. Classes were usually open air during the day and within a crude cinderblock-walled, thatched-roof room at night. Anyone who wanted could attend the lectures.

During the point at which I was busy blasting coyotes away from our chickens, the four of us went into the village for dinner one evening. We pulled folding chairs around our favorite table on the patio of Las Hamacas. Several students were there also. They were talking about the class to be given that night, a lecture by a young biologist who had been living in Baja and studying whales in their native environment.

After dinner we walked across the airstrip to the room where the lecture was in progress and joined the group. The boys were impressed by all the older youths. I wanted to hear, enviously, about a fellow who had been living for six months in an even more remote site than ours.

The speaker was a young man about twenty-five. His shoulder-length blond hair was bleached from the sun, and his skin was darkly tanned from many months out of doors. The point of his research was to study whales when they were on their own. This meant no boats following them. As a site from which to conduct this study, he had selected the easternmost point of Punta Soledad, a small finger of mountain jutting eastward into the sea, and a part of Punta Roja which formed the southern tip of Bahía de los Angeles.

He chose this isolated location because it was the narrowest open channel of water in the Gulf of California where whales commonly passed. From his deserted overlook he could peer down a thousand or more feet and watch the whales without disturbing them. For his lecture he had an abundance of slides of the huge sea beasts breaching and wildly churning the waters. The whales' behavior was unlike that which we had experienced with one or more boats around. When we were nearby, their attention was on us rather than their own activities.

The young man talked about his living conditions. He had only a tent and a small lean-to for the six months he'd been there. But he was outdoors all day, glassing the whales and recording their behavior in his ledger. Wasn't he lonely? I remembered Mary Ann and I, living nearby at the south end on the previous full summer trip in Baja, in 1974. We had, at least, Rochie and Dulcie and each other to keep us company. He had no one. But he spoke of a family of coyotes, a mom and newly born pups that had attached themselves to him—and he to them.

After living near them for an extended period and feeding them small scraps of food the mother was soon tame enough that he could approach within a few feet before she snarled. I could imagine him, in his lonely state, wanting a friend. I could feel his arm, arcing slowly out toward the wild animal, in a reach for friendship, with a deprived need few have experienced. I could sense the mother nervously searching for scents in the air that provided her with an overlay to her genetic makeup; man is not safe to deal with. She would watch for sudden movement, unaware of man's intentions, knowing sometimes they included a morsel of food that she would quickly consume, enabling her to better nurse her pups.

The young man talked about the bonding that had taken place between him and the coyote family. How wonderful a relationship this was, but it must have been hard on the young man. We humans want to touch everything we hold dear. Is this the way of animals in the wild? The wilder cats of our house in the mountains north of Los Angeles won't tolerate being touched, let alone being restrained in an embrace. Being held restricts their avenues of escape. Animals raised in the wild are very insecure when they are within range of other animals of the same or larger sizes. I wonder about close relationships. Humans have this luxury, at least in a family environment. I doubt that it exists, though, in the world of investments and business.

He went on to show us slides and tell us of his experiences. These included many warm and related vignettes into the rearing of the coyote pups by their attentive mother. Was I doing the wrong thing trying to blast them away from our water night after night? How far would the coyotes go if they got comfortable in our environment? How long would it be before they were stealing chickens—or taking other small lives?

Too soon the talk ended. We thanked the lecturer and the boys flirted with several of the more tolerant college students for a few moments and then we walked across the airstrip to the truck. Driving home I was compelled to review my interests in killing the coyotes attacking our camp. It was a difficult image for me to call up, of a young coyote mother doing what she could to stay alive and, executing her programmed demands, raising progeny in this waterless, nourishment-poor world of the central desert. In my heart I knew I would be wrong to interfere with this painting of life. I was the one out of place. Who was I to change a pebble of sand in that proverbial stream?

I imagined opening my eyes in the night on hearing noises around the water-trap I had set, rising in my bed, sheet falling away in the dark blackness and the breeze, grabbing for the positioned gun. I could imagine wrapping my hands around the blued steel metal and cool, oiled wooden stock, slipping a finger into the trigger guard, smoothly and effortlessly aiming and firing a single round of bird shot at the mother a few meters away. I imagined the shock of the pellets striking her, mid-body, knocking her fully to the ground. Pain was not involved. The tiny but deadly projectiles had passed deeper than the pain sensors located only on the surfaces of her body. She would feel tugs from deep within and try to stand, possibly staggering to her feet to leave a few red paw prints in the sand, indentations in smooth, round stones. She would think about her pups a mile distant in the desert. Her instincts would lead her to them, but she was weak and needed sleep. And she would lie dying as her mysterious life-bearing blood was pulsing and dripping, running and coagulating slowly over the stones and sand—soon to be diluted, carried away in wispy swirls with the flow of a rising tide.

Away in the desert her pups would wait, over the few days after their mother failed to return. They would whimper amongst themselves, frolic and wonder where was the thing that had made a warm home-place for them where they had first experienced consciousness. They would die slowly, starving and dehydrated, in the byways of the desert. They would not suffer; they had no concept of suffering. Life was simply whatever they were dealt. They had no power to cause change, and there was no reason to do that. Their small bodies, tender flesh, would serve as nourishment to other struggling life also trying to survive the guiltless desert.

We arrived at the hut. The boys, my pups, had fallen asleep over Old Rocking Horse Road and we carried them to bed. Mary Ann lit the lantern and sat reading quietly with the small waves lapping at the stones. I performed my nightly ritual. I don't remember the music I selected that night but it was warm and emotional and Spanish guitar was probably involved. Somewhere in my reflections of the lecture, the music, the rum and the fluidity of the day merged and were one. There is no room for pain or sympathy in the desert. There is only fact.

Before I lay down on my cot, I returned the shotgun to its case. I knew I would not need it again on this trip. But I remembered the lesson of the coyote: trust nothing that had the potential to threaten.

Barsam's Corner

I was usually the first one awake in the mornings. I read for a half hour or so and then tried to find something to occupy myself. Mary Ann or the boys would often still be asleep, and I had to look for something to do that wouldn't make too much noise.

We knew we would have visitors later in the summer so sometimes I would busy myself making simple improvements to our little alluvial fan. The road from the plateau to our hut followed the erosion that had cut into the earth's surface, growing deeper as it neared the beach, to a depth of about ten feet. Over the final fifty meters the walls were nearly vertical with several sharp turns. The cliffs were so close that there was little room to negotiate curves. It was a slow drive even in our truck. When Barsam and his family had helped us find this remote site earlier in the spring, we had worried that one place in this gnarly path would keep his thirty-foot motorhome from getting to the beach.

One morning, looking for something to do, I walked out to the road. The problematic corner was about a hundred meters from the hut, far enough away that I could use a pick and shovel without waking everyone up. This was going to be hard, hot work, even before the sun rose. I'd have to do small amounts of picking and digging early each day.

On this first morning, I examined the job: the corner was sharp but was negotiable, even with the overhang at the rear of the motorhome. The real difficulty was a large chunk of volcanic rock that blocked the roadbed on the right side and prevented a gradual right turn to enter the S-shaped twist at a reasonable angle. The lava could not be avoided on either side because the gully's walls were so close. If I removed this single impediment, Barsam's motorhome could make it through.

I started this small excavation of some two cubic yards of rock at about six the next morning, After clearing the loose dirt and rock from the lava outcropping, I swung the pick a few times to break away the rock in small pieces. After the first few swings I was drenched in sweat, but could see no change in the seemingly growing obstacle. I continued this sweaty effort for another hour until Michael came running out with a gallon plastic bottle of Kool-Aid fresh from the ice chest. We sat on a nearby rock and I polished off about half the bottle. There is something about drinking from a large container that I enjoy. It must be that I was really dehydrated; with the large bottle I was able to consume as much as I wanted with no concern of shortage.

"I want some too. Don't drink it all!" Michael yelled. I handed him the jug and he took a couple of swallows. Kevin came running up from the hut, wearing only trunks and boots.

"I want some. I want some *too*."

"*Here* Kev." Michael handed him the bottle. Kevin threw the heavy bottle against his mouth, upended it, blew a bubble into the liquid, swallowed a mouthful and handed the bottle back to Michael. Red sticky juice ran down his chest onto the dust of the roadway.

"Why are you *digging*?" they asked.

"I'm making a corner for Barsam's motorhome. See?" I pointed to the corners of the S-shaped curve and showed them it was too sharp for the motorhome. "So I'm going to get rid of this giant rock in the road."

"Okay," they chimed. "That's gonna be a lot of work."

They had had enough of the heat and sun and went running back to the hut, yelling.

"Mom! *Mom*! Dad's building Barsam's Corner."

Forevermore for us that twisted piece of ravine in the desert will be called just that.

Over the weeks, I worked on the ravine from time to time and, whenever I did, the boys brought me an icy drink and we would sit in the skimpy shadows of the early morning in the steep ravine and talk for a minute before I would go back to work and they would go to swim in the sea or play in the earth by our hut. These simple pleasures continued until I had reduced the lava to a pile of rubble lying along the sides of the ravine. There was, I thought, just enough room for the motorhome to make that sharp turn. We wouldn't know the results of this effort until our friends arrived later that summer.

Black Warrior

When we ran low on supplies or just wanted a change of scene, we would take a trip into the town of Black Warrior, Guerrero Negro, about three hours down the peninsula. This town was, back in those days as it is now, a supply hub for Baja's central desert. We left Las Cuevitas early in the morning with me rushing everyone to stick to the schedule. The time was important because siesta in Black Warrior was more formal than in smaller villages. Not much in the town was open except restaurants between one and four in the afternoon. If we left the hut at seven in the morning, we would get to town by ten and have time to do our shopping before the shops closed at midday. The town had just about all you could want or need on a basic level. In fact, all the building materials we had carried across the border were available here, and they were cheaper than they had been in the States. But Black Warrior was, and is, still an outpost, surrounded by hundreds of kilometers of desert on three sides and on the fourth by the Pacific Ocean, a desert in its own right. The town had several markets, auto parts stores, a furniture store, numerous clothing shops, a tailor, yardage goods, an ice cream store, several *dulcerías*, mechanics, tire stores, a toy shop even, and everything else that was required for rural living.

When we arrived in town, Michael and Kevin insisted that we visit the toy store first. Here, among the dusty boxes of packaged toys on the half-filled shelves, they would invariably find a small toy car or truck that they would employ in the nests of small tunnels they had dug behind the hut at Las Cuevitas. We grew to know the storeowner as a good fellow, and he was quick to recognize the two blond heads running down the street for his shop every few weeks. His store was just down the dusty way from the aging theater which seemed so out of place in this setting.

Next were the markets, each with their own products: meat, vegetables, fruit, bread, canned goods. It was a pleasure wandering through the stocked small markets of the town, the shelves and a few small chillers filled with goods not available at the bay: fresh fruits and vegetables, freshly baked pastries, large glass jars of Mexican drinks. We wandered the narrow aisles buying more than we needed just because it was available and abundant. The prices in Black Warrior were high, but the goods were available. In Spanish the word I had learned as a child for expensive was *caro*, which means dear—an interesting correlation between languages and innuendoes.

After we had visited the toy store and the markets, it was nearing siesta time and the stores began closing, one by one. Their owners and workers walked down dusty paths to visit their wives, children, and lovers for a sweaty reprieve from work in the midday swelter.

We stopped often at a restaurant near the highway we had discovered and usually all ordered *carne asada* and cokes. It always surprised us that at their young age the boys wanted something other than a hamburger or sandwich. Mary Ann and I would relax over lunch while the boys tore around in the heat kicking up dust outside the restaurant with their new cars, making motor noises, their naturally bleached hair and tanned faces reflecting the sun like natives.

By two in the afternoon, we were heading back to the bay, sometimes buying gas at Villa Jesús María, the turnoff for Laguna Manuela a few miles west on the Pacific coast. By the time we made the turnoff just north of Punta Prieta and wound down the Bahía road, the boys were asleep in the back seat, toy cars gripped tightly in their hands. The bouncing of the rougher dirt road to our bay woke them rudely and a half hour later we rumbled into Las Cuevitas just in time to round up Burlap and Billy before it got dark.

Solitude and Storms

If there were reasons in my mind for our trip this summer, it was to stop the world for a brief moment while the boys were young and for our family interrelationships to benefit from sharing almost everything together rather than each of us being out and about all day doing our individual work and school activities. From this moment in time, I wanted a freeze-frame of the four of our lives together that would last forever. I knew the tangles of our individual worlds in southern California would unkink in Baja and we would coalesce into the homogeneous entity. The predictable and unpredictable elements of our daily lives, together, undivided by the smallest interruptions, would become projections of our lifetimes when the boys and we, years in the future, inevitably went our individual ways. In Baja, although we were often threatened by external elements, we were never attacked from within ourselves. The more the wind raged and pulled at our fragile home, the more we worked together to control the environment. Like sailors, threatened by a storming sea, we learned to work together against the odds to solve our problems. The four of us grew to rely on each other, equally.

Great and threatening storms grew out on the gulf and attacked us unpredictably. We learned to read their arrival on the water before the wind and to take their pulse, to know when they had peaked and when we needed to take additional precautions. This taught us responsibility to each other and the need to each be counted on under the most trying circumstances. We watched the behavior of the wild and domestic animals and the ocean, and we watched the land to evaluate the damage it had withstood over the centuries, the millennia before our time there.

Sometimes during the day or night the wind rose suddenly with no warning. It could blow thirty knots without causing us any grief; we always kept the gear pretty well secured. If it was during the day, we took care of things with no major problems. But big winds often came during the night. It was difficult to wake to a rising wind, get dressed in the dark, unless there was a near-full moon, and determine what needed doing.

When the wind was over fifteen knots, the kitchen pots and pans, hanging close from the roof on their wire hooks, rang like heavy wind chimes. At anything over thirty knots, the walls of the hut would begin to lean, the upright posts being buried only in eighteen inches of sand. Mary Ann usually dealt with the troubles inside and I would go outside to see what the problems were there. If the wind rose above thirty, I would move the Land Cruiser to the corner taking the worst beating and tie a guy line from the truck to the upright at that corner. I would back the truck up slightly to straighten the hut and hold it in place for the duration of the storm. The boys helped their mom pick up inside the hut.

Three or four times during the summer the winds blew beyond the tolerance of the hut and we took significant damage: either the roof blew off or parts of walls blew away. The suspended gear rattled and banged and the storage crates on the walls spilled their contents onto the ground before falling themselves. The boys were awake and afraid; the animals were scared and restless. The wind howled and whistled and churned the black sea. We were wet with salt spume. Sand flew in sheets above the ground. The danger was very real, in part because we never knew the limits of the wind. Like an earthquake or a tornado, you never quite knew how bad it was going to get.

We held things together any way we could, and never suffered catastrophic damage, but there were many late night blows where I was sure we were going to. I had seen the damage the wind had done to our first hut at the south end, and I remembered clearly how strong it could grow. Eventually, we dug deep holes a few feet outside each corner of the hut and sank dead-man anchors that we could cinch down when a wind came. These helped to stabilize the uprights, but we still had to use the truck if the blow was really strong. These events became nothing more than an inconvenience after the first few storms and we worked them into our routine. All the threats served the purpose of throwing us together and learning the benefits of working as a team under pressure. The boys, even at their young ages, were learning to think on their feet—looking for something that wasn't getting done and doing it.

Friends

Before we left southern California, we hoped that our friends would come and visit us. This was a long time to be isolated on a remote beach. But Mary Ann and I also knew that, if we had friends around much of the time, we would defeat the purpose of the isolation. We were caught in a dichotomy.

The approach we decided upon was to encourage our friends (an independent lot) to come during a one-week window toward the end of summer. As we approached this period, we began to worry how many would actually make the trek. By late summer, this event was looming and we were making preparations to support a small number of visitors from the north. Many of our potential guests had never been to Mexico or Baja. We had told them in many stories about the lack of supplies, but you never quite know what to expect, so we wanted to be prepared for just about any eventuality.

In Black Warrior we bought additional supplies and stocked up on food, gas, and water. We spent several days cleaning up the area around the hut and along the shore where our friends would camp, moving large rocks and clumps of seaweed that had washed up on the beach. Once we were ready, we sat through interminable hours awaiting their arrival. But, of course, there was no schedule of arriving flights or any such like. I had thought earlier that it would be difficult to find our place with all the twisting roads leading north of La Gringa. Could our friends find us? Then I thought about Barsam and his family who had helped us find our isolated beach. I grabbed a stack of paper plates from a fruit crate and got Mary Ann to do a little calligraphy work while I gathered a few pieces of wood and a handful of roofing nails. I started the truck and headed off into the desert following our road back out to La Gringa. At the junction of our side road with the road from the village, I stopped and nailed a paper plate to a piece of wood and pounded the assembly into the ground beside the road. The plate read "Barsam's Corner, 3 miles" with an arrow indicating the direction to take. I drove back toward the hut, stopping and placing a similar sign at every intersection, reducing the distance appropriately. All our friends, originally coming from separate sources, by now knew Barsam. When they encountered the first signs they would know to follow them to our camp.

In the ravine where I had sweated so many early morning hours, picking and shoveling the tight lava flow that prevented free access to our beach, where my sons had brought me the quenching and rejuvenating, life-renewing, ice-cold Kool-Aid, I placed the final sign: "Barsam's Corner." From that point our hut was visible.

When we are old and feeble and our lives are done, and we can only look back at ourselves and our doings, what can we expect? The relationships we have formed with family, friends and affiliates will be our major accomplishments. We will reflect on how we have helped the world or humanity. It will be difficult for me to find a serious contribution with respect to the work I have done and taken so seriously most of my life: the American space program. No matter what I have done—written hundreds of technical documents, help organize many missions to planets and around earth, helped fresh-outs learn the ropes—nothing specific will be left for which I am warmly proud, nothing for which I will be remembered. But I was proud that our friends were coming to visit a place they would not otherwise have ventured without our being here. A number of people would experience something new because we were here, as Bill, John Treat, Nick and Peter Tompkins did on their trip to visit our first hut in 1974. Not all our friends would enjoy the threats and pleasures of Baja, but at least they were open to new experiences. Many of our current friends had such negative impressions because of the contemporary drug-smuggling problems across the long stretch of our common border and the news of *bandidos*. I was anxious to put these in perspective. We prepared for our friends with four pairs of eyes and ears turned toward the north.

Our area had been cleaned and arranged; we had attended to every thinkable detail. Now we hung around waiting apprehensively, not having a specific day of arrival. Assuming they would come for a week, leaving L.A. on Friday night, that would lead them (barring serious problems) to the village by late morning or early afternoon on Saturday. Having placed the directional signs, we continued to wait...

On a Wednesday late in summer, Barsam and his family arrived. Mary Ann and I heard the noise of a vehicle floating over the desert, went up onto the plateau to see who it was, and could see Barsam turning his motorhome into the gully that led to the hut. We scampered up the *barranca* to the road. The motorhome was about as wide as I had expected and could squeeze between the sides of the gorge, but, when it came to Barsam's Corner, it was going to be tight. Bar reversed direction, cut the wheels, checked his rearview mirrors, scudded back and forth and eventually made it through the passage. Pulling down onto the beach, he shut off the motor, and the Diradoorian family piled out onto the sand: B.J., seventeen; Brian, fifteen; Melody, thirteen; Bar and Marlene. The corner had worked and the signs had their desired effect. During the arrival of our friends over the next few days, no one failed to heed the clearly recognizable postings.

In the afternoon of the next day and after a long drive, the Gallos arrived from New Jersey. Jimmy and Carol had driven across the country and down Baja in four days and were ready for cold beers and a fishing pole. Beanie and Lisa, their daughters, jumped into bathing suits and headed for the water. The girls had grown up—Beanie was fifteen and Lisa was seventeen. Both had matured nicely into women since we'd last seen them. We all spent the evening catching up on the events of our lives and kids. The Gallo girls were great with the boys and they all wore each other out and fell asleep on the sand.

Sometime after dark, while no one was watching, Barsam snuck up the most prominent side of the Three Brothers with a hundred pounds of lye on his back. He opened the sacks and created, in the white powder against the dark, tanned skin of the hillside, a giant *H* (for Humfreville). It escaped our attention for some days' time until we were returning from a trip in the boat and one of us noticed the ten-foot-high letter on the hill from miles away. What a guy!

Over the course of the next few days, we had the best of everything, and the least, with the minimum of supplies we had on hand. But in this minimal environment we found magic. There were several days spent with the Diradoorians and the Gallos. The kids all worked together and joined with the adults whenever they wanted, and the adults joined with the children—there were no lines of division. We spent time all around, in nothings and everythings, talked about sense and nonsense, sat on the beach and made intelligible noises or were silent. We enjoyed it all. The men, young and old, took to the sea to reinforce and substantiate the tall fishing tales that we spun with each other. The women, young and old, shared stories about home, work, and family. Sometimes these stories included shady aspects of their husbands and male offspring and offered simple attempts at understanding things beyond anyone's grasp.

And life perpetuated.

The small waves of Las Cuevitas, the sand, the sun and the stones with their associated simplicity, and their lack of confusion cast their spells. The earth, the sky, and the sea became one, as did we, with the dolphins, the working bait, frigate birds, empty seashells, pelicans, and the warm and humid wind from the east.

By the end of the week many more folks passed through the *barranca* of Las Cuevitas and Barsam's Corner. We welcomed, over the next two days, at least forty friends. Several families brought small trailers, some brought tents, and some brought only sleeping gear and a few clothes. Two other families brought aluminum boats about the same size as ours. Our friends fell primarily into two groups: they were from JPL or they were from a group we had gotten close to in the Indian Guides, a club for Michael and Kevin and a number of other youngsters. So there were friends of all ages. And soon they all knew each other.

The area surrounding our camp had a hundred feet of beachfront on either side where everyone camped, strung out along the sand and stones in an assortment of funky campsites. The afternoon was spent setting up equipment and staying in the shade, adjusting to the heat and humidity and recovering from the two-day drive. Everyone gathered in and around the hut, Mary Ann and I showing off all our simple facilities. The boys took their friends through the paces: into the water, down to the beach caves, up into the hills, the Three Brothers, and onto the plateau.

The adults, dazed at driving through such desolate backcountry, settled in, guzzling beers and wine coolers to shake off the dust from the road and then settled into the beginning of a week full of promise and adventure.

The men were anxious to get the boats into the water and so they backed their trailers up to the beach in the gravel, pulling the gear out, mounting outboard engines, gathering fuel lines and organizing fishing tackle. The air rang with sputtering two-cycle engines all around Las Cuevitas. We caught yellowtail and tuna and marinated several sides in soy sauce and brown sugar for a day or two. We smoked and served these. There was *ceviche*, small cubes of raw fish marinated in Mexican limes for a few hours and mixed with diced tomatoes, onion and cilantro. We'd been lucky enough to catch octopus and it was boiled, and the skin was removed from its tentacles. It went into the *ceviche* also. Everyone fixed something and there was always food on the tables of every campsite as we all walked back and forth visiting on the beach.

That evening was the typical Baja scenario: great sunset over the desert and backlit mountains; jumping bait; several guys, poles in hand, surf fishing against the darkening sky; boys with a campfire even though the temperature was over eighty. The ladies sat on the patio of the hut or on the steps, talking, while the guys harassed each other regarding the small catches from the shallow water. When the light had faded enough to give us a bit of privacy we bathed in the ocean, squirting dish soap or liquid shampoo into our bathing suits and scrubbing as modestly as was appropriate. We rinsed in the sea and followed that with a cupful of fresh water poured over our heads to get the salt out. When it was completely dark, we watched the stars and the earth-orbiting satellites, with Bill and John from JPL telling us which were the military and spy orbiters and which were civilian based on their direction of travel.

Marlene set a Coleman lantern at the tide line as we sat in sand chairs in the shallow, clear, still water. She chummed the water with a few scraps left over from the omnipresent snacks. Soon, small fish were schooling in the six-inch-deep water along the shore. Within a few minutes a five-inch blue-point crab came on the scene. Later, a small octopus passed through. The search for life-sustaining substances was unending.

By late evening the line of aluminum chairs had appeared, filled with groggy men telling a few last stories and taking some abuse from the ladies on the stairs of the hut. The guys arranged their pecking order for the next morning and we went to bed by ten p.m. We had three boats which were enough for all of us that wanted to go fishing every day. The early mornings were always reserved for the serious fishermen. The kids slept in anyway and the women enjoyed reading and talking in the early morning before it got hot.

Fishing Buddies
(the Old Men and the Sea)

I woke up about five-thirty the next morning to the sound of footsteps in the gravel. Barsam was up and loading fishing gear into my boat and filling a small chest with cold beer. Above all he was American, but he had been raised by very Armenian parents fresh from the old country. It always bore watching when he worked. Into the chest with the cold beers he meticulously placed a few pieces of ice frozen in small containers in the refrigerator of his motorhome overnight. He didn't just reach into an ice chest and take a bucket of ice and throw it into the smaller chest, he was very conscious of excess. We always ribbed him because he was the only guy in our friend-set that clipped and shopped coupons. It was Barsam that was always the first up in the morning and prepared the boat for the day's fishing. He was the one to quietly leave the evening gathering for a few moments to prepare the boat for the next morning's run. His father and mother must have hung heavily within him, reflecting the conditions that prevailed in Eastern Europe earlier in the century.

In a few minutes those of us going fishing were all awake. We washed our faces and brushed our teeth in the ocean and within a minute or two were ready to go. All, that is, except our friend Peter, who was lobbying for coffee. He howled so loud and so long it was easier to pacify than deny him. We sat idling while he had his coffee and were soon enough off for the inside of Smith's with the three boats, each running at its own pitch and with its unique irregularities, of which there was an abundance.

Dropping down into the channel with Salas, we "yoyoed" the bottom for a while and had several moderate hookups which we threw into the back of the boat. By seven we broke out the first beer and wore out the "yoyo-ing" and moved to the northern point of Isla Coronado in the channel between the island and the islet called Coronadito. We bottom-fished with little luck, tried the north side of Coronadito, and then moved into shallower water in the bay on the outside of Coronado's north end beneath the volcano. When we left the shade of the island, the sun hit the boat with full force. Sweating in the heat, pulling our lines in, we were casting, sinking and pulling in again. Barsam was always the first to get his line in the water and the last to reel it in. He was competitive and operated on the surefire principle that the guy that kept his line in the water the longest would catch the most fish. He was almost always right.

A nominal catch for three guys in a boat on the average day in summer back then was between five and seven midsized yellowtail in the twenty- to thirty-pound range. If there were no yellows, we would fish for bottom grabbers. Our collective favorite of the bottom variety was what the locals call Cabazon. This is what gringos called jawfish, but we didn't know it. They seem to hang out in a hundred feet of water with a sandy bottom. When you are in their vicinity, they are easy but no fun to catch. But they are about the best fish ever for deep frying in beer batter.

The guys were full of laughs between the three boats. One of us would hook up only to be harassed by the others regarding the small fish that we pulled reluctantly from the depths. Peter was the pilot of one boat and, while we were all collected in an area but not catching much, he fired up his engine and headed a mile or two north to another hole or reef. After a half hour of catching nothing, our other two boats moved to Peter's location. As we approached his boat from about a hundred meters out, we could see the guys had hooked something unusual. Peter reeled in a sea snake, about three feet long and bright green. He hauled the evil-looking thing over the side and waved it at pole's length in front of his two boatmates who shrank into the extremities of the small craft. I was piloting my boat and pulled close to see what exactly he had caught. The head of the snake was the most noteworthy. It was bright green with long, bright red protrusions above its eyes that looked like shaggy eyebrows. It had the head shape that we are taught to be wary of, triangular, with large cavities behind the eyes for poison.

The three boats, seeing the snake, had all clustered within a few yards of each other. About the time we were all realizing this snake must be poisonous, a strange shadow crossed Peter's face followed by his Harrison Ford crooked and devilish grin and we knew he was up to no good. We jammed the engines into gear and pulled a safe distance away almost as fast as Peter grabbed the venomous beast by the tail and swung it around to throw it at us. But a fortunate swell from our hasty retreats threw him off balance and, as he struggled to regain his legs, he dropped the snake to the bottom of his own boat.

Peter's boat is not simple like mine. His boat has a bottom of slatted wood that runs from bow to transom. Into this false bottom Peter has built many storage cabinets and bait tanks and whatever else he could find use for in his fourteen-foot barge. It was into this morass that the slippery snake fell. That menacing, twisting and ugly, threatening and evil *thing* was loose in Peter's boat! The three people therein couldn't get out of each other's way fast enough.

Johnnie Boyd, Dave, and Peter rushed to grab any gaff, oar or stick they could lay their hands on being careful not to put their hands or feet where they couldn't see. From a safe distance, the rest of us were whooping and catcalling indiscrete suggestions about abandoning ship and swimming for shore which was miles away. Too soon they located the snake coiled in a crevice, snagged him with the gaff and flung him, hissing and spitting but unharmed, away from the boat and back into the ocean.

We were all having a great time fishing but were doing poorly in the *catching* department. While we were stopped in the water now that the snake had been disposed of, Bar and I were scanning the distance, looking for birds. From several miles away we saw a small swirling mass, black specks in the sky, working an area well north of Smith's. We shouted to the drivers and all headed north, outside the channel.

It took us a few minutes to arrive at the site. During this time, skimming over the water at top speeds of twenty knots, birds were passing us in their rush to get to the fish. We were all rigging our lines with whatever we wanted for casting into a boil. As we neared the boil, the birds were so thick in the sky that they shut out the worst of the sun. Thousands of gulls, goonies, pelicans, and frigate birds were flying in a circle at least three hundred meters in diameter. In any instant at least a hundred birds hit the water beneath their swirling airborne mass, each kicking up small spouts as they struck the surface, each adding to the turmoil. Thousands more birds were in the water swallowing fish, waiting for clearance to take back to the sky and dive again. The sea away from this violence was calm. No wind was blowing. Inside the boil the water was rough and churning. The bait was desperately fighting by the millions to avoid the attacking yellowtail and the birds.

Our three boats pulled into the center of this furor, cutting the engines and casting lures into the fish as the boats slowed. Within seconds several of us had solid hookups. Bang! Dive for the rocks to snap the line. Straight down they'd go until we thought we couldn't hold them. Adjust the drag. Bring in whatever line you could…another run downward. Crank it in—200, 150, 100 feet. It's coming up now—50 feet. Spot the bottom of the boat and make a final run. Do a long and slow retrieve required by our six-to-one ratio reels. Soon we were gaffing and hauling twenty-pounders over the hull.

This went on for fifteen minutes with "Hookup!" ringing frequently in the air. The guys in each boat had no time to spare; they worked quickly and as teams, bringing in line, gaffing, working fish to the back of the boat, keeping lines from tangling.

Gradually the boil widened and was less intense. The birds began to thin and the surface calmed. Activities returned pretty much to normal. We had three boats full of yellowtail. During that fifteen to twenty minutes we had caught three or four fish each. Coupled with the catch of earlier, we were going to be hard pressed to clean and process it all.

Pulling in our lines we headed for camp. Half an hour later we rounded the point of Las Cuevitas, powered across the smooth water of the bay up near the beach, cut the engines and coasted gently onto the small stones in front of the steps leading to the hut.

Barsam jumped out, retrieved his cleaning table and moved it to the water's edge. The rest of us gathered knives and cleaning boards, washed canning jars, lids and rings. Others fired up the Colemans and got the pressure cookers ready.

We filleted the first few fish, leaving the skin on. I mixed a simple marinade of brown sugar and soy sauce. These first fillets would soak, on ice, over night and would be smoked the next day. We spent an hour working quickly in the noontime heat, male torsos dripping sweat, filleting and skinning the remainder of the fish. We cut these into segments two inches wide and three or four inches long that would serve for dinner and for canning.

From the minute we threw the first fish from the boats onto the beach, birds began collecting. Some came so close we had to wave them away. The injured birds are often the most aggressive; they cannot catch food on their own. The pelicans and gulls rocked in the foot-deep water waiting for the fish skin, heads, and innards they knew we would discard. The gulls set off a loud, aggressive cawking, first one then others, until the entire collection was yech-yech-yeching a concert of close echoes. The pelicans sat, dignified and majestic, chins tucked, beaktips etching the waters surface, eyes sadly watching our every move, waiting pensively.

When we threw the first handful of gut, skin, and bone into the water several feet from the cleaning table, the scene turned into a feathered war zone. Every bird fought for every scrap. Soon all our children heard the commotion and came to help. They grabbed fish guts that we were tossing under the table, and threw pieces into the air. The gulls caught the morsels in midflight. In the shallow water, thousands of tiny fish worked to collect the pieces too small for the birds. The gulls quarreled over anything they could turn into an argument.

The women had the jars rinsed and set the rings and lids beside the jars. We stuffed quart, pint, and half-pint jars, which had wide mouths, full of the cleaned chunks of pale pink flesh, keeping the level well below the ring on the jar. We added water to just cover the tops of the fish, worked knives in to remove air bubbles, placed a lid loosely on top of each and twisted the rings on until they were beginning to resist. We put the jars into the pressure cookers, added an inch of seawater, cinched down the lids two-fingers tight, secured the pressure cooker lid and turned up the heat, waiting for the water to boil. The pressure inside the cooker slowly rose. As it neared ten pounds, we turned down the heat and sat down for an hour and a half's relaxing wait with nothing more to do than keep an eye and ear on the pressure, have a beer or two, and review the war of the morning.

During the lull, I started the charcoal briquets in the smoker. Within a few minutes this was burning nicely. I threw some damp citrus chips on the coals and put the chimney of the smoker over the base of coals. I set the racks into place and put the other fillets that had been marinating overnight, dark brown and covered with the sugar-soy marinade, onto the grills and covered the whole assembly with the lid.

While I was doing this and the guys were finishing up the cleaning chore, the ladies were cooking. We ate homegrown eggs from our chickens, scrambled and mixed with Spam or Brazilian canned corned beef, fried potatoes, frijoles, and tortillas. We ate lunch relating the morning to each other and those that had been left in camp, finished the food, cleaned up and spent the next hour or two napping, looking for shells, swimming, walking around the nearby hills and plateau or napping again.

By midafternoon we were regaining our strength. The canning was done and almost all the jars had sealed. Those that hadn't we would put on ice to make into tuna salad sandwiches later. Several of the diehards went out fishing. The rest of us re-collected in pieces of shade from the flapping tarps we had arranged randomly around the hut, talking, making jokes and laughing. Several of the children had picked up our poles and were casting Salas sixes with conventional reels from the shore, trying to outdo each other. Most of the adults wanted nothing more to do with catching fish.

Several of us decided to make a run for the village for ice and gas. There wasn't usually a problem getting ice in those days, but gas was a sure thing only right after the truck had filled the huge above-ground tanks at Patricio's then-flourishing Pemex station at the end of the airstrip in the village. In the early 1980s I was told that there were five Pemex trucks for the entire peninsula. This was not enough to keep the fuel flowing through the thirsty throats of the outboard carburetors that plied the gulf for fish.

For the run to the village, we rearranged ice chests, transferring contents from one to another, until we had several empties which we drained and tossed into the rear of the truck. Grabbing gas and water jugs, we piled into the Land Cruiser and threaded our way past Barsam's Corner and along the ravines and back to La Gringa. From here the road improved and we barreled along at forty miles an hour keeping ahead of the thick, rising, twisting column of dust we were throwing from the roadway. The movement of air from the open windows was cooling in the still heat of the afternoon. Hawks and buzzards perched occasionally on the tops of the cardón and cirio cacti. Their beaks were open and wings out, away from their body, looking like scarecrows on the dry desert landscape. We didn't see another vehicle on this fifteen-kilometer drive until we neared the village.

At the Díaz patio we parked in the shade of their single smoke-wood tree and carried the empty ice chests into the store where we replenished them with this most luxurious of provisions. Helping ourselves from the accessible Díaz coolers to *cervezas* of our choosing, we sat in the shade on the patio. With half an hour to waste before Patricio would return from siesta to open the gas station, we talked to the locals about the fishing that day. Everyone had had a good catch. At four we grabbed a bag of cookies for the kids, paid our bill, and bid adiós to Chubasco. Across a dirt field was the station. Patricio was just arriving and, thankfully, he had gas. We filled up the Land Cruiser tanks, then the jerry cans for the boats, and joked with Patricio about the few extra pesos that had mysteriously disappeared at the end of our purchase.

We drove up the road past Dos Pinos to the spring and filled our water jugs. A young boy came from a nearby house. It was his job to ensure the safety of the pump and make sure that water wasn't wasted. He helped us fill the containers and wanted to know where we had been fishing. When we were done, we tipped him a few *pesos* and headed north to Las Cuevitas. As we roared along the road, throwing dust into the air that was visible for miles, we knew the camp was watching and could see our column across the miles of desert. Get the beer ready we thought, we're coming home!

At camp I checked the smoking fish. The caramel marinade had formed a thick layer as the fillets had cooked slowly over the coals and the smoking wood. We passed plates around and it was gone in minutes. As the shadows lengthened, the few that had made an afternoon fishing run returned with a few bottom fish which they cleaned and put on ice. They had gone back to the place where we had caught game fish so well that morning, but had not had any luck. It was always a best-guess deal with the variables of lunar cycle, the weather, the water temperature, and who knows what other issues.

Stories

In the late afternoon we sat in the shade on the wide stone steps and shared stories and small talk, recalling incidents in which one or the other of us had been publicly humiliated or humiliating to others of us and laughed at the results. There were stories of great Indian Guides' adventures, camping with our boys in Alta California. The boys were laughing and related how, on a trip to a remote camp sight, the dads had, after a night of significant laughter, put the fire out by pissing on it. The boys were on-the-spot to join in this official activity. The memory would last them a lifetime—their dads were people after all. We joked about our Indian Guide names, chosen after prominent personal traits. Mine, for example, was Fierce Wind.

Peter preserved through ancient storytelling the manner in which the Mohawks (our tribe) made spaghetti: "You just put the dry spaghetti in your mouth and pour in the boiling water."

On the steps at Las Cuevitas we all laughed; Peter smiled and bowed. We reviewed other stories of various missteps in the world. Bottles of Mexican beer were tipped and tequila passed among the friends seated on flat rocks from the desert, brought to Las Cuevitas to meet the sea. Gradually families, couples, and children wandered off to their camps for the night. John McLeod, another JPL friend, Bill and I sat late into the night as always when we had the chance. This was a good time to evaluate issues from our work and JPL, when our minds were free to reevaluate decisions made under the stress of work. But alcohol was involved and sometimes the thought we chewed on all night was utter nonsense the next morning. Sometimes unique thought was the result.

Eventually all our friends were sleeping in their tents, trailers, cots and on the stones. Mary Ann and the boys were long gone in the hut. John and Bill had stumbled home and no doubt fallen asleep fully dressed. I walked to the water's edge to rinse my face. Lace on the water from a sliver moon floated silkily on the quiet surface, stirred by a breezy whisper, late in the evening. I sat for a moment in the small stones of the beach thinking about the day and our friends, of the events, the laughter, the equality of being one amongst peers.

Revenge on the Coyote

The next morning the fisherpeople toiled with the sea once again, extracting booty for another bout of cleaning and canning. We were winning; the fish were losing.

By midday we were collected on the steps of the hut eating the after-fishing meal. Mary Jo mentioned that a dog had chewed into some of their equipment during the night. Lassie was partitioned off in our hut after we went to bed. Other than Lassie, John and Devon Boyd had brought their tiny dog, Biff; they kept Biff in their tent at night. I suspected something other than dogs, but wanted to see what had been molested.

Mary Jo led me up a small rising ravine between our hut and their camp. Here they had enough privacy to position their portable toilet, alone, undisturbed and untended. Their boxy, plastic commode had been designed with a small compartment of fresh water to flush and another compartment into which the black water was deposited, so to speak.

I knew a thirsty coyote had sniffed the air, a mile off in the desert, and caught a whiff of clean and pure water from the reservoir on the toilet. He had followed his nose from a distance to the plateau and then down the twisted descending ravine to the portable toilet of Peter and Mary Jo.

After our war with the coyotes before our friends arrived, I understood how thirsty they got. I thought of this desperate coyote, smelling water, chewing through the hose of the toilet, teeth on plastic, tongue against teeth, gnawing until in a final clash of ivory against yielding pipe the coyote won and the walls of the pipe gave way. The coyote knew immediately he had succeeded and relaxed his jaws to allow the cool, sweet water to fill his thirsty mouth. Instead, he had chewed through the wrong side of the toilet. Into his mouth, at the height of his anticipation, drained the contents of the black and ugly side of the toilet.

It had to be a bad moment among the bad moments of the coyote's life.

Ian's Story

John and Laura McLeod's son, Ian, was a year old when this visit occurred. They joined our collection of friends, placed Ian on the safety of the steps of our hut where we were gathered and sat nearby visiting with us all. Ian could hardly walk, let alone stand on the uneven surfaces of our steps. He was so young he was rewarded with every step if he remained upright; he suffered awful defeats and kept trying. Ian had a minor diaper rash, so Laura permitted him to wander amongst us naked for the sake of clearing up pink spots on his bottom.

Ian took many steps with his air-dried butt exposed to the curing sun on the stairs in front of the hut, and was guided this way and that by the loving hands of adults and older children. He walked up, and down, and across from one side to another of our loosely collected group. After a period of time, Ian reached the top of the stairs and found the flat surface of our hut.

By design the floor of our home was smooth stones, gravel. Here, Ian was happy: it was all one level, a wide and flat place where he could walk without falling, unlike the steps. Here, too, he stepped, fell, arose and tried again. We could see him from below and he was safe.

Somewhere during this while, Ian felt a need. Maybe a child doesn't think of it as a need at that age. Maybe it just happens. And it did. Ian voided himself onto the porch of our house.

Spilling a noxious substance onto a homogeneous surface, hardwood, linoleum, is one thing. Even carpet can be cleaned. But small stones that are piled deep?

As soon as Ian had this unforeseen accident, we were aware of a really bad smell. There was only one likely culprit and the whole assemblage looked and shouted "*Ian!*" in a single utterance.

Ian had no idea that anything was wrong, in fact, had done nothing worthy of this condemnation. But he recognized his own name and could see all of us looking in his direction.

He panicked. Although, previously, so new at this walking thing that he had been unable to take two steps in the same direction, Ian took off down and across the steps and away from the awful mistake he had apparently made until he walked smack into the base of our fire pit. No fire had been lit since the day before; there were no roaring flames to consume Ian. There were no burning, red-hot coals to gnarl his tiny feet. He was safe from serious harm. But there was, still, from over night, significant residual heat in the fire pit. Ian's young and tender feet reacted to an already alarmed state of mind from the voices surrounding his unfortunate accident telling him he was hurt, and now, he actually was. After mom examined a howling Ian and determined there was no major damage, he again wandered through camp, still learning to walk, with both feet swaddled in white bandages.

Needless to say we removed a great number of stones from our patio later that day.

Continuing Days

There passed many more days in the warming rays of the sun sharing friendship and camaraderie. We caught and canned more fish; shared meals and sweated together in the midday heat; shifted our chairs from place to place to catch the best-flowing airs. We hugged our kids and listened to their stories and watched them all playing together on the beach.

One afternoon we were relaxing after our activities of the mornings fishing when the boys all came running into camp shouting about rattlesnakes in the small caves, *las cuevitas*, along the high tide line. We gathered and calmed the boys and together went back to investigate. Perhaps the slippery vipers had escaped. Perhaps the overactive imaginations of children had escaped. There were, perhaps, equal dangers in both.

No snakes were found. But this incident did lead us to inform our friends that there was a doctor available in the village. We had confirmed this when we had first arrived and were aware of the possibility of snakebite or other accident. There was an internist who operated a small facility beside the museum. If the doctor's office wasn't open when you had a need, how far could he have gone? (Many years after we'd met Abraham, the doctor, at Las Cuevitas, we re-met him at Camp Gecko. He is the originator of that camp, built on the same slice of beach where our first hut had stood in 1974. What a small world.)

Like another summer, ten years before, in another hut on a slightly more southern beach, with our friends here, we were filled with a sense of warmth and sharing, of humor and self-deprecation. Over the days our friends sank to the level of contentedness that Mary Ann, Michael, Kevin and I had achieved over the time we had settled into Las Cuevitas. The stimulations here were sensory and tactile rather than intellectual. Our minds came at last to a rest position from which we could see great distances in directions we were not accustomed to. Sharing an environment as intimate as Las Cuevitas and our hut was unique to most of us.

Of course, the discussion arose: why not all retire and move to Baja?

I've wanted to do this many times over the years. There were a couple of times when we could have done just that and been comfortable; it's so much less expensive and so much more accommodating than the U.S. But it was not the place, in those years and in my opinion, to make a financial investment of any kind. More importantly, the lifestyle is so different from what we're used to that most of us burn out after a brief period of infatuation.

But what a great feeling it would be to be surrounded only by your family and friends every day of your life in a sensorially enriched place like this with no outside problems introduced, with the world at bay, even unaware of the rest of the world. How wonderful to awake forever on vacation and to the gentle sounds of water lapping at the edge of a stony beach. To the magnificent sound of air flowing through the feathered wings of a vee of pelicans working south over the thatched fringes of a hut on an isolated beach. To open eyes for the first time of the day to the sun shining off the water in shards through the thatch. To awake to only the things in your environment that you had personally selected.

Suns and moons rose and set with prediction. Clouds formed and faded. Music and laughter came and went. In the evenings, gentle concertos floated across the stones in a fine mist like a fog clinging to the contours of the land. Days passed in that innocent and protected moment of time where we lived collectively in a single spirit, where there was no *I*, only *we*. We were, for a time, an indivisible *one*. I fell to thinking about the simplicity theory, the edge of a continent, a single piece of sea and sky with nothing else to interrupt us. This was the essence of Baja.

In the afternoons we took the boats out on runs to locate and mingle with the dolphins and whales. It was great to cut the motor in front of a million charging dolphins closing on us in a frothy wall, chirping, breaching, working with their young. They were as interested in us as we were in them. Given their intelligence and their lifespan, they should pass us by in another hundred millennia or so. We were just a drop in the evolutionary bucket.

Fueled mildly by alcohol, we drove trucks in the dirt to the village to show our friends around. Several stores had tee shirts with "L.A. Bay" or "Bahía de los Angeles" and pictures of a hot and sandy beach or dolphins stamped across the front. The old landing strip cutting through the heart of the village made an interesting story. The fact that, a few years back, you could land an airplane in the heart of the village, taxi to a gas station and then to a hotel all on the same dirt landing strip was unique.

Driving to the south end of the bay through the cactus forest surrounding Las Flores, we showed our friends the jail in the abandoned mining town. We drove east to the end of the road on the southeastern-most point of the bay past the scattered trailers and old mobile homes where a few folks spent modular pieces of free time. The road ended in a sandy arroyo halfway up the north end of Punta Roja. There, past the golden sand along Stingray Beach, beyond the end of the road, past an uninhabited mobile home that had been there for as long as I could remember, was a small thatched *palapa*. We sat in the same shade as we had, years before, with other friends. Once again, we had all brought folding chairs and we were so many that we just fit into the shade beneath the thatch. As we talked and sat and swam, we periodically moved the bank of chairs to remain beneath the shade as the sun cut a burning arc through the cloudless sky.

I can look into my most treasured moments from the beginning and know that they will be too fleeting. The visit of our friends was one of these. There are moments in life that I want to last forever, or almost. In the beginning, I looked into the future and saw the end before the beginning had started. And now the end approached.

As they had arrived, the Indian Guides, Jimmy, Carol, Bar, and Marlene were departing, en masse.

On the designated day, they uprooted themselves, shook and folded their tents, started engines, added lubricants and radiator fluids, drained ice chests, and passed us the unspoils of war in the desert.

They left us their unused cans and cartons of food. We were prepared for, but saddened at, their departure; they were gearing up for the attack on the desert and the unpredictable and inevitable problems they would face in real time. They were also going back to a real world while we were continuing in a fairy tale.

On their last night with us, we sat on the steps and mingled amongst the camps and shared the moments that only true friends share, of cocky humor and warm malaise spread on known prior mistakes. There is a line that friends cross freely where others could not venture. We listened again to the sounds of nature around us and finished the day with several changes of sweet and lofty melodies from several hard rock pals of Peter's, winding down to my eclectic solos of guitar, piano or flute. Again, a gentle and late night on the beach with moonlight, warm air, natural sounds, laughter and departing friends to share soon-to-be-lost moments with.

In the morning we said good-byes. There were tears and hugs and arrangements for get-togethers on our return home. Our thoughts were with them throughout the next several days, heading north toward the border, driving up the coast of Alta California through the increasing density of San Diego, La Jolla, Del Mar, Leucadia and Encinitas, Carlsbad and Oceanside, northward into the pressure-chamber of Los Angeles. I could smell the fumes of the smoke-pumping cars and trucks on I-5 as I imagined working past the Hollywood Freeway split, merging with the Golden State freeway, rushing to exit the cramping bowels of the freeways of L.A., splitting into smaller arteries working into the northern bedroom communities that define that side of the Los Angeles basin. Before I knew it we were left with dust settling in the arroyo that led to the plateau and back to La Gringa, Bahía de los Angeles and the pavement north. Our friends were gone.

Billy the Goat's Defining Moment

Several days after our friends left, we were finally enjoying the return to normalcy. In the late afternoon we decided to drive into the village for dinner. By the time we got back it was almost dark. Billy and Burlap were not in camp.

Over the summer we had learned that burros and goats do not have the same homing instincts that chickens have. We never had to put the chickens up; they took care of that all on their own. As soon as the sun started to set, they headed for the coop. But Billy and Burlap would wander far out into the desert and never seem to care that they were so far from home. Perhaps they had no concept or need for "home" as we know it. The chickens sure did.

There we were, trying to figure out how to track down our missing animals in the dark when we heard a bleating from one of the Three Brothers hills nearby. In the semidarkness, we climbed up the hill. As we neared the top, the crying was louder. Burlap had heard the bleating, too, as he came running from out of nowhere up the rise. These hills ran from west to east with the easternmost nothing but a straight drop of a hundred feet to the sea where the tides and storms had eroded the lava over the centuries. The earth fell in a sheer cliff into the ocean.

It sounded like Billy was down on this cliff somewhere, but it was so steep that we thought it was an echo. Then I saw the rope that we kept tied around his neck protruding just above the lip of the cliff. Mary Ann kept the boys back from the edge while I moved forward to see if it was Billy's rope and if I could see him. Before I reached the edge I was down, crawling, then slithering along on my belly. I was afraid the earth of the upper cliff wouldn't support my weight.

Reaching the end of the rope I clutched it without wrapping it around my hand—I didn't want to follow Billy down to the rocks below if it wasn't necessary. Peering over the edge, with almost no light, I could clearly hear Billy's cries for help. The little goat had gone down the nearly vertical cliff in search of something, but couldn't climb back up. He was stranded on a ledge a few inches wide above the ocean a hundred feet below.

I called back to Mary and the boys that he was stuck down the cliff and that I had the rope. But I had no idea how to get him back up the cliff. Billy was panicked. He must have been on his small ledge for some time and he was clearly glad to see me, throwing out a tremendous flurry of bleats the moment he heard us and saw me peering down at him. The rope was twenty meters long, so he was quite a way down.

I tried to maneuver him with the short length of rope I had, but nothing I did had any influence on him. Finally, I knew that the only way we were going to get Billy up the cliff was to haul him with the rope. But the rope was tied around his neck, and I worried that we would choke him. I expected that, under pressure and panic, he would help himself as much as possible crawling with his legs along the sheer cliff that he had climbed down. In addition to my hauling up on the rope, I expected that his hooves would be kicking, grabbing for traction on the stony face of the cliff whenever he could.

I shouted this hasty plan to Mary Ann and then started to pull. There was only a meter or so of the rope over the top of the cliff, and I was worried that, in my effort, I would go over with him if he lost his balance. Lying on the edge, I pulled using only my arms. I gained a small length of rope but I could hear Billy choking below. Pulling again, I got another small length, which gave me a small step back from the face. Once onto surer ground I could pull with all my might, hoping that Billy was, instinctively, keeping his hooves on the rocks as often as possible and trying to help climb upward.

Quickly I threw my whole body into the pull. I couldn't see Billy, but I could hear him choking. The sounds were so raspy that I could imagine him fighting to force air down a crimped esophagus. If I didn't have him up in the next few seconds, he'd be dead.

I now had about ten meters of rope above the cliff. Holding the rope tight, I moved back to Mary Ann and the boys. Throwing the loose end of rope to Mary Ann, I shouted to them to all grab a piece of rope and pull! All four of us dug our heels into the dirt and pulled with all we had. Soon we could feel the tension at the other end changing and knew that Billy had found a way to keep his feet on the ground. The uppermost cliff was less precipitous that the lower part. We pulled, moving away from the face and the resistance increased and we could hear Billy screaming like a mauled baby very near the top of the drop. Mary Ann and the boys held the line secure and I ran back to the cliff, extending my arms over the edge to lessen the friction between Billy's body and the cliff. As I did this, and as he caught sight of me, his hooves found which direction was down, and he worked with the rope to climb the remaining few feet to the top.

He was wobbling and coughing with a raspy hack for the first few moments. We moved him away from the edge and all collapsed in a heap on top of the lesser of the Three Brothers. Adrenaline does funny things to a body. Maybe I was the only one crying, but I doubt it.

We rubbed and patted Billy and massaged his throat. He was hoarse in every sound he made. But there didn't seem to be any permanent damage.

Listening to my music late that night with the rest of our family sleeping in the hut, I thought again about teamwork. If we learned nothing else this summer, we learned to work together when times got rough.

Billy and Burlap's Unexpected Trek

One night, not long before our summer was to close I had an attack of conscience. We got back late from some excursion and Michael and Kevin were putting Billy and Burlap into their small corral. I unilaterally decided that our favorite burro and goat deserved to make their own decisions about nighttime confinement. I positioned them near the corral, left the gate open and left Burlap's rope lying in the dust, unsecured on the other end. We watched them from time to time during the early evening and eventually we went to bed.

There were a few strange noises in the night, but there always were.

The next morning the goat and burro were nowhere to be found. We called to them, with no response. By around seven we were seriously worried. What had I done?

"I'll go look for them. They couldn't've gone far."

"I'll go, I'll go!" shouted Michael.

"Me too!!" echoed Kevin.

"It's too hot, boys," I said. "You stay here and guard the camp."

By seven-thirty I was hiking into the desert behind the hut. My plan was to follow their tracks and the trail in the dust left by the rope from Burlap's neck. This was easy at first because they walked in the loose dust up the narrow gully on the road leading to and beyond Barsam's Corner with the steep lava walls to keep them on the road. But, once they had risen to the level of the plateau, there was no restricting their wandering interests. The rope trail leapt from one grassy knob to the next, helter-skelter across the plain, invisible in the spaces of hardened earth. Where I could I followed their hoof prints. They always stayed together, pals forever, grown more friendly by living in the same radical environment for three months.

I managed to track them for miles into several small valleys and out again. After about two hours of slowly following the track, they seemed to turn back in the direction of home. Another half hour back in that direction, I lost them. The trail just ended. Circling around the place where I lost them in a spiral working out from their trail's end, I couldn't see another track anywhere.

I looked up into the hills around me. I called to them; I whistled; but there was nothing. I climbed into the nearest hill to get another perspective on the plains below; still there was nothing.

I had been in the direct sun on foot for three hours. I was dehydrated and tired and hot. I decided to go back to the hut, get a drink, rest a bit and try again. I started back, staying to clear areas so I could see a track if one was present, but I saw no sign of them. I looked up into the desert hills for movement; I wouldn't see them if they weren't moving because their colors were the same as the terrain.

About a half mile from camp I did see a small movement on a hillside to the north. I thought it was a bird; it was just some small movement that caught my eye as I scanned the hills from a distance. I stopped to examine the spot, but I couldn't see anything. I was tired and wanted an icy drink, but hope pulled me toward the hills where I had seen something I couldn't identify. I worked closer but I was still too far to see the spot clearly. The waves of heat poured off the land, upward into the air. My vision was not clear.

Finally, I was too tired to go on. I tried one last-ditch call to them, "Baahaa, baahaa," expecting nothing in return.

Immediately, Billy echoed my call. I couldn't see him, but I headed in the direction of the bleat. Within a minute or two I called again, and this time I could see Billy look up at me, with Burlap standing well below him on the hillside. I guess I was close enough for him to recognize me because he wanted to come down the hill. But Burlap was not so anxious. The hillside presented more luxurious dining than the plateau. Burlap was in burro heaven and not interested in me. If Burlap wasn't leaving, neither was Billy.

So I climbed the hillside, which took fifteen minutes. I halfway expected stubborn Burlap to balk when I neared his rope, but he didn't.

They were no worse for wear after being away from camp all night in spite of my worrying that they had been attacked by a band of coyotes or a lion. I was the dad whose children had not reported in after curfew. I led them back to camp to the happy cheers of Michael and Kevin. Lassie ran to Burlap, licking his muzzle. She had missed her morning routine.

"Here, Daddy! *Take this*." Kevin handed me the gallon of Kool-Aid, dripping icy water from the chest. I tipped it up and drew what felt like a half gallon.

"Don't drink it *all*, Dad! I want some too!"

"So do *I*!"

So we had learned one more lesson: domestic fowl like to roost in the same place every night if a place is provided to their liking. We really don't know too much about goats because Billy just echoed Burlap. But we could certainly question what goes on in the mind of burros. Burlap always had a mind of his own. He would take our arguments and pleadings under consideration, but he always wanted to make the ultimate decision. The night before he had and the two animals were no worse for the experience. Maybe we should have left them out from the beginning.

"Pass me that Kool-Aid young man. Now *you're* drinking it all."

Final Days in Camp

The summer was nearing an end. School was looming for the boys and we knew that we couldn't live forever without an income. During our friends' visit, Bill had told me about several people at JPL that knew we were coming home soon; there was work waiting for me once again. We all looked sort of forward to our other home, but it was hard to say we wanted to leave Las Cuevitas.

When we were near the two-weeks-to-the-end mark, we talked to Mari Elena at her home, the *tortillería*. She lived near the center of town and had several doe goats that her family tended on a mesa above the spring. We hoped she could take Billy and Burlap and merge them into her herd. She wanted Billy because she needed a buck to breed. What a happy ending for our favorite goat! We were not anxious to take them back to the house in the desert south of the village. That was a daylong trip and we were concerned to find them a place where they would be pets rather than dinners.

Mari Elena said she wanted the two of them and asked how much she should pay us for them. The price was not important but the fact that she was willing to pay something was. We trusted her family to treat the animals with respect and looked forward to seeing them again on our next trip. This is not to imply that they would be treated like pets. Rural Baja families can seldom afford that luxury to any but the luckiest animal. But they would be taken care of. When there was hay or grain available and affordable, they would be included; when there was none, they would be able to forage on their own. If we could have taken them home, we would have. But this was the best circumstance we could expect.

At the hut we organized and packed tools, clothing, and equipment. Over the week, we removed our makeshift cabinets and cupboards, closets, and pot hangers.

There were long and happy/sad trips into the gulf in the boat, the boys and I taking turns piloting. We passed whales in Canal de las Ballenas, dolphins in the channel between Smith's and Angel de la Guarda, and drove wildly through the masses of bobbing boobies, pelicans, and gulls sitting on the surface of the water offshore, sending them, burning scarce calories, swirling upward in a small tornado of squawks and cawkings. We caught fish and fed the sea lions.

Michael and Kevin put their boots on and climbed the Three Brothers. When they arrived at the crest of one or the other they would call down into camp. If the wind was right we could hear them. They would wave and we would call to them and wave back. Mary Ann and I would know that they were safe for another moment or two and relax just a bit.

Of course it was very sad to leave our home. There had been so many moments here that we could never expect from another place, anywhere, any time. We had achieved my freeze-frame; we had stopped the world and gotten off, effectively dropped out for a worthwhile adventure none of us would ever forget.

One of the practical problems during this emotional time was the hut itself. We were settled, it turned out, on Mari Elena's land. I didn't want to ask about this, but I had read about the value of land to Mexican citizens. I assumed that the government had distributed the desert hectares to everyone in the village or the *ejido* many years ago. The place we had chosen to build a hut happened to belong to Mari Elena's family.

When we discovered this near the end of our stay, we asked her son, Carlos, the boys' friend, what we should do with the materials that formed our hut. Could his family use them? He was excited that we would let him have these rather than take them back across the border. These materials, he said, could be used to improve the conditions in their home, the *tortillería*. This solved a problem for us and was a reasonable payment to Mari Elena for the use of their land for the summer even though she would never have asked for it.

In the village we visited with our friends and had several last meals. Driving south, to where we had spent the summer in a smaller and simpler hut ten years before, we showed the boys where we had lived before they were born—when Mom and Dad were first married. I told them about my discovery of a small seashell that revealed the values of Mexico for a young and aggressive man.

On the right tide we visited La Gringa, capturing a number of crabs in our nets only to release them to the rising waters of the lagoon. We saw the egrets pass through their rituals, jumping into the air and striking out at their opponent with their feet, and spent hours watching the blue herons padding patiently through the shallow marsh grass. There had always seemed to be three at La Gringa, and I wondered if it was the same three over the years. Even the distance between the birds seemed to be calculated and unchanging. The sandpipers waded the edges of the channel, filling with incoming water, probing the mud for sand crabs.

Sadly, we loaded up Billy and Burlap and the chickens and drove in to Mari Elena's. As we opened the back of the Land Cruiser in her fenced yard, the chickens scattered like leaves in the wind. Hot Stuff, our rooster, was quick to dominate every hen new to him. Billy immediately fell into lust with the doe goat. Burlap had no mate, but he was so sweet and stubborn it was hard to think he cared. He was just gentle and loving and happy to be around anyone he could seemingly ignore. It was more than difficult to leave Billy and Burlap there. Even knowing we would come back in a day or two to see them for the final time of this trip, we all cried and hugged, clinging to them, our partners in a wonderful, unforgettable summer.

And, as for me, I spent my last few late evenings sitting in the library reading, thinking, and listening again and again to the music that had brought me here. I had first become part of the scene that was Bahía de los Angeles late in my Baja experiences. But it was easy to become attached to such an uncomplicated and fetching place. With a John Williams soundtrack playing in the background and small waves washing smooth round stones in the foreground, it was very calming. I took long breaths knowing shorter ones would follow, to the north.

My two boys were asleep on their cots. Mary Ann was reading by the moth-covered lantern. Far off in the channel an old weather-beaten trawler pulled six equally battered *pangas* astern, puffing coagulated exhaust out its upright pipes like punctuation points in the fading light of evening, heading into Bahía de los Angeles just around the corner. I could hear the individual and precise, deep-chested pumps of each stroke of the diesel as the engine labored through the pulling, tugging water that supported so many of my friends, fishes and mammals, recently discovered.

I had made my first journey into the interior in 1968 hitchhiking with Epifanio Ybarra of San Ignacio. Mary Ann and I had found new depths to our relationship here during the summer of 1974. Michael and Kevin had filled the place with their youth and happiness in 1985 while we had formed new meanings of family and reliance. The events of these past and present times filled me with a feeling of…belonging. Of being in a place where I was meant to be, a place that was missing in my other life. Or, was it me that was missing from this place?

I could try to fight the battles of the space business with other minor players. Or I could come back here, refusing to play that mean and rough game. Here I was attacked only by the fundamentals that, at best, respected me and, at worst, didn't know I existed. I could easily return that respect.

On one hand, I was ready to return to an environment that was receptive to my work. But on the other I knew that southern California society tears at relationships, bombarding them, overwhelming them with such great intensity that there is little left for the members of the affair.

As the night wore on I wandered into the kitchen and poured dark rum into a plastic glass, added a handful of precious ice and a can of diet Pepsi. Through the slats of the split bamboo that we had slipped through the border three months before, I caught a glimpse of a fingernail Baja moon. I thought back over the many times that we had fought to keep the hut standing, and looked for missing animals, including Michael and Kevin, out wandering over the Three Brothers. The sliver of moon on the water as I returned to my chair on the stones threw a last silver ribbon for the trip, and I was duly appreciative.

Eventually, my chair melted into the stones, and I fell, sleeping, somehow, onto my cot.

A Gift for Mari Elena

On our last day the sun's early light slipped, liquid and flowing, over the volcano on Smith's Island and melted into pure gold on our beach and hut. We were already filling the Land Cruiser with boxes, gas cans, tarps, and food.

After our conversation with Carlos and his mom, we were donating the hut itself to their family. This was no great act of charity; what it really meant was that we didn't have to tear it down and figure out what to do with the remains. They could put the building materials to good use for their house in the village. More than half of their beds were outside the two-room house of three hundred square feet. The structure itself included only a kitchen and bedroom. The older children slept outside under a *palapa* cover. Of course, this was where the whole family would have preferred to sleep most of the year because of the heat.

When we finished packing, we went to lunch in the village going down Old Rocking Horse Road with the dust flying behind us, bouncing over the twists and turns along the beach. I let Michael, and then Kevin, ride on my lap and steer the truck. This was big stuff. Lunch was at Las Hamacas on the patio. It was hot but there was a breeze from the ocean. The small pepper tree they had planted when the restaurant first opened had grown into a shade-builder. They watered it over the years with dishwater and it was now strong and healthy. Nasty-looking crows sat atop the electrical poles that still looked foreign in the village. A scantly populated parade of 1950s and '60s American cars, all pocked with dents and dust, rumbled unmuffled along the oiled street.

A member of the Díaz family, Delia, had married José and together they owned and operated this small place. We had eaten here often since they opened, years before, and we were friendly with the family. I associated Las Hamacas, in corners of my mind, with Hemingway's *A Clean, Well-Lighted Place*. When we told them we were leaving today, it somehow made it true. After breakfast we climbed the road to the spring and filled a water jug.

On our final return to camp we made sure we'd collected everything and left the beach in clean shape. Michael and Kevin really wanted to take a plywood sheet that we'd used as a table—they had painted it with watercolors—so we found a place to tuck it in on top of the heaps of boxes and equipment.

Aloud, together, we said our good-byes to Las Cuevitas. We were happy and sad, sweet and sour, yin and yang. We were going north to another home we had not seen in an age of experiences, but leaving a place where significant events and tugs of the heart had been lived. The four of us had shared a single, mutual, together time, living in such a close and dependent environment, and emerged almost as one.

I remembered our experience from the mid-'70s, before the boys were born, of living another life on a beach twenty kilometers south at the other end of the bay. I remembered how Mary Ann and I had, alone and newly married, lived through another summer against the escarpment of our twin mountains, growing close in ways we would never fully recognize.

I hoped this would be true for Kevin and Michael, too, and knew intuitively that it would. They had certainly gotten to know each other as well as two people can, being alone together most of the summer here. Faced with nature's rages, they had learned to understand natural environments and how insignificant we humans can be. They had driven their first car along Old Rocking Horse Road; powered their first boat into a calm and unending blue gulf with light breezes and spume flying over the hull; seen their first pod of dolphins, thousands strong, and their first whales up close and personal; laughed as they ploughed through a gaggle of pelicans and sea gulls in the cove at Las Cuevitas, spilling them into the air like smoke from a windswept fire.

I hoped that they had absorbed some of the less spectacular experiences of the summer. I wanted them to soak up the mystery and beauty of music they heard subconsciously as they slept, quiet moments with the right symphony; to learn the routine of bathing and doing laundry and the time it takes to hand wash and sundry our clothing; to learn how a simple house could be built in just a few days, for our protection in the summer. Later in life these tools would help distance them from the ragged pack of souls competing for the meager scraps of common employment.

And if I failed in this goal, the least I could expect is to have participated closely with my family for an extended period, immersing ourselves in an environment that was unforgettable, even at face value. In the event none of the underlying subtleties struck home, the visual and tactile impact of Baja was unavoidable. The availability of the resource of time, coupled with the image of the individual vanes and barbs from a pelican feather attached to a long, flapping wing of a bird trying to grab fish from an unyielding hand is hard to miss. Water floating across the sand to strike you in the face during a *chubasco* when you're trying to hold the hut together is startling and rude. Hiking across the ridge-lines of the Three Brothers to happen upon a rattlesnake coiled and ready to strike your small and innocent boot-covered leg is a vision hard to forget. The vivid colors, reds, oranges, yellows, of the sunrises almost every morning burned permanent slides in your mind that you will carry throughout your life. When you lie down at night, will this image help relax you?

We said our final adiós to Las Cuevitas knowing we would be back for many other summers. The ghosts of Billy and Burlap were romping in the early morning mind, with Lassie licking Burlap's muzzle. Hot Stuff and the hens were wandering the beach pecking at the fresh kelp that floated ashore during the night.

The South and the North

We had planned a short trip to the south before we returned to Alta California. We were going to spend several days on the East Cape. We drove to La Paz and then on to Los Barriles near the coast. Here a small dirt road heads back north among the hills and atop the steep drops into the Sea of Cortez. Fifteen miles along, we encountered the hotel built on a promontory above Punta Pescadero. This hotel offered large individual cabañas, each consisting of several rooms and a common area. They are built of local stone and cooling fans stirred the air. The nearest restaurants were in Los Barriles and La Paz and were too far to travel for a meal, but The Pescadero offered meals with our rooms. We spent two days luxuriously relaxing in this wonderful comfort, eating the hotel-prepared food and lounging by the pool and on the beach of this isolated place. We allowed ourselves to be pampered.

From here we moved just a short drive north and spend two days at Punta Arena, at Hotel Las Arenas. It was nice to be in the midst of people and to hear stories of sport fishing from excited, sunburned tourists. We left Las Arenas on a morning in mid-September and drove north most of the day. By evening we were near Bahía de los Angeles.

We decided it was worth the detour and turned at the junction and bounced, later, into the village. We had dinner at Las Hamacas and rented a room from the Díaz Hotel for the night.

The next day we packed and left in the early morning. The boys wanted to visit Las Cuevitas one last time so we raced out Old Rocking Horse to La Gringa and wound our way to the beach of the little caves.

We were startled as we spilled out of Barsam's Corner onto the beach. There was nothing left of our hut, no sign we had lived there other than the stairs, now leading nowhere.

Carlos had done his job well and immediately after we left. The roof and walls of the hut were gone and there was no sign we had ever been there. This was depressing! But why? I guess I should have looked at our beach in the way I might a flower or a small, delicate animal, a moth. It is a difficult thing for a human to not want to reach out and touch everything we care about. But we can't always execute this want. I needed to learn to be able to love and not influence. I couldn't touch the flower; the oils from my hand were poison to it. I must learn to let the untamed bird avoid me; it is necessary to its survival. It is wrong for me to try to tame it. The beach, in a few days time, was restored to its rest position; the records of our time there were reversed in a few short, meaningless moments. Everything was back to another normal. The coyote tracks through the area were testament to that. The bastard must be disappointed I took my water with me. Or perhaps he now missed the challenge of attempted burglary on a nightly basis. I talked to myself and wanted to cry but kept a straight face, and we shortly left to go to another home.

On a spring day, many months later, we returned for a weeklong trip with our friends, Barsam and Marlene, and camped at La Gringa.

We decided to drive up to Las Cuevitas just for the memories it contained. There were signs en route that there had been a violent winter storm and wild surf. When we got there, the beach had been shifted about, forming a large berm further up the shoreline than when we had lived there. There must have been a spectacular outrage of weather. I was glad we hadn't been there when it struck.

The steps from the hut were gone. I looked in the beach stones for the boulders I had gathered from the desert. The average weight of these was about fifty pounds. I couldn't believe a storm could have moved them so far we couldn't find even a single one. Unbelievable!

I carried this thought of the strength of the currents of nature throughout my life. Everything we do is overwritten in such short and cold order by the basic elements. What chance do we have to leave our mark on earth? And, for that matter, why did I need to? Just like a male cat's spray, I guess!

Around 1998 or '99 we were on another trip with Bar and Marlene and other friends. Again we camped at La Gringa. Some of our friends had never been to the bay and wanted to see where we had lived so many years before. One day we drove out to the plateau in the late afternoon after the heat of the summer day was fading. Other storms had continued unleashing their power on the shore. How well they worked together in a relationship that had passionately existed for eons.

The boys were grown now, almost in their twenties, and stayed in camp back at La Gringa. Mary Ann and I and our friends took the Land Cruiser and wound up the road to Las Cuevitas. The plateau and desert hadn't changed at all over the years. Barsam's Corner was the same. We stood on the site where our hut had once been and told our friends about the summer, reliving the moments of our so-much-younger years when the boys were still our babies. We told our stories, remembering the events of times behind us, unrecoverable, gone. I left Mary Ann spinning a recalled sensitivity and walked up a hillside to see where we had hauled Billy over the cliff from a certain death. Really I was preventing my friends from having to deal with the fact that I was, as often, crying. I knew then that the most tender moments in my life were behind me.

The small, tight hugs of my tiny boys were gone forever. Now I would get handshakes and slaps on the shoulder. Never again would I experience that most basic of feelings, the father-the-protector. I knew at this moment my life had turned, once again, from a known course onto another path into the unknown and unpredictable future.

I sat on the hill above Las Cuevitas watching the rolling sea we had fished, through which we had been chased by dolphins and carefully scrutinized by whales. It was a clear afternoon and the breezes supported the gulls and pelicans hanging above the cliffs of the Three Brothers. The islands were beckoning. All this had become buried in the depths of our communal family soul years before. We would carry it forever as part of us. How much richer our lives were because of Las Cuevitas.

Mary Ann and our friends, wondering where I had gone, called and drew me down from my perch. I walked back to the beach. They were digging where our hut had been, moving handfuls of stones away from anything that might lie beneath, and I assumed they were looking for shells. Then I saw that they had found some large rocks under the smaller ones. Looking more closely I could see a gentle pattern of small waves in the gravel working toward the beach. There, underneath the gravel, were our steps just where they had been throughout the years. The storms hadn't destroyed them, they had covered and protected them.

In one moment, I had turned my boys free in my heart. In the next, I found that an important time of my life was, in fact, not so easy to erase from the face of the earth as I had thought.

In the long run there must be something inside all of us that wants permanence. We must want to leave an indelible imprint. To not be forgotten.

So I now had Mary Ann, Michael, and Kevin who would never forget me, for better and for worse, and there were enough of both to go around. And I had my family in return. And we all had Baja, the Bahía de los Angeles: the village, the south end, Las Cuevitas, and La Gringa. We had smooth round stones scattered throughout our life. What more could a guy want?

Another Home

We left Las Cuevitas behind us, and headed to another home, *al otro lado*, on the other side.

We soon arrived back in Glendale. It was time for the boys to start school, and we all fell back into our routines. On the weekends it was soccer, T-ball, basketball. It was up at 6:45 on weekdays. Michael and Kevin would get ready for school, we'd eat breakfast, then drive them the few blocks to the same school my mother had attended in 1917. It was Mary Ann's ritual to meet her friends for a morning walk. My custom was to return to the house and begin work for the day. I had called Bill, my lifelong buddy, and he had lined up several possibilities for work. Within a day or two I had work waiting and got started.

One morning, after our return, I was looking at my schedule for the day: build a project plan from 7:30 to 9:00; meet with the project manager at 9:30 to present the plan; present the results to the project team for approval; meet Bill and our group for lunch; meet with an engineering core team for another project, to gather, organize, and document software requirements for a spacecraft; get back to the house by three, in time to be there when Michael and Kevin got home. I'd work through the late afternoon; we'd have dinner and talk about our day. Then I'd get back to work again, until it was nearly bedtime for the boys.

My evenings, working at home, were punctuated by their bursting into the office with questions and silly stories and jokes from their minds and their friends at school. For a few minutes, before they went to bed, we had tickle time where I chased them around the living room. If I caught them, which they made sure I did, I would toss them to the floor and scrub their ribs with my knuckles to their excited whoops, snorts and shouts. Mary Ann would caution me that they would never go to sleep if we kept this up.

On nights when I was too tired for this rambunctiousness, I would call for a game of "freeway" which I had invented as a shallow decoy for a backrub. The game consisted of me lying belly down on the floor and them driving their matchbox cars all over my back. If neither of these worked, I put on their favorite album of the day, *We Are the World*, a collection of songs they knew was created by musicians dedicated to helping raise money and food for impoverished people in a distant place. During this scene, my assignment was only to observe while they performed wild and exotic dances, gyrating freehand on the soft carpet of our living room, in the air and prone and spinning. These were the days of break dancing and it had swept the young people across our country faster than a rumor in an office. As I watched them trying to kill themselves, sometimes my attention shifted just so, looking behind them, through a picture window that overlooked all of Glendale and a major part of Los Angeles, from a safe distance, thinking how lucky I was to have the opportunity to focus on only their images in the reflection, not ghosts of suffering and poverty.

When they wore themselves out, Mary Ann took them off to bed, and read them a story once they were tucked in. This was our traditional evening.

I wrapped up work items for the next day and stacked up the reports and documents that I would carry to JPL. When I was lucky enough to finish by ten or so, I would sometimes find time to sit in the living room on the couch facing the many large Spanish-style arches leading across the ground floor of our home, lit indirectly. I pushed the right buttons on our record or tape player to cause amplified sounds to emanate from the too-complicated equipment, and spent a moment selecting an album from among those of the hour. John Williams, Bob Dylan, or Barbra Streisand?

Whatever I chose, I would crank the volume up as loud as I thought I could get away with, feeling like a kid in a full cookie jar. Kevin and Michael were asleep in the far reaches of the second floor. Mary Ann was at the top of the stairway, watching television in the den, the door shut to filter the melodies that were radiating from downstairs. I poured a drink and evaluated the risk of increasing the volume another tick or two. If the stresses of the day warranted, I often tried. The worst I could get was a bawling out.

Gradually the music quieted and calmed my tattered mind, flowing into the secret places where panic and stress hid, erasing fears about my performance the next day, the bills, other problems. Over a few minutes shared with the right music, my mind began to slip from the push of the day. On really good evenings, I would hear some fine-tuned guitar strings I had absorbed on other occasions on a small beach well to the south. Sometimes I fell asleep listening to sweet music spilling over smooth, round stones.

Sunbelt's Baja California Booklist

"Adventures in the Natural History and Cultural Heritage of the Californias"
A Series Edited by Lowell Lindsay

Backroad Baja: The Central Region   Higginbotham
Twenty off-road trips to Baja California's beaches, missions and ranchos.

Baja Legends: Historic Characters, Events, Locations   Niemann
The author's extensive knowledge of Baja's colorful past and booming present.

Baja Outpost: The Guest Book from Patchen's Cabin   Patchen
Stories, reminiscences, and comments from the remote cabin's many guests.

Cave Paintings of Baja California, Rev. Ed.   Crosby
A full-color account of the author's exploration of world-class rock art sites.

Gateway to Alta California: The Expedition to San Diego, 1769   Crosby
The groundbreaking trek through northern Baja California. Color maps.

Houses of Los Cabos (Amaroma)   Aldrete
A stunning full-color pictorial highlighting architecture in and near the Cape.

In the Shadow of the Volcano: One Family's Baja Adventure   Humfreville
Two summers in a beach-side hut at Bahía de los Angeles in 1974 and 1985.

Journey with A Baja Burro   Mackintosh
Over 1,000 miles on foot, with his trusty companion, from Tecate to Loreto.

Loreto, Baja California: First Mission and Capital (Tio Press)   O'Neil
A comprehensive history of the small town that was California's first Capital.

Mexican Slang plus Graffiti   Linton Robinson
The hip talk and off-color eloquence of the Spanish commonly used in Mexico.

Mexicoland: Stories from Todos Santos (Barking Dog Books)   Mercer
These stories, ranging from satirical to dramatic, capture daily life in Baja.

Other Side: Journeys in Baja California   Botello
Over twenty years of traveling—a love story, adventure, and inner journey.

Spanish Lingo for the Savvy Gringo   Reid
The colloquial Spanish of Mexico, plus a guide to language and customs.

Tequila, Lemon, and Salt   Reveles
The border town of Tecate comes to colorful life in this collection of stories.

The Baja California Travel Series (Dawson)   Various authors
Selected titles in this hard-to-find series of histories.

We carry hundreds of books on Baja California, Mexico and the Southwest U.S.!
www.sunbeltbooks.com